Murder Movie Makers

ALSO BY OR EDITED BY
MATTHEW EDWARDS
AND FROM MCFARLAND

*The Rwandan Genocide on Film:
Critical Essays and Interviews* (edited, 2018)

*Twisted Visions: Interviews with
Cult Horror Filmmakers* (2017)

*Klaus Kinski, Beast of Cinema:
Critical Essays and Fellow Filmmaker Interviews* (edited, 2016)

*The Atomic Bomb in Japanese Cinema:
Critical Essays* (edited, 2015)

*Film Out of Bounds: Essays and Interviews
on Non-Mainstream Cinema Worldwide* (edited, 2007)

Murder Movie Makers
Directors Dissect Their Killer Flicks

MATTHEW EDWARDS

Foreword by
STEPHEN JOHNSTON

McFarland & Company, Inc., Publishers
Jefferson, North Carolina

LIBRARY OF CONGRESS CATALOGUING-IN-PUBLICATION DATA

Names: Edwards, Matthew, 1978– author. |
Johnston, Stephen (Stephen D.), writer of foreword.
Title: Murder movie makers : directors dissect their killer flicks /
Matthew Edwards ; foreword by Stephen Johnston.
Description: Jefferson, North Carolina : McFarland & Company, Inc.,
Publishers, 2020 | Includes bibliographical references and index.
Identifiers: LCCN 2020014998 | ISBN 9781476676470
(paperback : acid free paper) ∞
ISBN 9781476639666 (ebook)
Subjects: LCSH: Serial murderers in motion pictures. |
Motion picture producers and directors—Interviews.
Classification: LCC PN1995.9.S297 E39 2020 | DDC 791.43/6552—dc23
LC record available at https://lccn.loc.gov/2020014998

BRITISH LIBRARY CATALOGUING DATA ARE AVAILABLE

ISBN (print) 978-1-4766-7647-0
ISBN (ebook) 978-1-4766-3966-6

© 2020 Matthew Edwards. All rights reserved

No part of this book may be reproduced or transmitted in any form or by any means, electronic or mechanical, including photocopying or recording, or by any information storage and retrieval system, without permission in writing from the publisher.

Front cover: Michael Rooker in the title role of the 1986 film
Henry: Portrait of a Serial Killer (Maljack Productions/Photofest)

Printed in the United States of America

McFarland & Company, Inc., Publishers
Box 611, Jefferson, North Carolina 28640
www.mcfarlandpub.com

Acknowledgments

This book would not have been possible without the help of my family, friends and the contributors who participated in this book. I would also like to thank all the individual interviewees who gave up their own time to be telephoned/interviewed about their film and for agreeing to be part of the collection. Without them and their amazing films this book would never have been realized. So, a big thank you to Tom and Scott Hanson, Philippe Mora, Ian Merrick, Gerald Kargl, John Aes-Nihil, John McNaughton, David Wickes, Chris Gerolmo, Chuck Parello, David Jacobson, Clive Saunders, Paul Shapiro, Byron Werner, David Birke, Sebastian Niemann and John R. Hand. Thank you also to Stephen Johnston for writing the foreword for the book and for being interviewed for the collection. I also thank my contributor Marcus Stiglegger for the interview he provided for this book.

Thank you also to my Mum and Dad and my brothers Paul, Mark and Daniel for their support during the production of this book and my writing. Thank you to Doug and Rosemary, Mimi the cat, my nieces Lily, Poppy, Naomi and Eliza and Mandy and Kate. Thank you also to Patrick Prescott for his support in my writing endeavors and for continuing to support and spread the word about my books. I would like to extend my thanks to the editorial staff at McFarland for agreeing to publish this anthology and for their help in realizing the project.

Last but not least a huge thank you to my wife Johanna for her love and support during the writing of this book, for allowing me to watch a vast array of films connected to serial killers and mass murderers and for getting me interested in this area of history in the first place. I thank her for all her suggestions and advice during the production of the book and for contributing questions to the interview with Chris Gerolmo about his film *Citizen X*. Without her, this book would not have happened.

Table of Contents

Acknowledgments   v
Foreword by Stephen Johnston   1
Introduction   3

1. *The Zodiac Killer*: An Interview with Director Tom Hanson (with Scott Hanson)   9
2. *Swastika* and *Mad Dog Morgan:* An Interview with Director Philippe Mora   23
3. *The Black Panther*: An Interview with Ian Merrick   42
4. *Angst*: A Conversation Between Director Gerald Kargl and Marcus Stiglegger   54
5. *Manson Family Movies*: An Interview with Director John Aes-Nihil   59
6. *Henry: Portrait of a Serial Killer*: An Interview with Director John McNaughton   68
7. *Jack the Ripper*: An Interview with Director David Wickes   81
8. *Citizen X*: An Interview with Director Chris Gerolmo (with Johanna Edwards)   89
9. *Henry: Portrait of a Serial Killer, Part II, Ed Gein* and *The Hillside Strangler:* An Interview with Director Chuck Parello   100
10. *Dahmer*: An Interview with Director David Jacobson   118
11. *Gacy*: An Interview with Director Clive Saunders   130
12. *Ann Rule Presents*: The Stranger Beside Me: An Interview with Director Paul Shapiro   142
13. *Starkweather*: An Interview with Director Byron Werner   152
14. Killer Scripts: An Interview with Screenwriter Stephen Johnston   166

15. *Gacy* and *Freeway Killer:* An Interview
    with Screenwriter David Birke   176

16. *Jack the Ripper* (2016): An Interview
    with Director Sebastian Niemann   182

17. *Joel*: An Interview with Director John R. Hand   190

Chapter Notes   201
Bibliography   203
Index   205

Foreword
by Stephen Johnston

Of Men and Monsters (and Monsters Who Are Men)

The term "serial killer" is of reasonably recent adoption, credited to FBI criminologist Robert Ressler (specifically to define Ted Bundy, a subject I'll return to directly), although the pathology dates to biblical times and exists in Greek mythology. Indeed, many monsters we imagine in the collective consciousness, whether the vampire (Countess Bathory, Vlad Dracula) or the werewolf (Pierre Burgot), possess horrific—but otherwise quite human—origins. Perhaps it's easier for us to process the evil mankind is capable of if we simply compartmentalize it as the work of monsters.

Cinematically speaking, the first genuine representation was likely Peter Lorre in Fritz Lang's 1931 film *M*, about a psychotic child murderer and the resulting manhunt, although one could argue that Battling Burrows in D. W. Griffith's 1919 film *Broken Blossoms* was more than a bit of a psychopath. As an adjunct, a scene from Lang's *M* was later used in a 1940 Nazi propaganda film, perhaps giving us further insight into the nature of human evil.

My own route to the world of serial killers was somewhat mundane, if not a little circuitous. I was the prototypical movie-loving kid who grew up fascinated with monsters. One of my first tangible movie memories was watching *Abbott and Costello Meet Frankenstein* on late night television. I was hooked. I had no idea how movies were made, but I was damned certain I was going to figure it out.

Flash-forward to film school in Chicago, where I stumbled across the legend of Wisconsin killer Ed Gein. I was familiar with the name, as he was the inspiration for well-known movies such as *Psycho*, *Silence of the Lambs* and *The Texas Chain Saw Massacre*, and even lesser-known stuff like *Deranged* and *Three on a Meat-Hook*, but what intrigued me was why nobody had told the story as it existed. I mean, if the guy could serve as inspiration for all these dark tales, surely he warranted his own movie. So, I dove into research, including a visit to the small town of Plainfield where Ed's adventures took place (and where, oddly enough, people had little interest in talking about said adventures).

Up to that point, serial killer biopics tended to take a "procedural" approach to the material, and were frequently focused far more on the detective(s) tracking the killer than the actual killer. There is nothing wrong with this approach, of course, but I wanted to take a more elliptical, biographical approach, and tell the story of this man who was haunted both literally and figuratively. The resulting film, starring Steve Railsback in the eponymous role, produced by Hamish McAlpine and Michael Muscal and directed by Chuck Parello, proved to be a success, critically and financially.

Hollywood being Hollywood, whenever you have success, you immediately try to duplicate it. If the movie *Ed Gein* was a do-wop song, then *Ted Bundy* was meant to be rock and roll. For that movie my approach was less elliptical and more linear, but still very much focused on telling Bundy's story, warts and all. Michael Reilly Burke played Bundy, Matthew Bright directed and McAlpine and Muscal again produced. Horror legend Tom Savini even made an appearance! You'll find that we filmmakers frequently aren't fans of our own work perhaps because we've seen behind the curtain and little about the resulting product comes as any real surprise, but I consider *Ted Bundy* to be the most fully realized serial killer flick I've written. It just seems to fire on all cylinders, and successfully replicates the same weird combination of charm and grotesque deviance that defined Bundy.

If *Ted Bundy* was rock and roll, then *The Hillside Strangler* was the darkest death metal. C. Thomas Howell and Nicholas Turturro star as the sadistic serial killing cousins, and they both inhabit their roles so completely, it possesses a genuine power to disturb. (And I wrote the damn thing!) Chuck Parello returned to direct, applying a different touch to the material than he did with *Ed Gein*, which suited the project. As it evolved, I think *Ed Gein*, *Ted Bundy* and *The Hillside Strangler* served as a sort of serial killer trifecta, representing three different pathologies in three different cinematic (and storytelling) styles.

Separately I was approached about writing *Starkweather*. Produced by Mark Boot and directed by Byron Werner, it's a propulsive punk rock ride that really sort of serves as a coda to my time spent in the world of serial killers.

For better or worse, the success of these movies seemed to usher in a rash of serial killer biopics of varying standards (I'm not taking credit nor accepting blame), and ironically, they over-saturated the market to such a degree the licensing fees dried up and the market effectively died. But, like zombies and taxes, it's safe to say serial killer cinema will always be with us.

This brings us to *Murder Movie Makers*, Matthew Edwards's respectful but irreverent book on the subject of killer cinema, including interviews with a few of us who've dabbled in the genre. It provides a concise overview of the creative process behind these sort of movies, and also hopefully reveals that those of us working within the genre are artisans trying to craft thoughtful (if horrific) films and that we aren't (for the most part) the homicidal monsters we seek to create in films.

As a final note, and although I've felt the accusations, I've never accepted the notion these sorts of movies somehow glorify serial killers. Surely nobody would suggest that movies about World War II glorify Hitler or the Nazis. The thing is, no matter how evolved we imagine ourselves, evil will forever walk amongst us, and if monsters there be, they are undoubtedly us. Never forget the abyss, because even if we live in light, the darkness man is capable of is never really confined to shadows.

I continue to believe that the bright light of a movie projector is the best antidote to the darkness.

Stephen Johnston *is an award-winning scriptwriter of numerous films, including* Deadly Charades, Officer Down *and* Detention. *He is best known for his screenplays based on real-life killers, including the groundbreaking films* Ed Gein *(2000),* Ted Bundy *(2002) and* The Hillside Strangler *(2004), all produced by Hamish McAlpine and Michael Muscal. His film* Starkweather *(2004) was released by ThinkFilm. He is working with Hamish McAlpine for* On the Moors, *about the infamous Moors Murders in the UK. He lives in Los Angeles.*

Introduction

Filmmakers have long sought to create cinematic monsters and creatures as a way of inducing scares and flights of fear in audiences, even from the medium's infancy as shown through films such as *The Lost World* (1925), *Haxan* (1922), *Vampyr* (1932) and *Nosferatu* (1922). Then, with Fritz Lang's grim psychological thriller *M* (1931), considered cinema's first serial killer hunt, the cinematic lens was used to study one of the most terrifying monsters of all: the human condition, the beast in man. Over the intervening decades, a handful of films based on real-life killers were conceived, filmed and unleashed onto the public, usually to a wave of controversy and public outcry. Earliest examples included *The Boston Strangler* (1968) and *10 Rillington Place* (1971), starring Richard Attenborough as British serial killer John Christie, before the seventies heralded in a new era of films inspired by the crimes of notorious killers such as Jack the Ripper and Charles Manson. One filmmaker, Tom Hanson, who is interviewed in this book, even went as far as to make a film in order to catch the Zodiac Killer, all the while creating one of the most enjoyable, zaniest and craziest exploitation films of the era! While seemingly rooted in fiction, films such as *Psycho* (1960), *The Texas Chain Saw Massacre* (1974) and *The Hills Have Eyes* (1977) were initially bred from the real-life crimes of infamous killers. The aforementioned *Psycho* and *The Texas Chain Saw Massacre* were inspired by the murderer Ed Gein, who, despite only killing two people, has a vast number of films inspired by his crimes (the best being *Deranged* [1974] and *Ed Gein* [2000]). The latter, *The Hills Have Eyes*, was based on a bloodthirsty 16th-century Scottish clan headed by cannibalistic Alexander "Sawney" Bean.

By the late seventies through to the early nineties, independent and exploitation filmmakers, along with television studios the world over, became increasingly keen on greenlighting projects based on real-life mass murders, spree killers, serial killers or bloodthirsty outlaws. Producers and television executives saw that there was money to be made as well as high televisual ratings to gain in audience's grim fascination with psychotic killers and folk who slunk to the lowest forms of depravity. For the most part, the films/TV movies followed a very similar staple in that they were police procedural dramas focusing on the detectives' manhunt to catch the "in-human" monster(s) inflicting wounds on an otherwise seemingly genteel society. These killers were usually portrayed as sub-humanoid monsters, or maniacs, devoid of emotion or empathy with little or no characteristic traits shared with the rest of humanity. They were monsters, akin to a vampire or a creature that had emerged from a black lagoon. Emphasis was on the hardworking police force tracking down and ultimately apprehending the sicko on the streets. Lip service was generally paid to what made these killers tick. Some showed their wicked deeds on screens, others were more tasteful and respectful. For me, the true horror and fascination in such movies, has always been that the killers are very human, yet few were ready to shine a light on this initially. Instead, many filmmakers/studios chose to present these killers as monsters, odd-balls and freaks unlike the rest of humanity, whereas in truth, the films that stand out for me are the films that shine a light on the darkest recesses of the human condition, showing that man is capable of the most extraordinarily violent, sadistic and brutal acts. Though the human condition has many positive attributes, history has shown us to be an equally violent, wicked, sadistic and bloodthirsty race that has razed, raped, murdered and pillaged for its own gain, religion, ideology, interest and, in some cases, enjoyment. Our history is populated with people, usually men, who have committed the most atrocious and violent acts.

Serial killers pick at the holes and edges of our society's moral fabric and, unsurprisingly, for cinematic audiences, films based on their crimes garner the most traction in terms of morbid curiosity. Why is this? Why are audiences drawn to such a dark and grim subject matter? Why does it make compelling viewing? The truth is, as the cycle of serial killer films shows, these films are profitable and find a worldwide audience. Yet there is an anomaly here, as some audiences who harbor an interest in such fare almost stipulate, or have a defined notion of, a set trajectory that the film must follow: the formula invariably follows two good guys (usually detectives) hunting down the deranged killer who ultimately gets his (as is customarily the case) comeuppance, usually in the form of death or, at the very least, is put behind bars. For such audiences, for the film to end without the killer being punished was taboo.

In terms of violent content, serial killer/mass murderer/spree killing films can be divided into two parts. On one side, with bigger budgeted Hollywood films and TV movies, the films tend to employ an element of restraint in terms of depicting the crimes of the killer, perhaps showing just one or two of the killer's handiwork, but overall exercising a conscious decision on the part of the filmmakers to be not overtly graphic in terms of the violence on the screen. Both in the U.S. and in the UK, some of the best examples of killer flick movies have played out in the televisual format intended as movie of the week, or as a mini-series, where the primary concern was not on gratuitous violence but on the drama of catching the perpetrator. On the other side of the coin are exploitation films that have not held back on depicting the savagery of the crimes that killers such as BTK, Bundy, Gacy and Dahmer have committed. Both are legitimate ways of exploring this subject matter, if they are handled intelligently and do not stray into the murky territory of glamorizing such killers.

Resultantly, the cinematic output during the seventies, eighties and nineties ranged in quality, with films falling into both of the aforementioned categories. On the TV front, there were some fine examples of true-life crime movies focusing on the murderous deeds of some of America's most infamous serial killers or mass murderers. *The Atlanta Child Murders* (1985), starring Jason Robards, James Earl Jones and Rip Torn, was an excellent mini-series on the brutal child murders by Wayne Bertram Williams, who terrorized Atlanta between 1979 and 1981, killing between 23 and 29 children. That the series has slipped into obscurity, despite its great cast, is an unfathomable shame. Other notable TV movies during the eighties included the soviet thriller *Citizen X* (1995) on the Rostov Ripper, who claimed the lives of at least 52 women and children, and Marvin J. Chomsky's *The Deliberate Stranger* (1986), which depicted the life and exploits of Theodore Robert Bundy and was considered by critics to be the best movie about Bundy's crimes. The Manson cult still haunts and fascinates the American psyche to this day, yet it was Steve Railsback's astonishing performance as Charles Manson in the brilliant *Helter Skelter* (1976) that is still considered the greatest film on Charles Manson and the horrific Tate–LaBianca mass murders to date. In Britain, David Wickes celebrated the 100-year anniversary of the Jack the Ripper slayings with a memorable mini-series of the same name while Bruce Seth Green's TV movie *Manhunt: Search of the Night Stalker* was a decent stab at putting the killings of Richard Ramirez, with particular emphasis on the LA detectives who sought to track him down, on-screen. Jud Taylor's *Out of Darkness* (1985), starring Martin Sheen, and *Ann Rule Presents: The Stranger Beside Me* (2003) were fine examples of quality filmmaking on a modest TV budget yet both slipped into relative obscurity. The former, much like Spike Lee's *Summer of Sam* (1999), dealt with the hunt and capture of New York serial killer David Berkowitz, while the latter was another examination of the crimes of Ted Bundy (see interview for more information). Eric Till's *To Catch a Killer* (1992) proved to be another good example of the staple TV movie covering the murderous antics of John Wayne Gacy. Gacy's crimes would be filmed numerous times with varying degrees of success, the most underrated of which is Clive Saunders's version, which was butchered by its producers (see interview for more details). *Judgment Day: The John List Story* (1993) was a decent TV movie starring Robert Burke and David Caruso about the infamous family man who snapped and killed his entire family before absconding, only to be apprehended decades later. Directed by Bobby Roth, the film boasts a good central performance by Caruso but the picture lacks a gritty edge which is ultimately undermined by the TV sheen. Also, Roth fails to direct Burke adequately because in his portrayal of List for the best part he comes across more like a bumbling gurning fool than a man pushed to his snapping point by his mounting debts, eventually lashing out by murdering his entire family.

This trend continued into the new millennium as serial killers and mass murderers invaded the living rooms on both sides of the Atlantic, where they provided fertile ground, and stories, for commissioners and producers. With violence levels toned down, these series/TV movies both satisfied viewers' morbid interest in these killers and entertained them with the hunt and capture of these fiends. In the UK, ITV churned out a number of dramatizations including *A Is for Acid* (2002) about 1940s acid bath murderer John Haigh, *See No Evil: The Moors Murders* (2006) on the brutal killings of 5 young children by Ian Brady and Myra Hindley, a case that still haunts the nation's psyche to this day, and *Harold Shipman: Doctor Death* (2002), which dramatized Shipman's turn from family doctor to mass murderer (with 218 killings being ascribed to the beardo weirdo). *This Is Personal: The Hunt for the Yorkshire Ripper* (2000) was a gripping and gritty examination of the hunt for Peter Sutcliffe, aka The Yorkshire Ripper, a British serial killer who murdered 13 women in Yorkshire, England, while *Appropriate Adult* (2011) was a dramatization of serial killing duo Fred and Rosemary West, who found infamy the world over when they were arrested for murdering and raping at least 11 young girls at their home on Cromwell Street, burying them in the garden or the cellar of the house. A fellow teacher at one of my schools in Swindon, England, regaled me with a tale that her dad went to Fred West's house because they needed to dig up a gas maintenance pipe that ran through the back of his garden. Fred West politely told them he was happy to do it for them! No wonder why he was so keen on doing the work himself! *Appropriate Adult*, starring Emily Watson and Dominic West, focused mainly on the aftermath of his crimes, with his arrest and subsequent suicide. Harrowing and tense, this mini-series forgoes showing the crimes of West, instead focusing on the relationship between Watson's character, the Appropriate Adult (who helps children and vulnerable adults) and West. While Dominic West puts in a decent shift, he never really delivers the scummy, demonic evilness of Fred West. Then again, who could?

On the film front, *Bonnie and Clyde* (1967) and *Badlands* (1973) were well known in cinematic circles for their portrayal of what would become later known as spree killers. Though inspired by Charles Starkweather's infamous killing spree, *Badlands* never acknowledges its inspiration, unlike other films inspired by his case like *Stark Raving Mad* (1981), Tim Roth vehicle *Murder in the Heartland* (1993) and *Starkweather* (2004). Meanwhile, while there were plenty of exploitation flicks like *The Town That Dreaded Sundown* (1976) or cult entries like *The Honeymoon Killers* (1970) and Shohei Imamura's masterful *Vengeance Is Mine* (1979), the big game changer from this author's point of view came with John McNaughton's seminal *Henry: Portrait of a Serial Killer* (1986), a film that moved away from the police procedural formula adopted by many filmmakers and instead focused solely on the killer in its grim examination of his crimes as it bored deeper and deeper into the protagonist's fractured psychosis. Hereafter, more filmmakers adopted McNaughton's approach with more films emerging focusing directly on the killers as opposed to the race to catch them by the police authorities. David Jacobson's *Dahmer* (2002) was another excellent study of one of America's most infamous killers as well as Chuck Parello's *Ed Gein*, who opted for a truthful cinematic account of Gein's crimes instead of drifting into fictional terrain.

In Asia, especially Hong Kong during the nineties, with the advent of CAT III rating, a whole array of sexually violent, or downright offensive, films based on their local killers hit the cinemas. Such infamous titles emerging from its rotten woodwork included perverse classics *Dr. Lamb* (1992), *The Untold Story* (1993), *Final Judgment* (1993) and *Human Pork Chop* (2001), which became well known in the West. Recently, South Korean films such as *The Chaser* (2008) and *Memories of Murder* (2003) have been critically lauded. In terms of the aforementioned Hong Kong films, these films were a hybrid mix of extreme graphic violence, at times sexual, mixed with goofy, slapstick moments of comedy as the usually hapless detectives on the case attempt to track down the killers. For fans of Hong Kong cinema, these films featured standout performances by the leads, Simon Yam (*Dr. Lamb*) and Anthony Wong (*The Untold Story*, *Human Pork Chop*), who lifted the films firmly out of the cheap exploitation mire they could have so easily have been left languishing in. Interestingly, Danny Lee, best known for his role in Ringo Lam's *City on Fire* (1987) and John Woo's *The Killer* (1989), directed both *Dr. Lamb* and *The Untold Story*. Both are fabulous pieces of extreme cinema but be warned, they are not for the faint of heart! The CAT III films failed to shy away from depicting the extreme acts committed by the respective deviants. In *The Untold Story*, we see Anthony Wong tie up and graphically murder an entire family. The mother is stabbed repeatedly in the stomach and the dad is stabbed in the neck while the four young daughters meet the same fate (one mercifully off-screen), with throats cut and one decapitated. To hide Wong's knife wielding deeds, the corpses are butchered and served into tasty *char siu bao*, or pork buns to you and me! *Dr. Lamb* is equally as violent and based on Hong Kong serial killer cabbie Lam Kor-wan, who was apprehended when he took his photographs of his dismembered female victims into the Hong Kong equivalent of Snappy Snaps! Simon Yam gives an astonishing performance as Lam Kor-wan and the film pushes the envelope of bad taste to the limits, though some viewers may find the shift from dark, psychological crime drama, to excessive misogynistic violence, to slapstick comedy most unnerving.

David Fincher's brilliant film *Zodiac* (2007) was deserving of its plaudits while Tom Hardy's *Child 44*, another cinematic version of serial killer Andrei Chikatilo's crimes, underwhelmed (unlike *Citizen X* and *Evilenko* [2004], which were based on the same case). *From Hell* (2001) was a grand failure that never came close to matching the brilliance of Alan Moore's epic graphic novel and was pretty boring to boot. *Monster* (2003) and *Snowtown* (2011) proved to be other notable high-profile films that turned their cinematic lens onto serial killers from Daytona Beach and Brisbane, Australia, respectively. Meanwhile, at the other end of cinematic spectrum, in direct-to-video realms, cheap cash-ins became the norm throughout the nineties and noughties with disposable films such as *The Alphabet Killer* (2008), *Speck* (2002), *Kemper* (2008), *The Gainesville Ripper* (2010), *Freeway Killer* (2010) and zany classics such as Matthew Bright's *Ted Bundy* (2002) and forgotten gems like *Killer: A Journal of Murder* (1995), the James Wood–starring film about turn of the century killer Carl Panzram. In some territories the film can be seen on Netflix.

During the research of this book, one of the most satisfying elements was uncovering forgotten gems from beneath the mediocre and trash films that fell under the umbrella of scope of this book. William Friedkin's *Rampage* (1987), about the story of Richard Trenton Chase, who was known as the Vampire Killer, was a key find, along with *The Deadly Tower* (1975), a dramatization of the shooting spree of Charles Joseph Whitman, who killed 16, and Cédric Khan's harrowing drama *Roberto Succo* (2001), detailing the infamous Italian serial killer. Scott L. Flynn's director of *The Grey Man* (2007), about serial killer Hamilton Howard Fish, was an unexpected delight and a shame that it has proved to be his only film before seemingly disappearing without trace. The Australian exploitation film *The Chant of Jimmie Blacksmith* (1978), about a man of Aboriginal ancestry who's pushed to the breaking point by the British colonial rulers, where he violently kills his employer's family, was another excellent find.

This book is a compilation of interviews I conducted with film directors and scriptwriters over a two-year period from August 2017 to July 2019 in an attempt to compile an oral history of the pressures and hurdles that go into making films based on true-life killers. I deliberately centered the project on film directors (with the exception of a couple of interviews with screenwriters), as they have an overarching perspective on the cinematic process of making, financing and screening films which by their very nature are controversial, violent and contentious in terms of subject matter. With horror and exploitive/true-crime cinema now gaining close scholarly attention in the field of academia, this book aims to speak to the filmmakers at the heart of these challenging and critically acclaimed films. The interviews not only delve into the filmmaking process but also the moral considerations the filmmakers had to wrestle with when making films about serial killers, particularly opposition from the victims' families or national sensitivity around crimes that have shocked communities. What considerations must a filmmaker factor in when making such a film? How historically accurate must these films be without offending the survivors or the victims and stemming a tidal wave of backlash? Did the filmmakers encounter opposition? What levels of research went into the making of such films? Such themes are explored in the interviews herein.

Equally, I felt it was important to interview filmmakers who I felt had made films of distinct merit to this cult sub-genre of crime and horror cinema. I was deliberate in not diluting down the product of the book by interviewing directors of films that were cheap, exploitation cash-ins or films of such low artistic quality that they would be an insult to the reader if it was seen that I was recommending such tawdry fare. A prime example of this is the films of Michael Feifer, who sadly made a spate of dreadful, shot-on-video tosh during the mid- to late noughties. As much as I would have wanted to cover *B.T.K.* (2008), staring Kane Hodder, and *Boston Strangler: The Untold Story* (2008), his films are so poor that they border on embarrassing. And lest I get started on some of his other serial killer films, notably *Bundy: A Legacy of Evil* (2008) and *Ed Gein: The Butcher of Plainfield* (2007). The late Ulli Lommel was equally as guilty, with a plethora of terrible, micro-budget exploitation flicks based on some of America's most infamous killers including *Nightstalker* (2009), *D.C. Sniper* (2010), *Green River Killer* (2005) and *Killer Pickton* (2006) (to name but a few of the turkeys that were spawned from his video camera). One cannot believe that these nasty little films were made by the same man who made the brilliant *Tenderness of the Wolves* (1973), based on the gay serial killer Fritz Haarmann, a true classic of the sub-genre of killer cinema. Sadly, some of the film directors I would have loved to have interviewed have passed away while others remain elusive. I was equally conscious of not interviewing too many directors around one particular killer, such as Ted Bundy, and all the films featured in this book I consider worthy of scholarly study and artistically/culturally appropriate for discussion and exploration. All the interviewees spoke openly and candidly about their films and the struggles and, in some cases, hostility their visions caused when released. Some of the interviewees have not been interviewed in print before or little has been talked about their films for more than 30 years. One hopes that the interviews inside this collection will encourage further scholarship from academics and writers into this sub-genre of serial killer cinema and true-life crime films.

During the writing of this book there has been a new interest and surge in films relating to films about killers. *My Friend Dahmer* (2018), *Extremely Wicked, Shockingly Evil and Vile* (2019) and *Once Upon a Time in... Hollywood* (2019) show that this interest in such killers as Dahmer, Bundy and Manson remains unabated. Beneath the top layer of such high-profile titles such as these you will uncover a number of smaller titles: *Cabin 28* (2017), *I'm a Killer* (2016) and *Strangled* (2016). So just as mass murderers, serial killers and spree killers are here to stay in this world then so are its cinematic counterparts.

1

The Zodiac Killer
An Interview with Director Tom Hanson
(with Scott Hanson)

Northern California saw, during the late 60s and early 70s, the local populace terrorized by one of America's most notorious serial killers, the Zodiac Killer. He was a man responsible for a slew of violent slayings in Benicia, Vallejo, Lake Berryessa and San Francisco who evaded capture and whose identity remains a contentious issue even today. The Zodiac Killer was not only content with embarking on a murderous spree that rocked California; the killer also mockingly taunted the police and community with a series of cryptic messages that were sent to the local Bay Area press, the actions of which were detailed in David Fincher's superb film *Zodiac* (2007). As the police desperately tried to solve the cryptograms, and with the body count rising, an outraged and shocked community prayed for the authorities to catch the perpetrator. Some folks even devised their own ways to catch the serial murderer. Enter pizzeria entrepreneur Tom Hanson, who hit on a rather ingenious idea of catching the killer. Did Mr. Hanson form a vigilante mob and prowl the Northern California streets looking for the perpetrator? Nope! Without a pizza in sight, and in a cinematic first, Tom Hanson decided to apprehend the bastard by channeling all his hard-earned dough (pun intended) into producing and directing a feature film with the sole purpose of entrapping the deranged serial killer! The content mattered not a jot. Shoot the film. Get it in the can. Get the killer in the slammer! Simple, eh? Surely such an egotistical maniac would show up to an exploitation flick showcasing/detailing his handiwork and dreadful crimes. Surely he couldn't avoid the temptation to witness his deeds on the big screen in the company of others? That's what Tom Hanson thought! With this in mind, theatrical screenings became the setting for a stakeout to catch the killer. But how would Hanson capture him? Easy. Hanson employed an assortment of tools, ranging from elaborate theater traps and rent-a-cops to a raffle for a motorcycle in order to catch the killer! That the elaborate plan failed is irrelevant. Kudos should be given to anyone who sinks a pocketful of cash into a movie with the sole purpose of making the streets of California safer for the wider population and putting a psychopath behind bars!

That the film is a zany piece of exploitation cinema is irrelevant as the film is a fictionalized account of the Zodiac Killer's crimes and actual historical facts, loosely based on what was known at the time. In the film, the Zodiac Killer (Jerry, played by Hal Reed) is shown to have a normal day job as a postal carrier. He is shown as a polite, charming, rabbit-loving dude but with an unsavory side to his character; a man who dabbles in Satanism and displays flashes of pent-up anger. The first half of the film follows his friendship with the troubled misogynist Grover (Bob Jones), a toupee-wearing drunk who is stuck in a loveless marriage. The pair make for a swell team and the kind of folks you'd love to share a few beers with ... not!

After a night at the local drinking hole, Grover's false charm is exposed to all. While trying to impress four lasses, one of the women in the bar accidentally pulls off Grover's ludicrous wig, much to his consternation. As the women laugh hysterically at our balding protagonist, Grover flips into a violent rage and vows to get even with the girls. Here, Grover is presented by Hanson as one of society's unhinged people who has the capacity of inflicting violence on our streets or, even worse, murder. Hanson sets up Grover as the Zodiac Killer but he is soon bumped off early on in the film when his own family issues

Original poster artwork for Tom Hanson's zany, serial killer flick *The Zodiac Killer*, 1971 (courtesy Tom Hanson).

push him over the edge and he takes his daughter hostage. After a shoot-out with the police, Grover is shot dead. Before the bullets slug into Grover, sending him spiraling into the family swimming pool, Grover proclaims himself to be the Zodiac Killer. Thinking they have got their man, the detectives seem pleased to close the file, which infuriates the real Zodiac Killer (Jerry). After letting the detectives know the real-life killer is alive and well, detailing his crimes with stunning accuracy, the Zodiac Killer begins a new murderous campaign before a hilariously zany finale sees Hanson speculate on the motivation for our killer's violent spree.

With its trashy script (which was written in a day and a half), hammy acting and shot-on-the-fly filmmaking, you'd think this film wouldn't have anything going for it aside from the aforementioned production history. You'd be wrong, as this is one strange, surreal and bizarre cinematic grindhouse classic with enough murderous mayhem to keep even the most jaded of gore hounds happy and enough over-the-top acting

1. *The Zodiac Killer*

Director Tom Hanson in a photograph taken during the production of *The Zodiac Killer* (courtesy Tom Hanson).

to send you giddy to the stars. Hilarity is never far away either; in one scene a little crooked-teeth lad yells out at Jerry in a park, "I don't like him!" and sprints out of the frame, after Jerry says hello to him and his mother. The little brat clearly isn't fooled by Jerry's false charms and senses his murderous desires towards his mother. Levity is also never far away in Hanson's world/film. Take the scene when Jerry crushes some old dear's head with the hood of his car or when the film's clueless detectives consult a psychic called Koslow to help them solve the case! Yet all of this is topped by the hilarious scene when Jerry's hospitalized friend is pushed down a hill in his hospital bed in a scene of sheer lunacy! You don't get stunts like this in Fincher's *Zodiac*, folks!

Purists will argue that there is little to gleam from Hanson's exploitation romp and fictionalized version of the Zodiac killings, especially as it presents a fictionalized character as the killer and a slew of fictionalized deaths thrown in in order to bump up the death count. Yet such an accusation is unjust as the film does attempt to accurately portray some of the known facts about the killings at the time. Firstly, Robert Avery was known to Hanson and used as a consultant during the making of the film. Equally, the film touches on the letters/ciphers that were sent to Bay Area newspapers at the time and are accurate renditions of those ciphers. Furthermore, the known killings of the Zodiac Killer are depicted accurately throughout the feature, especially the grisly Lake Berryessa attack, which is particularly grueling and harrowing as we see the killer tie up his victims and stab them repeatedly. It is a jarring moment, thus making it all the more effective after the lighter, zanier moments in the film. This scene is both graphic and disturbing and you are reminded that this horrific act is based on actual events. Hanson films the attack with such ferocity that our busty actor's breasts almost pop out of her bikini as she wriggles frantically on the grass as the Zodiac Killer's knife penetrates into her flesh. As he daubs his signature sign on their car and flees, you are quickly reminded by Hanson not only of the brutality of the Zodiac Killer's crimes but that the killer was still on the loose for those audience members watching it at the time.

The Zodiac Killer is an enjoyable exploitive romp that was made with the best intentions to catch a violent killer that was terrorizing the state of California. While it did not succeed in its aim, Hanson did succeed in giving us one of the craziest true-crime films ever committed to celluloid and a snapshot of the crimes committed by the Zodiac Killer. Sleaze, horror, comedy and surrealism are all thrown into the mix along with a spoonful of fact with a large dose of fiction. Ultimately the film attempts to analyze the mindset of those capable of committing such acts. The Jerrys of this world can lurk and exist anyway as the eerie final denouement in the film suggests.

In January 2018 I had the pleasure of interviewing the director of this grindhouse classic, Tom Hanson, along with his grandson Scott Hanson, about *The Zodiac Killer* and his attempts to catch the killer. In this revealing interview, Tom speculates that he may have actually met and identified the Zodiac Killer, how they set about trying to apprehend the murderer and how they pulled off some of the zaniest stunts seen in the

For all *The Zodiac Killer*'s off-beat moments, Hanson's portrayal of the Lake Berryessa scene packs a powerful, disturbing punch (courtesy Tom Hanson).

film. I thank both Tom and Scott Hanson for sharing their tales about the production of the film.

Matthew Edwards: *What was your background prior to making* The Zodiac Killer*?*
Tom Hanson: My background was in the fast food industry and I worked in all kinds of food operations, such as KFC and my own chain called Pizza Man. I had about sixty-seven stores, I think.

ME: *You had worked in the film industry prior to directing* The Zodiac Killer. *Is that correct?*
TH: I did stuff like *Divorce Court* (1957–1969) and lots of those kind of TV shows. I also did something for Universal set on a ship, but I can't remember the damn thing! I worked on several low-budget films with Manny Cardoza, like *Night Train to Mundo Fine* (1966), which was about The Bay of Pigs invasion.
Scott Hanson: Have you seen that one?

ME: *No, but I have seen* The Hellcats *(1968).*
SH: Great. Actually, *Night Train to Mundo Fine* was featured on *Mystery Science 3000*!

ME: *I love that show.*
SH: It's great. Tom has a couple of great scenes in that film. It is funny. I haven't seen *The Hellcats* yet. [Laughs.] Maybe I should!
TH: When you are working on a low budget you can't really make a decent film. I knew that. This is why I thought about doing *The Zodiac Killer* because he was still up there in the San Francisco area. He's got to go and see it. So, I set that very elaborate trap to catch him. Then all the killings stopped for a while.

ME: *Had you always wanted to direct a film?*
TH: I always wanted to direct a film and I always enjoyed the process of it. As you well know, it is a tough business. The unions give you a lot of trouble, like SAG. I always told them to go to hell. They tried to stop the shooting a couple of times.

ME: *What was the climate like at the time in San Francisco when you set out to make the film/trap? You wanted to make the film in order to catch the killer. Were people in San Francisco frightened during this time with this killer on the loose?*
TH: They knew that he was somewhere in the area which is why I thought that I'd better get the movie out fast. Having worked on low-budget films I knew every trick in the book to get it knocked out. I figured I'd have a second film, too, so I made *A Ton of Grass Goes to Pot* (1972), which they changed to *The Big Score*. That way I had two films and I knew the low-budget guys would run them in the theaters, which they did.

ME: *Was it easy to fund the films?*
TH: Real easy, because you never pay anyone, otherwise you are never going to get it done! [Laughs.] But I burned up all my cards. I had about three or four credit cards and I used all those up. By the time I was done with the film I was pretty much broke and I had to start all over again.
SH: Sadly, he lost the rights to all of those films. Those films are not part of our purview. The film has been rereleased in America by AGFA. We worked with them but legally it is their property.

ME: *That's the nature of the business, isn't it! How did you go about casting for the film and securing locations?*

TH: I had worked a lot on low-budget films and knew a lot of people doing the same thing. For instance, the Smothers brothers who did *Another Nice Mess* (1972). Billy Fine screwed them over like he screwed me over.

SH: Billy Fine was the distributor at the time. He had a well-documented reputation which was very negative. In terms of locations, a lot of that was done by a guy called Manny Nedwick, who is still alive. However, they never got a permit for any of them. They did all that kind of shit. Manny and Tom went around areas in Los Angeles that could double for San Francisco. That in itself is hard to do because Los Angeles doesn't look like San Francisco. They found Franklin Canyon Reservoir, off Coldwater Drive in Hollywood Hills, and that doubled for Lake Berryessa. If this had been shot six months later it wouldn't have worked out as it would have been brown everywhere. San Francisco never gets like that; it is always green. It was shot in the wet season in LA. They only had a couple of months where they could have even possibly shot it here in Los Angeles and gotten away with it.

ME: *How did you set about writing the script? Manny Cardoza is listed as one of the scriptwriters.*

TH: There were about three or four guys interjecting different phrases and this and that. We were trying to do things in a hurry, so we had to change things in a hurry, too. So it wasn't just Manny Cardoza and Ray Cantrell. There were others working on the film. We were always readjusting because we had to get the damn thing done and into the theaters while the Zodiac Killer was still active in the area.

Original advertisement of Tom Hanson's *The Zodiac Killer* at the RKO Golden Gate Theatre. Note in the bottom right-hand corner the opportunity to win a free Kawasaki 350cc motorcycle (courtesy Tom Hanson).

ME: *You set up the film to catch the killer. I understand that you persuaded Kawasaki* *into giving you a motorcycle to give away at the screenings. In order to catch the killer, you handed out little yellow cards to everyone who bought a ticket and then you got the audience members to fill it in. It was with these cards that you would check the handwriting samples to see if they matched that of the killer!*

TH: Yes, that's correct.

SH: I have a sample card here. [Scott fetches the card and returns.] When we did the rerelease here in Los Angeles we redid the gag and got people to fill out the reproduction cards of the time. The original card read: "I think the Zodiac Killer kills because…."

ME: So originally, Tom got the audience members to fill in the card and you were hoping handwriting experts were able to match the handwriting.

TH: Well the idea was for the Zodiac to fill out the card to win the motorcycle and drop it in a box that was on top of a specially built stage. It didn't look like anyone could be underneath that box, however there was a guy under there and if a card looked suspicious, or seemed quite significant, the idea was for this guy to press a button that would alert all of us, whether in the freezer, the office or the theater. There was a guy in a hollowed-out freezer and a couple of others in the theater. The guy in the freezer looked through a vent and if the guy under the display beeped his button, the idea was for the guy in the freezer to watch to see who dropped it in! On the fifth or sixth night, we got a strange card through the box saying, "I think the Zodiac Killer kills because … I was here, the Zodiac." That's what it said.

ME: Did you interview many suspects?

TH: I think we interviewed about five people. The only one that really stood out was the guy from the restroom. The others weren't quite there. There was one guy that seemed to be like an ape! I couldn't get over how hairy he was. [Laughs.] His shirt was open and he literally had the most hair I have ever seen on a human being! There was a drug dealer who was a little off the wall, but I didn't get anything out of that.

SH: Needless to say there were a lot of characters that made an appearance to the showings!

ME: But it was the guy you encountered in the restroom that concerned you the most?

TH: One of our guys had figured out where this guy was sitting. We found his seat and found two more cards crumpled up. They weren't signed. How the hell he got hold of three cards, I don't know. Every night, I told the girl outside the theater with the cards to not give more than one card to each audience member. He had three! I learned to memorize people's faces, ears, hair. That's why when the guy turned around and saw that guy in the restroom I panicked. That was the guy I thought was the Zodiac!

ME: I loved the way you set the trap using rent-a-cops to apprehend the killer!

A sample of the "I think the zodiac killed because…." cards that were handed out at the rerelease of *The Zodiac Killer* in Los Angeles. During its original theatrical run, the yellow cards were used as part of the elaborate plan Tom Hanson had devised to capture the real Zodiac Killer. He arranged for handwriting experts to be on hand to identify the unsuspecting criminal (courtesy Tom Hanson).

SH: [Laughs.] They were just cast and crew.

TH: There were four or five of us and I said that if I point at him we have to grab him! The one I saw in the bathroom was the most suspicious. He scared the living shit out of me! When he came out of the bathroom I pointed at him and two of the guys grabbed him. He then entered the office. When he went in he was not panicked at all. He was very calm. All of a sudden I am looking at him and I see the paratrooper boots. I see his face and I'm thinking, "What the hell is going on here? My guys are having a conversation with him as if they are old war buddies, or something!" Finally, I stepped on in and I moved in real close. I was about 8 inches from his face and I said, "I want to say something to you, my brother Paul Stine [the cab driver who was shot by the Zodiac Killer] was killed by the Zodiac." I was looking for some change in his personality, a little panic or something. He said, "I'm sorry to hear that." He was totally and normally calm. He was not upset and he didn't ask why we had grabbed him. He denied putting the ticket in the box. After a few seconds I said, "We obviously made a mistake, you can go," and he left. In the end I had to give up as it was a pretty expensive journey. The next day was our last showing and I was in the office alone and all of a sudden I hear, "Were you looking for me last night?" I had tried calling him at his hotel but he was never in. He told us he was staying at the Astoria Hotel. I tried at 9 o'clock, 10 o'clock, 11 o'clock and finally I said, "Let's darn well break into his apartment!" We were just going to go and then he called. I don't know, he showed up and there wasn't much more I could say to him. He was on his way to get something. I think he was checking to see if we still suspected him.

ME: Do you think he was the Zodiac?

TH: Do I think the guy we pulled in the office was the Zodiac? Sure, I do. I have always thought that. Again, because I have always memorized faces. When he turned around in that bathroom and for me to go "Ahhhhh," you know, Christ, I don't shock very easily but I got to tell you that scared me. That's why I fumbled for some kind of words, zipped up and got myself out of that bathroom! Maybe I thought I was next!

ME: I understand that you premiered the film at the Golden Gate Theatre.
TH: That's correct.

ME: I understand that the Golden Gate Theatre is close to the Paul Stine murder location.

SH: We'd have to look at it on a map but the Paul Stine murder would probably be the closest murder to the Golden Gate Theatre.

TH: Yes, it wasn't very far at all. It was about five blocks away. He could have walked it. He had a cab drop him off there and then he shot the cab driver. He would have had to walk back because he had no vehicle, unless he had planted one before that. The guy who came down the street where the cops were going up said he had heard shots. He went up to the cops voluntarily. He was walking down the streets. He didn't take off and run. He walked right over to the car. Those two cops didn't even question him and they got into deep trouble. They never got an identification or his name. In one of his letters he brought it up and said he walked right over to the cops. I don't know if that was bullshit or if that was him. It sure got the two cops in trouble.

ME: Your film does draw on historical elements of what happened at the time. How difficult was it marrying what actually was happening with the killings into a fictional context? The killings were still going on, weren't they?

TH: Yes, the murders were still going on at the time. I was in such a hurry all the time that I got it made because I was convinced he would have to go and see his life's story.

SH: Some of the murders, like the carjacking killings, were made up. But the Lake Berryessa murders were super accurate. They recreated the murders with information that was given out to the public, like newspaper clippings. The other deaths they just had to embellish.

ME: You mentioned that some of the deaths were made up, yet one of the elements that stands out for me in the film is how accurate, haunting and terrifying the death scenes are, especially with regard to those based on the actual murders perpetrated by the Zodiac Killer. I felt they were very disturbing and powerful, especially after moments of comedy. Was that deliberate?

TH: I don't know because I had to get it shot and done. Everyone fell under that concept because it was important to get the film out while he was still there. I think there was a letter sent a week before we finished. So we had to hurry.

ME: I particularly found the attack on Bryan Hartnell and Cecelia Shepard very graphic and grueling, especially the moment when she is being stabbed. Did you deliberately make that as disturbing and explicit as you could?

TH: The girl in that scene is my wife's sister. They are family members.

SH: That's true. When Tom talks about the film he mentions how fast he had to shoot it, and that's obviously how it went, but if you look at the time, money and the props, you can see with that murder they clearly spent the most effort on it. That prop knife kicked around the house, my dad remembers that growing up and playing with it. It seems talking to them [Tom and the crew], their goal was always to make the film as quickly as possible but the emotional impact of that scene had to work. They had to focus in on that for the Lake Berryessa murder, right down to the lipstick on the door. When you look at it, they kind of had comparatively limited things to work with that they know happened. They poured a lot of detail into that. With other stuff, like the whole thing about the killer's father, there is a slight explanation as to why he does the killings. They pitch why the Zodiac Killer would be who he is. "Maybe he has a sick dad" kind of thing. You can see other places where it is totally fictional but the few things they had public knowledge of they poured a lot into because they didn't have a lot of subject matter to work with, other than making up murders ... which they did, in a couple of cases! You get this thread throughout the film. It is meant to piss him off. It doesn't show the Zodiac Killer in a good light. The film is trying to get his goat in some way. And those death scenes were graphic with the plunging knife! It came out well.

ME: I thought the emotional impact of those scenes were well done and seemed to draw on the facts of the time really well.

TH: Except the Zodiac Killer in the bathroom, when he was standing at the urinal, he said to me "real blood doesn't come out like that!"

SH: That was the conversation that started in the restroom with that guy, which we spoke about earlier.

TH: That's what he said to me before I turned around.

SH: Also, on an unrelated note, with the rerelease of the movie, and through the attention we have received, we got the suspect's name. We did chase after this guy for many decades afterward and we are essentially trying to reopen it now. We are currently putting together our own book and announcing who we think the suspect is. We have a literary agent. If we get a chance we hopefully would like to publically name who we think the suspect was and see if we can get some closure one way or another.

ME: Currently, the general consensus is Arthur Leigh Allen was the Zodiac Killer.

SH: There's a grand debate about that. The most popular book is Robert Graysmith's book that lays out Arthur Leigh Allen as the Zodiac Killer and the 2007 movie *Zodiac*, with Jake Gyllenhaal, says the same thing. However, Arthur Leigh Allen was cleared by DNA evidence a couple of years ago. Since then, Robert Graysmith has come under a lot of scrutiny for embellishing facts. Now the consensus is that it is not Arthur Leigh Allen. That was what was put forward by Graysmith but that has been disputed by DNA evidence. I don't want to throw shade at Graysmith but in the film research of the *Zodiac* movie a lot of shade is thrown at Graysmith. I don't know if that's because he is the most successful in terms of telling the story of the Zodiac Killer or for getting it out there. Graysmith does reference Grandpa in his book and he spells his name wrong! He spells Grandpa's name wrong! It is such a simple thing—"Oh, man! If you are missing details like that!" So right there he misspells Grandpa's name and then he makes reference that Grandpa's suspect was caught masturbating in the bathroom. We have never heard that reference anywhere outside of the Graysmith reference book.

TH: A total lie.

SH: It certainly didn't happen in the bathroom. Graysmith never reached out to Grandpa at the time of the publishing.

ME: And Graysmith became so obsessed with his own theory that he was trying to find answers when maybe they weren't necessarily there.

SH: That seems to be the running hypothesis. That Graysmith couldn't see the forest for the trees. He started to push his own idea. That's probably true for us. You start to push your suspect because you want it to be true. That is the super danger fall in all of this. We talk about this. From our perspective, something is amiss. Hence, there is a curveball somewhere in this equation that has been missed. Whether that was information that was in the hands of the police, that didn't get into the right hands of the right people at the right time, or whether it was multiple murderers and not just one murderer, or maybe it was multiple individuals ... something is amiss. Something isn't right. You can tell by the way it has been gone over again, and again, and again. Something doesn't feel right. Perhaps the actual perpetrator was able to get themselves cleared off, somehow. Perhaps they had a false alibi. Something like that. As time goes on it is going to get harder and harder and it seems there is at least one curveball—maybe more—that have been largely missed and why none of this makes sense, quite frankly.

ME: Interestingly, in David Fincher's film Zodiac, *Paul Avery, whom you worked with on* The Zodiac Killer *as a production consultant, is not presented favorably, is he?*

SH: No, he is not.

ME: Tom, how did you find working with Paul Avery as he is not portrayed well in Zodiac? *He is portrayed as a man whose life is ruined by the Zodiac killings, which, from my research, is not strictly true.*

SH: It sounds like that was a bit of an exaggeration.

TH: I would meet Paul Avery for coffee right around the corner from the theater.

I would see him across the street and there was an alley and he would wait for me to go in, I guess. Then he would come in. We would talk about this and that. I met him two or three times for coffee, but he was scared to death because they had put that sign over his bedroom window: *Paul Sleeps Here*. So, he was a little jumpy about running into the Zodiac.

ME: What kind of character was he? In the film Zodiac *they show him to be an alcoholic, taking cocaine, etc. Was that the person that you knew or again a fabrication?*

TH: The feeling I always got was that he was always scared because of that Halloween card he got sent saying he was next.

SH: Another interesting overlap, the couple at the Lake Berryessa murders met Charles Manson within a few months of the shooting of that scene. They were invited by Manson to a party he was holding but they didn't go.

TH: They were staying near Charles Manson's ranch. They were hippies, too, and they were lucky to not get involved.

ME: The Zodiac Killer *is a bit like your* Jack the Ripper, *isn't it?*

SH: Yes, and Grandpa always makes that reference. Grandpa tried to take it a step further and this is a letter he wrote to the Metropolitan Police in Leeds, West Yorkshire, UK, trying to help them catch the Yorkshire Ripper [Peter Sutcliffe was the Yorkshire Ripper and responsible for the murders of 13 women. He was finally caught in 1981] by using the same trap he had used to catch the Zodiac Killer! They politely declined his offer.

ME: What happened when the film was released?

TH: The guy that distributed the films (*The Zodiac Killer* and *A Ton of Grass Goes to Pot*), well I can tell you that I never got a dime from him. I was not here in California [at the time of the release] and good job, too, as I would have gone into his office and beat the hell out of him. I think Manny Cardoza got some money, as he took him up to the magic castle. I think the distributor was stealing from everybody, not just me.

ME: I find that a common experience of many low-budget filmmakers of this era, where they were screwed over by the distributor.

TH: Yes, that is basically what he did to me and he did it to others, too. That happened to the Smothers brothers, as I mentioned earlier. There wasn't a hell of a lot I could do. I was trying to get back on my feet in Wisconsin, trying to figure out what the hell I should do next.

ME: How did audiences react to the film when it was originally released?

TH: I don't know. It played in some big drive-ins in California, but I really don't know. I do know that the distributor shipped the film across the country and it played everywhere, both films.

SH: I think it is worth noting now, when we can look back on it, that the information that the film was set as a trap to catch the Zodiac Killer did not really come out at the time. I have not been able to find any references or newspaper articles about it. The original purpose of the film was to catch the killer, right? Their original intention was to film some of that, to film some of the catching. So, having not caught the killer, and the public not being informed of it, it seems to be universally received as an exploitation film. The film certainly fits that bill. Knowing it was made to catch the killer shows

WEST YORKSHIRE
METROPOLITAN POLICE
Millgarth Street, Leeds, LS2 7HX
Telephone: Leeds 35353, ext.300

Our reference: J/PH/kma
Your reference:

1st December 1980

Dear Sir

Your letter dated 19th November, 1980 addressed to the North Yorkshire Police has been passed to me for attention. I thank you for the offer of your services in an attempt to entrap the "Yorkshire Ripper" and I have read with great interest the scheme you have outlined for that purpose.

However, I do not think that the time is appropriate to embark upon a project of that nature and feel I must therefore decline your kind offer.

Yours sincerely,

P. HOWARD
Chief Superintendent

Mr T Hanson
rewdco
1115 SO Flower,
Burbank,
California 91502,
(213) 841-2203

Letter from West Yorkshire Metropolitan Police in the UK in reply to Tom Hanson's suggestions on how to apprehend the Yorkshire Ripper (Peter Sutcliffe), who was terrorizing Northern England during the late seventies and early eighties. Sutcliffe murdered 13 women and attempted to murder an additional seven (courtesy Tom Hanson).

the film in such a different light whereas at the time that didn't come out. So, I think that was lost on most folks and it was largely distributed as a low-budget exploitation film.

ME: But it wasn't an exploitation film, it was a trap!

SH: Exactly! Even now that it has come out as a trap it seems the film gets seen in a different light.

TH: The police tipped me off that they were going to do a John Doe warrant on my suspect's hotel where he had something in his storage. A package, or something. He had been staying there at the time of the Paul Stine murder. So, my wife and I stayed over in San Francisco. But then that night they discovered those letters sent to the *Chronicle* about Dave Toschi [the detective in charge of the case who was later removed from the investigation after he admitted writing and mailing anonymous fan letters to the *Chronicle* praising his own work. Toschi died on the day of this interview, 11 January 2018]. So, they never did the John Doe at the Astoria Hotel. I don't know what the hell my suspect had stored there. Later he got married and moved out to Daly City into a house with a garage. When I finally tracked him down he came out of his house dressed as a mailman and I though Jesus Christ, that's how I portrayed him in the film! It went on and on and I finally gave up.

ME: I thought it was a brilliant trap yet there is still so much to enjoy in the film. I particularly like some of the other cast members. I liked the character "Doc" played by Doodles Weaver.

TH: He was a friend of Bob Hope's! He was so pissed off with the unions because they couldn't get him work that he would do anything. However, he could never remember his lines! He kept forgetting them! So, I just had to take what I could from him and run. He couldn't memorize his lines at all.

ME: I also liked the psychic (Aaron Koslow).

TH: He was a good actor. He always wound himself up in fights, here in LA. He should have made it in the film business as he was one hell of an actor.

ME: I also liked the stunt at the end of the film where the guy is pushed down the hill in his bed!

SH: That's the scene where the guy rides the bed down the hill at the end.

TH: I forget who played that part.

SH: Manny Nedwick was the guy driving the car during that stunt which sees him almost hit the guy on the bed. So, they did do that stunt. That bed on wheels did have a steering mechanism that is underneath the blanket. It had two ropes that was used as a steering mechanism. That's why his hands are under the blankets because he is steering that bed down that hill! That was one of the steepest hills in LA and they used it to make it look like San Francisco. Every street in San Francisco looks like that but nowhere in LA looks like San Francisco so goodness knows how they found that spot! I think the guy in the bed told Manny to try and hit him! He figured he would have enough control to swerve out of the way and I think that was the shot that they kept.

ME: It was fantastic. The bit when he goes down the steps as well! [Laughs.] *Was it fun to film that scene?*

TH: [Laughs.] It was fun to film every scene we ever shot. I always loved working in the film business. Too bad I couldn't get other projects off the ground, otherwise I think I would have made it in the industry.

ME: There are some good stunts in the film. I like the one where you push the car down the hill.
    TH: We stole that car!

ME: You did what?! Can I print that?
    TH: [Laughs.] Well, it wasn't working. It wasn't really a theft … we were just helping to get it off the street!

ME: I liked the death scene where Jerry jumps on the hood of the car and crushes the old lady! I like the way you juxtapose the elements of horror and comedy in the film. However, the film ends on a very eerie note, I think. The killer states that he is still loose and that he'll be seeing you.
    TH: I firmly believed throughout the filming of the film that we were going to catch him and that he would slip. I had access to all his letters, through Paul Avery. That was a very unstable mind, like the guy I caught in the bathroom.

ME: Are you pleased that the film has lasted the test of time? Even though it was made as a trap to catch the killer, are you still proud that people around the world still fondly remember the film?
    TH: Yes, because I think it still might trip something. I don't know if my suspect/the Zodiac Killer is dead or not. We shouldn't let it go and let him get away with it, like Jack the Ripper.

ME: The thing is, everyone now assumes it was Arthur Leigh Allen, especially after Fincher's film.
    TH: It is still unbelievable that they didn't trip on something definite with all those murders. The police should have been able to find something definite. They claim they have the fingerprint from the cab when Paul Stine was killed. I don't know if that is true or not.

ME: Hopefully you will be able to uncover new evidence and pinpoint the suspect you think it may well be. So, you have a name?
    TH: Yes, and you'll be wanting me to give it! [Laughs.]

ME: I'm guessing I'll have to wait for the book! [Laughs.]
    SH: When it gets to that stage we will give you a call! You will be the first to know.

2

Swastika and *Mad Dog Morgan*
An Interview with
Director Philippe Mora

Film director Philippe Mora is a familiar name to those purveyors of cult, exploitation, sci-fi and horror cinema, with a body of work that includes such B-movie titles as *The Beast Within* (1982), *Howling II* (1985), *Howling III* (1987) and *Communion* (1989), starring Christopher Walken. In a career that has seen him tackle a magnitude of different genres and films, it's unsurprising that he would have at some point delved into the world of real-life killers. To dismiss Mora as merely a director for hire would serve as a great injustice. An accomplished documentarian, Mora's first foray into the world of mass murderers came with the brilliant documentary, *Swastika* (1974), one of the first films that showed the rise of Hitler and Nazism in Germany. Compiled from footage taken from newsreels of the time and propaganda films shot by the Nazi party, the film is an invaluable document of both the party and Hitler, and how Hitler was revered by sections of the German population. The film is both a chilling chronicle of how the German people were sucked into the Nazi party's warped ideology and propaganda and how that escalated into one of the most horrifying and shameful events of the 20th century: the Holocaust. Powerful, disturbing and haunting, it is a documentary that lingers in the mind long after the credits have rolled. Yet the film's biggest coup (at the time) was the use of 8mm footage obtained from Hitler's wife Eva Braun. What emerges from this grainy silent footage is Hitler the man and glimpses of his private life; Braun's footage manages to humanize Hitler, an aspect of the film many find troubling. Like all the killers in this book, it is easy to demonize Hitler and dismiss him as merely a monster. Yet the true horror comes when we acknowledge that they are human and their actions can be considered humanistic traits. *Swastika* is a film of astonishing horror, yet an invaluable insight to the inner workings of the Nazi regime.

Having found critical acclaim with his documentary work, including the aforementioned, Mora sought a return to feature filmmaking (his debut film being the little-seen *Trouble in Molopolis* [1969]). His choice of subject would be a film about one of his adopted home's most infamous outlaws: Dan Morgan, aka Mad Dog Morgan.

Considered in Australia to be one of the most bloodthirsty ruffians who ever traversed the bush, Dan Morgan was an Ozzie violent criminal and armed robber who terrorized homesteads in New South Wales. In the year of 1864, Morgan's terrorizing finally caught up with him during a botched raid on Round Hill Station. Intoxicated, Morgan's booze-induced raid ended with one man dead and two others injured. On the lam, and now with a considerable bounty on his head, Morgan continued his killing spree across the state, gaining instant notoriety in his native Australia, where he was dubbed Down Under's answer to Billy the Kid. Not before killing two more people, the Australian police finally cornered Morgan's sorry hide and put an end to his terrorizing ways once and for all.

Morgan's tale became that of legend in Australia. Seizing on this fascination, director Mora took the opportunity in 1976 to create a Revisionist Western in his native Australia of Morgan's exploits. At the time blacklisted in Hollywood, Dennis Hopper was cast as the titular Morgan and brings to the screen all of Mad Dog's idiosyncrasies and bubbling violence. Like Hopper, Morgan is presented as a misunderstood soul whose bad luck and conspiracy has led him down the path where he now finds himself. Mora portrays Mad Dog as a man driven to his brutal crimes—robbing and murder—as a result of abuse suffered by authority, the British and the rich land-grabbing landowners. Mora depicts Morgan as a ranting, rum-guzzling outlaw. A man more at home stargazing in the outback than living under a wooden roof, a rebel unwilling to sell his soul to conformity and, most damning, a man who has suffered injustices. And Mora does not shy away from depicting these injustices: imprisonment, penal rape (a scene Hopper was less than thrilled with) and authority willing to shaft him. His violent spree becomes less surprising in light of these scenes and in many ways it can be considered as Morgan's attempts at rebelling against the system that has abused and disrespected him for so long.

Mad Dog Morgan (1976), with its liberal bloodletting, maddening protagonist and sweeping vistas, lends itself as an Ozzie stab at the Spaghetti Western genre. Like those pictures, it mixes the brutality of the West with the beauty of the landscape, juxtaposing them beautifully: the violence of man with the beauty of nature. Hopper is a revelation in the role of Morgan, a part he clearly identified with, while David Gulpilil

Original poster artwork of the Ozploitation flick *Mad Dog Morgan* (1976), directed by Philippe Mora and starring the irrepressible Dennis Hopper (courtesy Philippe Mora).

puts in an excellent shift as his aborigine companion. While there are a few confusing jumps in time and place, it still remains an excellent slice of the Australian exploitation/Revisionist Western film genre that, amidst pangs of explicit violence and scenes of extraordinary beauty, features a standout performance by one of cinema's most maverick and renegade actors.

In November 2018, I had the pleasure of interviewing director Philippe Mora about both incredible pieces of work. I thank him for the generous amount of time he afforded me to conduct this interview.

Matthew Edwards: Your documentary film Swastika *is one of the most interesting films relating to the rise of Nazism in Germany. I understand that you initially intended to make a film about Albert Speer's book* Inside the Third Reich?

Philippe Mora: Actually, it wasn't, but producer Sandy Lieberson's, who brought the rights for *Inside the Third Reich*. I was very interested in it and I asked him whether I could document the making of the film. He said, "Sure." So, I started researching the film—which became *Swastika*—and he couldn't get the film made. It was David Puttnam and Lieberson who were partners and they couldn't get the film done. However, because they had brought the book I got to meet Albert Speer and Lutz Becker at Lieberson's house. When that film fell apart, by that time I had done a lot of research with Becker and I said to Sandy, "Can we just make the film *Swastika*?" In fact, we had enough material for two films, the other being *The Double Headed Eagle: Hitler's Rise to Power 1918–1933* (1973, director Lutz Becker). That is the film about the rise of the Nazis and I made the film *Swastika*. The original title of the film—which explains it much better—was *The Nazification of Germany*. That was the idea, to show how they took over Germany. So that was the birth of the film.

ME: I really like the opening of the film with the Swastika coming through space.

PM: There is a bit of a story behind that! [Laughs.] I thought it would be good to call the film not *Swastika*, but the symbol of the swastika. That main credit is actually the title of the movie. What happened was that newspapers wouldn't print the swastika symbol as the title of the film, or they didn't understand that was the title of the film. They wrote it out as *Swastika*. So, by default, that became the title of the movie. The opening scene of the swastika flying through space is the main credit with the original title. That was filmed, I think, at Pinewood Studios, with this gadget that had been developed for *2001: A Space Odyssey*, where the camera revolves at the center of the lens on its axis, so the whole camera turns around 360 degrees. That was quite complicated. The first time we shot it there was a janitor from Pinewood in the shot turning the swastika around! He wasn't supposed to be there, and it was the funniest damn thing. I wish I had kept it. So, I told Sandy the concept of the shot—and we didn't have that much money to make the film—and he liked the idea and he agreed that we should do it. So that is the origin of that shot.

ME: How did you get access to the footage, in particular the private footage shot by Eva Braun?

PM: First of all, when I started the film I had no idea that I was going to find, or use, that Eva Braun footage. I had no idea. However, I was after private footage. It turns out now that there is a lot of private footage. The Nazi Germans were big home movie buffs and they loved cameras. They had a system called 9.5mm, not 8mm, which was their home movie system. Anyway, Lutz was in charge of research and I kept annoying him by asking whether we could obtain any private footage. There were rumors of these home movies and it turns out a couple of years after the war that *Life* magazine had photos from the home movies. They were black and white. There had been limited release of the photos after the war and limited release in newsreels—only a few shots had been used. What triggered me was a photo that I saw of Eva Braun with a 16mm camera. I immediately thought as a filmmaker, "Where is that film?" It turned out that the film was in the Pentagon and I called them up in Washington and they put me through to a colonel. During this era there was no paranoia so they simply put me through. I just said I was a filmmaker from Australia, which they thought was very interesting! I asked, "Did you capture any film at the Burnhoff?" I had found out that the marines and the signal core—which was an intelligence division—had been the first into the house. The colonel said, "Let me find out and I'll call you back." When he called back he said, "Everything we captured is logged here under data capture and not content capture." He said, "If you can give me some dates I can check it out for you." So we got into the *New York Times* morgue and found the dates of when they went in—April 1945—and he called back to say that there were eight cans of 16mm color film captured in Eva Braun's bedroom and private garden. "Is that what you are looking for?" Jeez, Jesus Christ, that was unbelievable. So there was eight cans and because we had helped locate them, Bill Murphy, the director at the National Archives in Washington, called the Pentagon and said those cans should be here at the National Archive. As we had helped locate them they allowed us to make a copy of the footage. It was amazing. It was footage personally edited by Eva Braun. It had her splices in it. It was mind blowing seeing it for the first time as there was very little footage of Hitler in color, if any. There is a scene in *Swastika* where there is a huge rally—a harvest festival—and that was in color. It did creep people out when we showed people in Cannes. Hitler, in color, in close-shot, shot handheld. That was another thing, no one had seen Hitler *cinema vérité*. Hitler shot by his mistress. It was disturbing for people. "Oh my God, he is an actual human being and not this black and white propaganda figure!" It is still amazing to me when I see the footage.

ME: I thought the footage was astonishing.
   PM: I agree with you. One shot in particular had an effect on me. The shot when he comes out of the house in a dapper suit. It seemed like another person and that is the real Hitler. I should add that they said that swastika was controversial, but it wasn't to me. What was strange about the reaction was that it never occurred to me when making that film that there was an issue whether Nazi Germany was the worst thing that ever happened. To me it was the worst thing that happened in the 20th century. It was a shocking tragedy. It never occurred to me it would be open to debate. With that assumption, I thought that anything on the private life of Hitler was naturally very interesting. It had to be because of what he'd done. People said that I shouldn't have shown him like that and that I shouldn't show him playing with children. Of course, that was the whole point, because if you didn't see him as a human being you aren't going to see the next Hitler coming. Guess what, he was a human being. A terrible one. An evil one; a disastrous person.

ME: It is the humanization of killers that people find difficult, isn't it?
   PM: Yes. That is right. It is the same with serial killers. It is difficult to understand because they are aberrations and when you get these aberrations running a country you

are in real trouble. These individual killers, the police catch them and so on. However, when they are running a country that's when it becomes a disaster. It is irrational to think that horrible people aren't human.

ME: In Swastika *you humanize him. We see him reading the papers, he likes dogs and music. We see him with his mistress—all the things we do—and that shot when you see him in his dapper suit, he resembles a normal middle-aged man. You are not presenting him as this inhuman monster but as ultimately a human being.*

PM: Look, the point is Hannah Arendt said, "The banality of evil." She pointed out how banal these Nazis are. The ordinariness of it is much more terrifying to me, but I get what you say. The ordinariness of the killers like that is really frightening. If the guy had horns and was breathing fire, or came out of a spaceship, some people would find it easier to understand. But they are not. They are the guys next door who suddenly turn. I find it very interesting that most serial killers are generally good-looking and charming guys. They have to be, to do what they do and seduce people into trusting them to that extent.

ME: Or they tend to be respected people in society or affiliated with the local church, for example Denis Rader.

PM: Exactly. If you don't understand this about Hitler then you don't understand what happened. The Hitler the Germans saw was this nice guy playing with kids. The Nazi party made a big effort to normalize Hitler to make him seem like your everyday guy. He wears lederhosen and goes hiking. They really emphasized the ordinariness of Hitler because they knew that was important. So no one suspected him. Even after the war some Germans thought Hitler couldn't have known about the camps because he was too nice of a guy! If only he had known he would have stopped it! That's how convinced they were about him.

ME: That comes across in the documentary because there are scenes when you see the local people revere him as a God-like figure.

PM: Yes, they do. They had visiting days when the local people would come up and walk past him. That's what you see in *Swastika*. That was all part of the brilliant, but evil, propaganda effort. It is hard to believe, and it is distasteful to even say it, but he was a sex symbol as well. Women would go crazy at these rallies. They were like rock concerts.

ME: You showed that in the film.

PM: Yes, there are shots with women going hysterical over Hitler.

ME: It just goes to show how much the German people got sucked into the ideology and propaganda.

PM: They got completely bamboozled and, by the way, there is no excuse for what happened, but there are reasons. One of the reasons was the barrage of modern technology and media that no population had been subjected to before. Radio, print, theatrical spectacle, movies, records … every single thing was directed by Goebbels with the one message: Hitler, the messiah. Hitler, the unknown soldier. Hitler, the saint. Every single thing in your life touched on that, and people didn't say hello, they said "Hail Hitler." A simple thing like that is pretty diabolical and clever.

ME: He used propaganda well and played on the fact that the Weimar Republic was treated harshly after the First World War through the Treaty of Versailles.

PM: Totally, he felt they had been screwed over, so they played heavily on that. It was a huge effort by the Nazis to get the German people to blindly obey. One of the interesting things here is that the top Nazis were literally Pagans. One of the conditions of joining the SS was that you had to give up any religion. You had to be an atheist to join the SS. Your overall allegiance was to Hitler, personally. Hitler was literally becoming God.

ME: That comes across in the documentary with the footage that you show.

PM: Terrifying! One interesting thing is that when they got to power, Hitler had a meeting with Göring and Goebbels and he said, "OK, it is 1933. That's bullshit. That is such a Judo-Christian calendar which is the curse of civilisation." So, they wanted to start with the year zero and change all the calendars in the country. They said no, as they felt it was too soon. They still had a lot of voters to get on their side, like the Catholics. Then during the war, Goebbels tried something else. He changed all the crosses in churches to a swastika. Inside and outside of churches. He changed the stain-glassed stations of the cross to show the rise of Hitler. The SS was reading everyone's mail, which was part of their control, and part of the propaganda, and they saw these women writing to their husbands on the front, alarmed, saying, "Oh my God, they have taken Jesus down and they put the Führer up in the church." They were upset about it. So, they had to take swastikas down, the stain glass down, and put Jesus back! Again, it was considered too early. Hitler was the most radical out of all of them.

ME: An interesting aspect of your film is that there is no commentary and you let the images and footage speak for itself. What made you approach the documentary in that manner?

PM: Well, I wanted to put you in Nazi Germany. I wanted to do to you what basically the Nazis did to the Germans and show at the end the camps like a slap in the face! "Look, this is what happened." I felt if you were subjected to what the Germans were subjected to you would have a better understanding of what happened. I felt that a conventional narration was alienating, or put it this way, it distanced you and tells you what to think. I still think that documentaries that have a voiceover are telling you what to think. I didn't want to do that. I wanted you to experience Nazi Germany and not be lectured. That is a pretty big step and this is where I have to give Sandy Lieberson credit as he totally backed me on the idea when I explained it to him. I said, "No narration," and we are talking 1972 here, so this was a pretty gutsy move as a producer on his part to let me do that.

ME: You touched on it in the last response, the last twenty minutes does feel like a slap in the face. There is a fundamental change in tone, isn't there? Suddenly, the violence is revealed. You have that harrowing footage from the concentration camps. I felt that was a very effective move by you.

PM: Well, thanks, as that was what I was trying to do. When I explain it to you now it seems rather simple yet at the time there was a bit of an uproar! One interesting thing is that I found that song, "Don't Let's Be Beastly to the Germans" by Noël Coward. I felt it was tremendous and I felt it captured the sarcasm that I felt myself. I couldn't find the song anywhere. I found the lyrics. Finally, we tracked down Noël Coward in Switzerland and I called him. I thanked him for speaking to me and then I said that I would like to use his song in *Swastika*. Then Noël Coward paused, and said, "My dear, boy, are you completely mad?" He explained that he got into a whole lot of trouble when he did it. He said a lot of people don't understand satire and a lot people thought that he meant it literally! There was an uproar in England about it. They thought he was telling everyone not to be beastly to the Germans. They were at war with them! The song was banned. The BBC wouldn't play it. There was protests. That's why it disappeared. Churchill, who was a friend of Coward, said, "What I suggest you do is go on a tour of North Africa to the troops and sing to them. That will overcome all of this. People just don't get it." So he said to me, "You are welcome to use it but you are going to get into a lot of trouble. I am just warning you. What happened to me will happen to you." He was right! At Cannes, people were freaked out by seeing Hitler in color and they started yelling at the screen and everything (especially the French). The lights went up and we had to stop the screening! Then they really went nuts when "Don't Let's Be Beastly to the Germans" came on! [Laughs.] That was subtitled ... in French! So you lose the irony! The French were going bonkers! We left it on again—and Sandy Lieberson really stuck by me on this—and I remember film critic Alexander Walker, of the *Evening Standard*, said to me after one screening, "You should really take that song off, it is really inappropriate." Even he was offended. I said that my yardstick was "What would Hitler hate? I think Hitler would hate that song so that's why it is on there."

ME: Clearly people misinterpreted the song and caused upset in the UK. I am also led to believe that the film was originally banned in Germany. Is that true?

PM: That's right. It had an informal ban as opposed to a legal ban. The German distributors were at the screening in Cannes and freaked out. They backed out of the arrangement they had with us. It was just too early for the Germans. It was finally shown in 2009, in Germany. By which time they had seen the home movie footage in other documentaries. The footage we found was first shown in depth in 1973, since then that stuff just about appears in every documentary you ever see about the Third Reich.

ME: You used footage from the concentration camps in the film. Was that a big decision for you to make, especially back in the early seventies?

PM: It wasn't a big decision insomuch as I wanted to show how all this ended up. I wanted to show how the dapper guy in the suit, with his servants and bimbo girlfriend, had ended up with bodies being bulldozed in mass graves [the footage is from the Bergen-Belsen concentration camp]. The British were actually the first into Belsen and they couldn't believe it. It was just unbelievable. By the way, I have been researching for a different film why we didn't bomb the railway tracks into Auschwitz. The Allies knew. There had been photos smuggled out. But no one could believe the extent of it. There are even horrible memos to Churchill and FDR complaining of the whining Jews about the camps. No one believed you could kill six million people like that. By the way, it was accelerating near the end of the war. They were taking trains off the front to take people to concentration camps. That's how insane it was. They were losing the war and they were using trains to ship people to the camps.

I met Nazis after I had shown *Swastika* to them. One was Albert Speer and another Arno Breker. Because we had dubbed the voices—I decided to get lip readers in and try to put some dialogue on the home movies—and I was concerned about that from a historical and authenticity point of view. I didn't want to be criticized for doing that. So the only two people we had contact with who were there were Albert Speer and the architect Arno Breker. So Speer saw the film and he said, "That is exactly what it was like, except that the voice actor you have doing my voice has a cold. I never get colds." I thought if that's the only criticism that I am going to get on authenticity then I have done a pretty good job with the voices. It was really *Dr. Strangelove*: "I never really get colds [affects German accent]." Then we showed the film to Arno Breker—and I don't know if he believed what he was telling me—but he said, "Speaking as a sculptor," and these are his exact words, "I can tell you that those bodies being bulldozed are fake bodies. They are models. Corpses don't move like that if you push them with a tractor. The only place you can have the money and make films like that is in Hollywood. Those are films made in Hollywood." I don't know if he believed that but he was trying to convince me it wasn't real. It was obviously Nazi BS.

Of course some Nazis didn't deny that it had happened and just said that they didn't kill enough. But this issue of authenticity came up at the Nuremberg Trials. They showed a one-hour compilation of atrocities from the concentration camps—and they showed this to all the defendants—and they asked them what they thought. Göring was unapologetic and said similar to what Breker said and how anyone could make a film like that. He said all you would have to do is dig up bodies and shove them back in again with a tractor. That was his reaction. Others were sobbing and crying. But at the beginning of this one-hour compilation film there is an affidavit from the Head of Special Effects at Twentieth Century Fox addressing the authenticity. In it he states that he is a special effects expert and vouches for the authenticity of these films and that they are not fake. The issue of it being fake came up immediately at the Nuremberg Trials.

Saucy, original lobby card from *Mad Dog Morgan*.

ME: Your first feature film was the brilliant Ozploitation flick Mad Dog Morgan. *The film is based on the real-life bushranger and outlaw Dan Morgan. What inspired you to make a film about Morgan?*

PM: A couple of things. First of all I wanted to do a feature film. Though *Swastika* and *Brother, Can You Spare a Dime?* (1975) were feature films—albeit documentaries—I wanted to make a film with actors. I was in London and a family friend called Margaret Frances Carnegie had written a book on Dan Morgan called *Morgan: The Bold Bushranger*. As a kid growing up in Australia, I loved bushrangers. Since *Ned Kelly* had been made it interested me that there was this guy called Mad Dog Morgan. It was also interesting that there was a political aspect to this as well. It turns out that a lot of these outlaws were political—Ned Kelly was as well—against the British colonial powers. Some of them were Irish. There was much more to it than simple gangster stuff.

My closest collaborator on that movie was Mike Molloy, who worked on Kubrick's *A Clockwork Orange* (1972) and *Barry Lyndon* (1975). He had been a newsreel cameraman in Vietnam. My father helped me raise the money and Jeremy Thomas—my editor and close friend—I asked him to produce it. That's how the film came about.

Actually, in those days there was no Australian film industry. As I like to say, cooking on that movie was cooking a whole sheep! There was no caterers on the movie, other than the people who cooked the sheep for us, which, by the way, was bloody good! [Laughs.] It was all uncharted territory. Actually, *Mad Dog Morgan* was one of the first Australian films to get a release here in the States and helped break the ice. It opened in forty cinemas in LA and forty cinemas in New York. That helped start the interest in Australian films, along with other films like *Caddie* (1976), *Picnic at Hanging Rock* (1975) and *The Devil's Playground* (1976). I am proud that *Mad Dog Morgan* was the first Australian film to get a proper release in America. However, they thought the film was too violent. My films polarize people and I don't do that on purpose! That said, Nigel Andrews of the *Financial Times* called *Mad Dog Morgan* a masterpiece. He loved the film. The *New York Post*—who hated Dennis Hopper—said that everyone involved in this movie should be locked up and the key thrown away!

ME: What?!

PM: [Laughs.] Yes, that was the review! So I am going with Nigel Andrews. Generally, the film got very good reviews. *Variety* liked it and Kevin Thomas of the *L.A. Times* said it announced the beginning of the Australian film industry and that something was going on down there. Personally, when I watch the film now, what I really love is the contrast between the violence of humans and the beauty of the landscape.

ME: I wanted to talk about that juxtaposition.

PM: I was very aware of what I was doing. I described it at one point as Francis Bacon figures in a Sidney Nolan landscape, which I think describes the film perfectly.

ME: I think the film captures that beauty.

PM: My cinematographer Mike Molloy had come out of the Kubrick school so the cinematography and landscapes just pop. There are some shots there where we used polarizing filters to make the clouds against the blue sky pop. That stands up for me.

ME: The cinematography and the acting are standout points in the film.

PM: Yes. I love Frank Thring in the film, as well as Dennis Hopper. He seemed to

Dennis Hopper (*left*) on the set of *Mad Dog Morgan* with director Philippe Mora (courtesy Philippe Mora).

be in movies forever till his death. He started the chariot race in *Ben-Hur* (1959). He chopped Kirk Douglas's hand off in *The Vikings* (1958). He was always the decadent Roman leader. He was a lot of fun and I put him in every film I could!

ME: *Am I right in thinking that Morgan is a cult historical figure in Australia, akin to Robin Hood? What is the fascination in Australia with the Dan Morgan story?*

PM: Not as much as you may think. He is regarded as a little bit outré because he killed cops. He was a hero to other bushrangers, by the way. He was a hero to Ned Kelly. The Kelly Gang used to yell out, "Long live, Dan Morgan." It is still historically controversial because he did kill people. He is not a hero to a lot of people. He certainly isn't a hero to the police. Like Ned Kelly there is an ambivalence there.

ME: *Is it his anti-authority stance that has helped fuel the myth/folklore around him?*

PM: Definitely. That scene in the film where he makes the owner of the station give money to the workers, that is true. That's true. He also had aboriginal helpers which was very unusual at that time. He had three or four helpers and I combined them into one with David Gulpilil's character. When I made the film even that was controversial in Australia. The fact that an aboriginal actor had a major part in a film. On one occasion the crew went into a local bar after filming and they wouldn't serve David.

ME: *Really?*

PM: Yeah, and we are talking 1974. Dennis was there and he said, "If you don't serve him then none of us are ever coming back," which would have cost them a lot of money. So they served David and that was the end of that.

When Dennis puts his arm around David's character in the film and says, "I love you, man," that caused puzzlement. Actually, that caused puzzlement as recently as five years ago when the film was shown at the Montreal Film Festival. I did a Q&A and the first question was "Was Mad Dog Morgan gay?" [Laughs.] I said, "I have no idea?! Why?!" Then the guy said, "Well, he puts his arm around the aboriginal and says, 'I love you, man.'"

ME: *What? That's kind of crazy.*

PM: Yeah, I know. So, all that is kind of amusing, but he is still quite a controversial figure. The business about turning his scrotum into a tobacco pouch is true. They make tobacco pouches out of kangaroo scrotums. Basically, they were showing that he was an animal. I get into that a bit in the movie with the Darwinian theories. In those days they thought that criminals were a different species, or it was biological. That's all true. All those names were true, like Professor George Halford [after his death, Dan Morgan's body was put on display by the police before being cut up. His head was sent by a Dr. Henry to Professor Halford for a medical examination at Melbourne University. Such was the outcry by the public at the violations against Morgan's body that a government inquiry was launched.] The film helped bring attention to Mad Dog Morgan and the political aspect of all the bushrangers.

ME: *When you set about writing the screenplay, one of the stories I have heard is that you wrote it on a boat trip from the UK to Melbourne!*

PM: That's right. [Laughs.] It was the most peaceful experience I have ever had writing a script. There was a ship that sailed to Melbourne, via South Africa. We stopped in Cape Town. Each day I wrote that script.

Another interesting historical aspect to the film is that the British Establishment were furious at losing America during the War of Independence. They didn't want that to happen in Australia, which it so easily could have happened. That is one of the reasons why the British were so brutal on these Bushrangers because they wanted to snuff out any trouble immediately. There was the Eureka Stockade [in 1854 there was a rebellion by miners against the colonial forces at Eureka Lead] and there were black Americans working in the gold fields and they were in this rebellion. They arrested a few African Americans and in the transcripts one of these men was dismissed because the judge said that blacks were too dumb to know what was going on! That was the climate!

ME: *Did you try and put in as much authentic detail as you could from Margaret Frances Carnegie's book?*

PM: Yes, I did. If you ever read her book you will see that. Her book is very dry and I did enhance it with stuff. There is no evidence that Mad Dog Morgan read stuff on Abraham Lincoln, yet on the other hand the papers were full of it, so there is no reason why it couldn't have happened. There are a couple of scenes that I cut out. One of them was to do with cannibalism and I can't remember why that was cut out. There was one scene that I do regret cutting out of the film. I cut it purely to keep the length of the film down. The assassin of Lincoln (John Wilkes Booth), well his brother was an actor who came over and acted in Australia. I had Frank Thring playing him as well. I had a scene of him doing Shakespeare in the bush. The remnants of that is the funny scene of the guy dressed in armor. I like those historical juxtapositions.

Bill Hunter was very good in that movie. He is the police officer that is after Dennis. He's the one with the tear tattoo on his cheek. Apparently in those days if you had a tear tattoo on you then you had killed someone.

ME: *Over here, if you have a tear tattoo on you then you have been to Borstal.* [Borstal was a youth detention center in the United Kingdom run by HM Prison Service as a means of reforming violent and seriously delinquent young people.]

PM: Is it? That is interesting.

ME: *With finance in place, how did you go about casting for the lead in the film? I understand that Dennis Hopper wasn't your original choice of actor? How did he become involved in the film?*

PM: He wasn't the original choice. We were quite close to using Jason Miller (*The Exorcist*) and we were very close to getting Martin Sheen. All the actors were really keen on playing the part, by the way.

ME: *I can see the appeal as the character would be interesting to play.*

PM: You are right. Actually, what we liked about Dennis was the fact that he was also a rebel. I didn't know that he had been blacklisted. We called his agent from Melbourne, Robert Raison, and we said "Is Dennis Hopper available?" and Raison almost came through the telephone like in a Tim Burton movie! "He's available, he's available!" We had to meet him, so we flew to New Mexico and there was Dennis, positioned very dramatically at the end of the runway, holding a rifle. As the plane lands I thought, yep that's Mad Dog. The shot of him with the rifle confirmed that. So we got out of the plane and into his truck, which was completely shot up with bullet holes. I said, "What's with all the bullet holes in the truck?" He said, "The Indians have been shooting at me and by the way stay in your hotel after midnight as that's when they start shooting." So all this is in my mind now that this is Mad Dog! We are living it! And sure enough, it was pretty wild around there at that time in the seventies, and sure enough after midnight these Indians began hollering, screaming and shooting! I hid under the bed! The next day I saw Dennis and he had read the script overnight—which we had presented to him the previous day when we arrived. He read it carefully and said he would really like to play the role of Mad Dog Morgan. So it was a combination of method behavior and this guy was wild. It was a good fit. The only technical question I had for him was the accent. I asked him whether he was able to do an Irish accent. I shouldn't have said that because for the rest of the trip he spoke in an Irish accent! [Laughs.] Dennis was a very interesting guy. He was an artist. He did photography. I was an artist, too. I was a painter. So we got on immediately and because I wasn't the Hollywood type, nor was he.

ME: *He had just done* Easy Rider *and he was a maverick and a rebel, wasn't he?*

PM: That was a watershed film. Actually the reason he had been blacklisted was because he did *The Last Movie* and Universal said it was unrealizable. Lou Wasserman, who was God in Hollywood, told him it was a piece of shit, or something to that effect. And Dennis said to Lou, "Get fucked." Well, that was the end of Dennis's career in Hollywood. It took years for him to get back but I started him back on his journey! I'll take credit for that because I got a call from Francis Ford Coppola and he asked me about Dennis and how I had shot the movie on time and on budget. I said we did, and Hopper was hired for *Apocalypse Now* on the back of *Mad Dog Morgan*. If you like *Mad Dog Morgan*, and watch *Apocalypse Now*, you will see that the character he is playing is still Mad Dog. His mannerisms ... everything! The photographer character he plays in the film I see as Mad Dog. Coppola called me again later and said, "Did you have problems with Dennis?" I lied and said no. I asked why. Coppola said, "He's not saying the lines.

He has to put his hands on an ox and say 'Hiroshima mon armour' and he keeps saying 'Nagasaki mon armour!'" I'm thinking, "That's pretty good, what's wrong with that?" Anyway, the story goes—and confirmed to me by Marlon Brando many years later—that Hopper arrived in the Philippines and sees Coppola and Brando talking to each other. By all accounts Hopper said loudly, "Hey, guys. If you have something to say, say it to everyone. We are all making this movie together. Say it to everybody." And Brando turned to Coppola and said, "I don't want to see that asshole again. I am not doing any of my scenes with him and you can sort it out." If you watch *Apocalypse Now*, they never appear in one shot together. It is always with a double. In those dialogue scenes they are not together.

ME: Talk us through the production of the film. You intimated earlier that Hopper was a real handful and that you lied to Coppola.

PM: Look, he was a handful. If I had been an experienced director I probably wouldn't have been able to deal with it. As it was my first feature, I just assumed that they were all like this! It was my first Hollywood star. I would go into his hotel room in the morning and he would be smoking joints and drinking rum. Method acting, as Mad Dog Morgan drank rum. I thought this bastard was going to die. No one can drink like this and live and act in a movie! I wound Jeremy up by saying that Hopper was going to die and destroy our career but I had an idea, which was to cast his face in plastic so when he dies we will have the mask and we can do long shots of him on his horse and schedule all his dialogue immediately and get it out of the way! We were really convinced that he was going to die. I had never seen anyone drink that much. Anyway, Dennis says to me, "What's this shit about casting my face?" I said, "Dennis, I have had this idea of you riding along on your horse and you look up in the sky and you see your own head and it blows up." And Dennis goes, "Far out, man. Far out. That's fantastic. I love it." Anyway, cut to four weeks later and Dennis is as healthy as any of us and I am exhausted, and we have every groupie and pot dealer on the set asking for Hopper. At one point I asked the crew to turn the roadsides around as we were having so many visitors. I said to Dennis that he was fantastic in the film—which he was, as he was always professional once the cameras were switched on, regardless of the state he was in—and he said, "Wait a minute, you haven't shot that scene where you see my head in the sky and it blows up! I love that." So we had to film that and I said, "Thanks, Dennis," and he said, "Wait, there's the scene when I am dead." I said, "Well, don't worry about that as we have the mask. It is a long shot anyway." He said, "No, no, no man, no one plays me dead, man. I play me dead, man." That should have been the title of his autobiography!

ME: You did that scene so well. When I first saw it I thought is that a photograph of Dan Morgan dead or is it Dennis Hopper!

PM: We matched the real shot of Morgan dead.

ME: How did he find Australia?

PM: He loved it. He said that making *Mad Dog Morgan* was one of his great life experiences. Actually, it was invigorating shooting on location. The cave in the film was the real cave where Morgan hung out.

ME: So you looked for actual locations associated with Morgan.

PM: As many authentic locations as we could. We wanted to shoot where Morgan actually ran around.

ME: I loved the performance of David Gulpilil, as Billy.

PM: Personally, I thought he was magic. There is something magic about him. We used him prior to making a lot of movies. He is still a great actor, but when we used him he had only done *Walkabout* (1971) and a couple of TV shows. He is just a natural. There is something magical about his presence in front of the camera.

ME: He did the music as well, didn't he?

PM: He did, yes. He did the didgeridoo. That's all him playing.

ME: I felt that added another layer to the film.

PM: Absolutely. He was a little bit concerned at doing a couple of things in the movie. Apparently, that dance in the film is a dance that no one other than his tribe is allowed to see. I discussed it with him and said, "You are playing a character in a movie who is on the run from the white guys, his tribe and obviously an outlaw, so he is not going to be worried about that sort of stuff." Margaret Frances Carnegie lived in that area and she had an incredible collection of aboriginal artefacts. She showed them to David and he became freaked out because white people weren't supposed to have this stuff. He grabbed this ancient boomerang and pulled out his knife and started carving it. She freaked out! "Don't! David, that's from 1850!" God bless, in the end she said go ahead as he wasn't destroying it, he was trying to fix it.

Original lobby card showing Dennis Hopper (*foreground*) as the outlaw *Mad Dog Morgan* and David Gulpilil as Billy (*background*).

ME: Did he get on with Hopper?

PM: Not initially. He didn't understand Dennis at all. Two weeks into the shoot David disappeared. It was really serious. He had gone walkabout. We called his wife in Sydney and said he had gone walkabout. He just took off into the bush. We were told that the only way to find him was to get aboriginal trackers to go after him. These two incredible old aboriginal men came to see me with long white beards, which were around 2 feet long. They spoke with thick Aussie accents and I took them to the hotel where he was staying. I took them to his room and they started doing weird stuff like smelling the floor, scraping the glass, turning the taps on and off, tasting dust ... they did this for half an hour before they said they were going to find David. So they took off and went into the bush. A day later they came back with David! We had to reschedule shots as this had been a major crisis as one of our stars had disappeared. I said to David, "You can't just walk off in the middle of a shoot. You have caused us an enormous amount of trouble and we were worried about you. Why did you do that?" He said, "I had to talk to the kookaburra and the trees about Dennis." I said, "Really? What did they tell you?" David replied, "Well the kookaburras say that Dennis is crazy!" I said, "David, I could have told you that, mate." [Laughs.]

Anyway, I told Dennis the story and he was mortified because of the trouble it had caused and he went out of his way to be friendly to David. He insisted David sleep in his room, which he didn't, but after that they were fine. Look, none of us had met someone like Dennis before, let alone David. After the shoot Dennis invited David to Taos and David went to visit him in New Mexico.

ME: One of the interesting aspects of the film is that you try to humanize Morgan. You present a flawed but likeable character who is a victim of a violent society and a repressive colonial administration. In fact, he is wrongly jailed.

PM: I think that's the story. I think I was pretty explicit about how I felt the system was and how it created monsters. If you treat people like that then that's what is going to happen. I tried to get some of that into the dialogue when the Doctor and Frank Thring's character Superintendent Cobham talk about criminal minds and how these criminals were viewed as animals at the time. If you treat people like animals for long enough then they will start behaving like it. At that time I was very concerned about social justice and issues like that—I still am. It is not the most popular subject matter to make a film. Most films are made by committee and you can see it, especially in America. They are boring movies. The European system is different because there is more respect for the director as the author. In America, the corporation is the author.

ME: They have so many executive producers on these movies and TV shows now.

PM: It is a joke! Fourteen producers on some films.

ME: Where does the vision from the director come out from that?

PM: I don't think it does. The bigger the budget the more pressure there is, the more frightened everyone is and the more formulaic it becomes.

ME: That's why some film fans love to hark back to eras like the '70s, when film makers were free to make films like Mad Dog Morgan.

PM: Definitely. I didn't know another way, of course.

ME: There are controversial aspects to the film, like the torture and rape scenes, but they are crucial to the plot, wouldn't you agree?
   PM: Crucial to the plot and that is still only one of the few male rape scenes in cinema. It is OK to rape women but it is not OK to rape men, apparently.

ME: Was Dennis Hopper comfortable shooting those scenes?
   PM: Oh, this is funny! He was totally on board but he really wanted to know in detail how I was going to film the rape scene. I said, "Well, they will hold you down and then what I would like them to do is pull your pants down and then Max Fairchild will fumble with his belt and then I will cut." Dennis said, "Okay, so they hold me down, they pull my pants down and Max fumbles with his belt and then you are going to cut?" "Yes, that's it," I replied. So we say action, and Max fumbles with his belt and I say "Cut" and Max looks at Dennis's bare butt and says, "Oh Christ, mate! That is the fucking ugliest thing I have ever seen!" Dennis looks up and says, "No one is more pleased to hear that than me, Max." [Laughs.]

ME: Talk us through the filming of the torture scenes in the film when Hopper is tied to the rack and branded with "M."
   PM: Yes, he is on the rack and he is branded which, by the way, was what they were doing back in the day. They would brand you "M" for malefactor. And that goes back to the point I was making about treating people like animals. They would brand you like cattle.

ME: No wonder he did what he did!
   PM: Yeah! That really is an explanation, I think. I think that is partly why he turned into a monster. Also, at the end with the family when he is feeling sorry for himself, I think Dennis is particularly good in that scene. I liked it when he improvised the line "I'm so lucky to be Dan Morgan." I think Dennis meant his career.

ME: Did you allow Hopper the freedom to improvise on set?
   PM: Yes, absolutely. Though it had to be within the confines of the scene. Look, I even do that now. Many actors aren't trained to improvise. They can't do it. They need to learn the dialogue. The truly, in my opinion, artistic actor can improvise within the context of the scene and often it's just better because it was more authentic. Marlon Brandon got to the point where he refused to learn lines. He would stick the lines on people's foreheads and look at the lines and read it. He felt that was fresh, and it was. There is an acting philosophy where they say "you have to be in the moment." Dennis Hopper was that.

ME: I remember reading a review of the film on the Guardian website and, while they were glowing about the film, I felt they were rather harsh about it when the author commented about the way you directed Dennis Hopper, especially the way you shot him. [The review complained of a lack of close-ups and implied Mora was not experienced enough to have directed Hopper effectively.]
   PM: The thing is, because of the stories about Dennis and how crazy he was, it has distorted people's perception of the film. So, if they read, "Oh he was drunk and on acid," they think he must have been out of control and the director couldn't handle him. That's not what happened at all. This emphasis on scandal and drugs is actually total bullshit in this sense. Everyone in the sixties was doing drugs. I don't mean literally everyone,

but the intelligentsia, the bohemians, the artists … everyday people were doing drugs and drink, just like today. However, none of them made *Easy Rider* or acted in *Mad Dog Morgan* or took great photographs or did great paintings. It is irrelevant. What the artist does when he is not creating is all rather irrelevant. I think it is a red herring that Hopper was out of control because he wasn't at all.

What I did do, in discussion with Hopper, was get him to walk around because I could see that he liked to do that in a scene. I said to Molloy that we need to change the lenses to make the film look wider so Dennis could walk around more. In a tighter set, or with a more uptight director, where it was scripted as a close-up, then you couldn't walk around and you wouldn't get the performance.

One of the best things Hopper did, since we are speaking about improvisation, and that I kept in the film because it was so great, is when he gets onto a horse and falls off and he is still hugging the horse. He slips down underneath the horse and he is still holding on. You couldn't write that! You would have to get a stuntman. I thought that was terrific and it was moments like that that were magic. I was at a dinner where Orson Welles made a speech. This was in New York many years ago and he said, "People ask me what is a director? A director is someone who presides over accidents." I love that.

ME: Were there any other examples of Hopper being difficult on set?

PM: There was another take that caused problems. There is a scene we were shooting, and we had a wind machine going, and Morgan gets disorientated and shoots someone by accident. It was a long take. It was early on in the shoot and I said, "Dennis that was great. Let's do another one." Suddenly he started screaming at me! "What do you think I am, a puppet or something? Do you see a piece of string coming out the top of my head? Do another one? What am I, Pinocchio?" He was going off like this and I was thinking, "Jesus Christ, this is embarrassing in front of the crew." So, I said to Dennis, "Let's discuss this privately," and we walked off into the bush. He put his arm around me and he said, "Do you love me, man?" I replied, "Of course I do. I love you as a person and as an actor. You are a great guy." He said, "OK, let's do another take." I walked out of the bush and we did another take. That was one of the few times he blew a gasket but I think he was testing me.

There was another scene we shot at the end of the movie when he is dying, and he is gurgling. Actors like death scenes because they can milk it. Dennis was gurgling and dying and gurgling and dying. There was an old guy as the doctor and he had one line and he had to lean on Dennis and say he was dead. Anyway, this guy kept saying Dennis was dead when he was still gurgling! So I said, "Saying he's dead doesn't make any sense if he is still gurgling. You have to wait till he stops." The guy then replied, "I needed the job and I didn't tell you that I can barely hear or see. I have ten percent vision." So I said, "What do you suggest we do?" He said, "Get a really long stick and when you want me to say the line poke me with the stick." I said, "That's a bloody good idea!" So we got this bloody long stick and we shoot. Dennis starts to gurgle, gurgle, gurgle and stops and we poke the old guy when Dennis is dead. Perfect. Then Dennis jumps up and went nuts. He starts screaming at me, "I've worked with some motherfuckers in my time. I've worked with Henry Hathaway, motherfucker. I've worked with many motherfuckers, but I've never worked with a director who pokes actors with a stick!" [Laughs.]

ME: One of the most memorable scenes is the dream sequence that is shown in reverse of a man on fire leaping from a cliff into a river. Where did that idea come from?

PM: That is inspired by Cocteau's *Orpheus* (1950). I loved the simple use of reverse motion and cheap tricks used in a special way, as Cocteau did. I was thinking of that and I had the idea of setting a guy on fire and having him jump in water and filming it in reverse. How surreal would that be? I put that in as a piece of artistic license as Morgan's nightmare, which turned out to be a very dangerous stunt. If you watch the making of the film, *To Shoot a Mad Dog*, you see the stunt went wrong and the stuntman got burnt a bit. I hate stunts because they are dangerous and the simplest of things can go wrong. It is a very strange scene because you see fire coming out of water.

ME: *I understand the film's violence was censored?*
PM: Yes it was.

ME: *Were you annoyed with that?*
PM: Of course. It is a nightmare when television stations edit them. The film has been shown all over the world but you have no idea what they are doing. You can't monitor it and they butcher films, mine included. The very important scene is when Mad Dog Morgan witnesses the man's head being blown up at the beginning. That is terribly important because it traumatizes him. It also traumatized the audience at the time because it was unusual to see that kind of violence. That particular scene is cut out of a lot of versions, though I am pleased it is now being show in its original version. The film was shortened originally in America as some distributors like to do that. I did the

Original lobby card of *Mad Dog Morgan*, showing Dennis Hopper as the titular killer.

cuts myself. So the American version is slightly different from the European version. The version in the UK is the longer version.

ME: Upon completion of the film I understand Hopper went to visit the grave of Morgan and got himself deported!

PM: Yes, that is true. For some reason my mother was with him! I can't remember why, but she must have visited the set. She liked him and he liked her. Hopper wanted to visit Morgan's real grave and pour a bottle of rum on it. My mum witnessed all of this. Hopper got two bottles of rum. One for him to drink and one to pour on Morgan's grave. He was still dressed as Morgan as we finished shooting. He drove off with my mum to the grave but the Victorian police—who were the police force who killed the real Morgan—were keeping their eye on Hopper because they wanted to nail him again. The Victorian police stopped Dennis when he crossed the border into Victoria—just like in the movie—and he was arrested. The next day in court the judge said, "I am looking at your alcohol report here and I can tell you that you are clinically dead!" He was also told he will never be allowed to drive a car in the state of Victoria again. Shortly after he had to leave. Actually, it must have been sorted out years later because he came back to Australia to play Frank Sinatra in a little film about Sinatra coming to Australia and fighting the Unions. It was called *The Night We Called It a Day* (2003). But that story is true about Hopper and he did pour a bottle of rum on the grave of Dan Morgan.

3

The Black Panther
An Interview with
Ian Merrick

As this book demonstrates, the United States has a long tradition of tapping into true-crime stories for the sole purposes of commercial gains, exploitation, cinema or even entertainment. Films like *The Boston Strangler* (1968), *Helter Skelter* (1976), *Henry: Portrait of a Serial Killer* (1986), *Summer of Sam* (1999) and *Zodiac* (2007) are just a few examples that support this idea. In the last few years there has been another boom in films relating to killers, as seen with *My Friend Dahmer* (2018), *Extremely Wicked, Shockingly Evil and Vile* (2019) and *Once Upon a Time in ... Hollywood* (2019), to name but a few. Over the last thirty and forty years, U.S. cinema has seen sudden spikes in films being made about killers such as Gacy, Dahmer and Bundy before fading out of fashion only to spike again a decade or so later, just like we are witnessing now. U.S. television regularly looks to true-life crimes for inspiration, with many TV movies being green-lit and produced since the eighties. Films and series such as *The Atlanta Child Murders* (1985), *The Capture of the Green River Killer* (2008), *Citizen X* (1995), *To Catch a Killer* (1992), *The Deliberate Stranger* (1986) and *D.C. Sniper: 23 Days of Fear* (2003) are just a few examples of content produced for home-viewing. In the U.S. there is a fascination with serial killers that goes way beyond their crimes: a fascination to understand these killers and the dark underbelly of American society they operated in. In the U.S., serial killers are marketable. Serial killers, or infamous killers, have become iconic characters that appeal to large swaths of the movie-going public, as shown with the latest film released on the Bonnie and Clyde story, *The Highwaymen* (2019).

In contrast, Britain has only produced five feature-length films that delved into the murky world of mass murderers or serial killers (if you exclude the Jack the Ripper films): *10 Rillington Place* (1971), *The Black Panther* (1977), *Cold Light of Day* (1989), *The Young Poisoner's Handbook* (1995) and *Peter: A Portrait of a Serial Killer* (2011). On the small screen, British producers have been more open to mini-series about killers, yet the results tend to be de-sanitized accounts of the crimes of killers such as Fred and Rosemary West, Harold Shipman, Ian Brady and Myra Hindley and usually told through the eyes of the investigative detective leading the inquiry. Yet, unlike America, the notion of depicting (serial) killers as a form of entertainment is treated largely as taboo by mainstream audiences. Even 40 years after the crimes of Ian Brady and Myra Hindley, some audiences were still repulsed at the notion of watching a drama based on their crimes (the two-part *See No Evil: The Moors Murders* [2006] and *Long-*

ford [2006]). While such shows as the aforementioned, and works like *Harold Shipman: Doctor Death* (2002), did ignite criticism in some sections of the media and with nothing-better-to-do-with-their-lives-other-than-complain *Daily Mail* readers, such TV movies did pray on audiences' morbid interest in this subject matter. Though the material had to be tame in content and, more importantly, seen from the viewpoint of detectives, relatives, penal reformers or social workers, with none being told through the eyes of the killers themselves.

Many British moviegoers enjoy serial killer flicks, especially fare created across the pond (as Chuck Parello pointed out to me during our interview), and the influx of television productions in the last 20 years is testimony to this. However, there is a vocal proportion of British society that in the past has felt the need to get into a moral panic the moment anything contentious hits the screens (whether televisual or cinematic). If played straight, and not too controversial, then any controversy is short-lived. Dare to make anything gritty, realistic, hard-hitting and disturbing, and you'll be vilified, hunted down and forced to flee the country with a torrent of abuse ringing in your ear. That's exactly what happened to director Ian Merrick after he made the disturbing and unflinching biopic *The Black Panther* in 1977, based on the mass murderer Donald Neilson.

Neilson was a ruthless armed robber who terrorized Britain between 1971 and 1974 with a series of burglaries and violent robberies that culminated in the killing of three sub-postmasters and the brutal beating of a sub-postmistress. Neilson's greed and violence went to a new low when he kidnapped seventeen-year-old heiress Lesley Whittle from her bedroom and kept her captive down a drainage shaft in Kidsgrove, Staffordshire. When the $50,000 ransom was not paid, the police located her hanging naked from a wire, though there is some conjecture as to whether Neilson killed her deliberately or by accident. Neilson was caught and arrested in 1975 in dramatic circumstances. Two

Original poster artwork for Ian Merrick's controversial thriller *The Black Panther*. The film caused a wave of controversy in Britain at the time of its release, with Merrick publicly attacked and vilified by the British media, leading to his eventual emigration to the U.S. (courtesy Ian Merrick).

police officers saw him acting suspiciously and called him over to question him. Pulling out a shotgun, Neilson took the officers captive in their police car and demanded to be driven to a town called Rainworth. During the journey, the officers managed to distract Neilson and attempt to overpower him. Coming to a halt outside Junction Chip Shop in Rainworth, members of the public came to the aid of the officers and helped apprehend Neilson. He was later sentenced to life imprisonment and died in 2011.

At the time, the case sent shockwaves through the UK, so when Ian Merrick decided to make a film about Neilson's crimes he had no inclination of the backlash he would face. Told with accuracy and with attention to historical fact, Merrick's film follows the life and crimes of Neilson as he lives the double life of a family man and serial robber before progressing into a full-blown killer.

Although accused of exploitation by the tabloids, the film is anything but exploitative. It is gritty and uncompromising, and Merrick avoids exploitation tropes, instead painting a picture of a disturbed and unhinged man, who, as an ex-solider of the British army, took his military fantasies into the domestic realm. Merrick and his writer, Michael Armstrong, adhered to Neilson's story as accurately as possible by using witness testimonies, court documents and known facts relating to the case. Even Whittle's death is not shown, due to the ambiguity of events that resulted in her tragic demise. Though the film is graphic in its portrayal of the murders that Neilson committed on the sub-postmasters, they are shot by Merrick without sensationalism and are scarily realistic. Merrick's view of Britain is like the titular character of the film; a crumbling shell of its former self. Neilson, like Britain, reminisces about his former military glory, glories that have now faded.

Shot with beautiful contrasting images of the English countryside and the decaying, grey drabness of England's towns during the '70s, and coupled with minimal dialogue and a standout performance from Donald Sumpter (now seen in *Game of Thrones*), who barks his minimal lines as if still in some private army, this brilliant, faithful dra-

A masked Donald Sumpter (*Game of Thrones*) holding up a sub–post office in Ian Merrick's *The Black Panther* (courtesy Ian Merrick).

matization of Neilson's crimes became the victim of a vile witch-hunt upon its initial release. An angered media sought about not only to destroy the film, but to ban it and ensure it would be a commercial flop. Derided by Sue Lawley on BBC's *Newsnight* even though she hadn't seen the film, Merrick became a pariah in his own country. Local councils jumped on the hysteria caused by Lawley's comments and banned the film in their jurisdictions.

Merrick escaped the mauling by heading to America, and the film sunk into obscurity until it was rereleased by the British Film Institute (BFI) thirty-five years later to much critical acclaim in the UK. A fabulous work, I had the pleasure of talking to director Ian Merrick about his superb crime thriller and the fall out upon its release. I thank him for talking so openly about not only the film but the painful memories that followed the film's release.

Matthew Edwards: The Black Panther *is a wonderful piece of British cinema and I am glad the British Film Institute rescued it from obscurity.*

Ian Merrick: It was a tragedy that *The Black Panther* was my first film. I did a fantastic job. I didn't know I had that capability or talent. Perhaps if I had stayed in England I would have had a career eventually but at that time no one would touch me after I had made *The Black Panther*. I would try and get an agent, for instance, and some of them would give me an appointment and I'd go to their office, sit there for half an hour and someone would come out and say, "Are you Ian Merrick?" I would reply, "Yes," and they would walk away. That happened twice. There was one guy called Ken Red [agent] and he did that to me. It was cruel and stupid. I doubt I could have got another film going anyway because the country was dead at the time [Britain was undergoing a severe economic crisis during the late seventies] and nothing was going on. I just wanted to get back to America as I was burned out! [Laughs.]

ME: I understand that you were based in America prior to returning to England to make The Black Panther.

IM: I had done an apprenticeship in photography in London, on Fleet Street. I went to America because I had just started skydiving and California had plenty of sunshine and I had broken up with a girl! So I left for the U.S. and while there I bumped into a chap called Barry Mahon and they had based *The Great Escape* on him. He was in New York making low-budget children's films and exploitation films and he met me out of the airport and asked me why I was thinking of going back to England? I was on my way back as I had moved from California to New York. He said, "Come and work for me!" So that's how I got involved in film.

ME: You produced a few films in America and then you tried to employ that low-budget guerrilla-style/method of filmmaking by forming your own film company. How easy was that at the time?

IM: Forming a company was OK. I had a colleague that I had known from skydiving that had run a couple of companies in England and he came in to help me. He put in £10,000 and I put in £10,000, and that's what we started up with. He did it as an act of friendship. He wasn't involved in making the films but he had a banking background and we were able to get a further £15,000 from the bank. So once we got £75,000 from a private investor we had £100,000 to make the film. That was probably a lot of money in 1976, though it was still low-budget.

ME: *The Black Panther was originally intended to be a fictional piece called* The Park Keeper *about a commando assassin that slips back into society. How did that morph into a true-life drama based on the killing spree of Donald Neilson?*

IM: That happened because I had *The Park Keeper* about a fellow who had been in the Army Special Services as a trained commando assassin and slides back into society as the park keeper who eventually kidnaps a girl. It was similar to the book *The Collector* by John Fowles. That's what inspired my original idea but I couldn't afford to make that. So I went to Stanley Long, who I sold a number of American films to, and he told me he had started a new distribution company called Alpha Films with his brother Peter. He listened to my idea and read the synopsis and he said he would give the film distribution but only if I did the real story of *The Black Panther*. I knew a little bit about what had happened so I decided to bite the bullet and do it otherwise I would run out of money and I'd be dead. [Laughs.] At least if he gave me distribution and with my £20,000 I could go to a studio. At the time, the country was going down the tubes, Elstree was dead. It had no films in there and they were going broke. I said to them, "What's your overheads?" I asked them for two studios for four months for £5,000 and they took it! I had a whole studio to myself. I took that money and I built the scene with the tunnel. I was sitting at the top of it, looking down with the cinematographer, Joe Mangine, and I thought this was a fantastic shot! We had put a pan of water down there so it sparkled a bit. We also built Donald Neilson's lair in the house that he lived. Actually, we did the front room of the house on location in Sheppard's Bush. The house was for sale so we rented it from the estate agent. The lead into the tunnels was a real sewer and then we cut into the studio tunnel. So that's how we did that.

ME: *How did you and Michael Armstrong approach writing the script? I understand that you went to great lengths to ensure accuracy and that it was legally sound?*

IM: We were concerned about the legalities but we needn't have been worried. You can't libel anyone if you tell the truth. Michael says when writing the script that he wanted to be meticulous but he took some artistic license, not in the story itself but in the way Donald Neilson acted, but it was fairly near to him. That was the other condition that made me go for it was that Stanley said, "We have a writer [Michael Armstrong] and we will pay for him if you use him." That's how they introduced me to Michael. He got to it and he went off at a tangent. We agreed to look at the first twenty pages and he had written something from a more exploitation angle. I said to Michael that this was no good and that we had to stick to the story. I said the first five pages are great but then he lost it. So he went back and did it again and it was perfect the second time. He did do a great job. It was a little overwritten but I prefer that than being underwritten. He is a great writer though a bit on the dark side! He has done stuff like *The House of Long Shadows* and *Mark of the Devil*. He did a few naughty and dark subjects! He's a great guy and I like him a lot.

ME: *I think it is commendable that you didn't fall into the trap of making a cheap exploitation cash-in on the case.*

IM: That's part of my make-up. You can only do what you are thinking. You can only do what you are. I knew I could do something as equally good as *The Collector*. Something that was well shot with great cinematography, and I knew with Michael's screenplay that flushed out the elements, which I wanted, which was the truth. It was a huge discovery for me that I had this talent and I could pull the film off. I was very lucky getting Donald Sumpter as Donald Neilson because he gave the film gravitas. I was ten days away from shooting—or when I planned to shoot, because I didn't have all the money, though I kept telling everyone that I had. I believed the money was somewhere out there in the universe and I wouldn't allow any negativity to come in and that a miracle would happen and I'd get the money. So, I still didn't have an actor. So I called up Mary Selway, who I originally wanted for my casting director, but she was busy doing another film. She said she couldn't help me and said, "Sorry, goodbye." Then, twenty minutes later, the phone rang and it was Donald Sumpter. He sounded like a sinister guy on the phone and I asked him to come on around to my place in the West End, in London. He said he could come over in an hour! Sure enough, I waited with trepidation but when I opened the door I saw Donald Neilson "The Black Panther" standing there. Donald Sumpter had thought it through and put on the clothes. I invited him in and I didn't want to give him a test but I got him to pretend to look at his maps on my table and he snapped right into the part! I said, "Don't do anymore, you've got the part!" [Laughs.] That's how I got Donald. It was a sure stroke of luck. It was one of those gifts that come out of the blue. It was thanks to Mary Selway. She knew real actors. It is all about luck and who you know.

Money I didn't have, but I had a crew. We had a pre-production crew. My cinematographer hadn't arrived yet. He had called up asking if I had the money and I said, "Yes." Joe said, "You are not bullshitting me, are you?" And I said, "No." But I didn't have it! So he came over. Before he did so, I had this location guy who kept asking me whether I had the money or not. I thought, "Why does he keep asking me this?" The location guy said he knew someone who has money to invest in the film. I said, "No, no, no, I've got the money." I thought he was trying to test me out because if I said I hadn't, he would tell the crew and they would all be gone. The next day, about the fourth time of asking me, he quit. It was two days before we had to start the operation. He had given me the number so I called the number—the location manager had gone so I thought I couldn't lose anything now—and he was straight up. He was a broker. I said I hear you are interested in investing in the film and he said, "Yes." I said, "Look, I need £75,000 and I have four people who want to do it and I am starting shooting on Monday and if you have all the money then that's what I want. Someone with all the money." I said he needs to have two things: all the money and he had to take the meeting on Monday morning. He said yes and that he would be there. So I knew this lovely Indian Princess—a real Indian Princess, too—and she asked me who this guy is. I said he is an Irishman. She said, "Are you having any whisky there?" I said, "No, because I don't drink." She said I was a crazy idiot. She came around with a bottle of whisky and I got the money by lunchtime!

ME: *That's amazing.*

IM: Yes, it was amazing. I did a good presentation. Money was burning a hole in the guy's pocket and the money invested was hot money, that's for sure! However, he cut me short by £5,000 at the end. That was the reason why I lost the film to the liquidator in the end. I went about a year waiting for the film to open up in 300 cinemas with EMI. We opened it at the CIC cinema and it ran for twelve weeks. We made money there. We were just £5,000 short of paying back all the debt to the suppliers, etc. A distributor wouldn't give it to me. I said, "Look, you can make foreign sales, can't you?" They said, "No." But do you know what they were planning? They wanted me to go down. They wanted me to crumble and they knew that video was coming along. About six months later video opened and I went broke. The film went into liquidation and Stanley Long and his brother, Peter, went to the liquidator and bought the film for £2,000. They made three million pounds with video. The film had all this publicity and then video came along and everyone bought it. That was my money!

However, I did buy the film back. In 1985, Stanley Long was in trouble and so they sold it to me for $50,000. Can you believe that? I had to buy my own film. I didn't have a partner and I immediately sold it to Vestron, and I got my money back.

ME: It sounds like you had a tough time during pre- and post-production. How did the shoot go? Did you encounter any problems?

IM: What was lucky, because everyone was out of work due to the economic crisis, I ended up with good people. I got Teddy Darvas, an Academy Award winning editor, I got a brilliant assistant director called Barry Langley and the most professional crew. That was my biggest lesson in filmmaking: surround yourself with professionals. I had one challenge from Donald Sumpter. I already had it in my mind how I was going to film a particular scene and cut it and he got all stroppy and said he wanted to shoot it the way it says so in the script. I said, "No, Donald. I have this scene already figured out. You don't have to do this shot." He said, "I want to do the shot." I said, "Look, I am the director. If you want to do it your way I'll wrap the set right now and we will all go home and that will be the end of the film." And I meant it! I knew I had to say that otherwise I'd lose and it was right in front of the crew. He thought for a second or two and then said, "All right."

ME: What was the shot?

IM: It was something to do with getting in the car. I can't quite remember the details but I recall it was something to do with getting into a Morris 1100. Actually, that

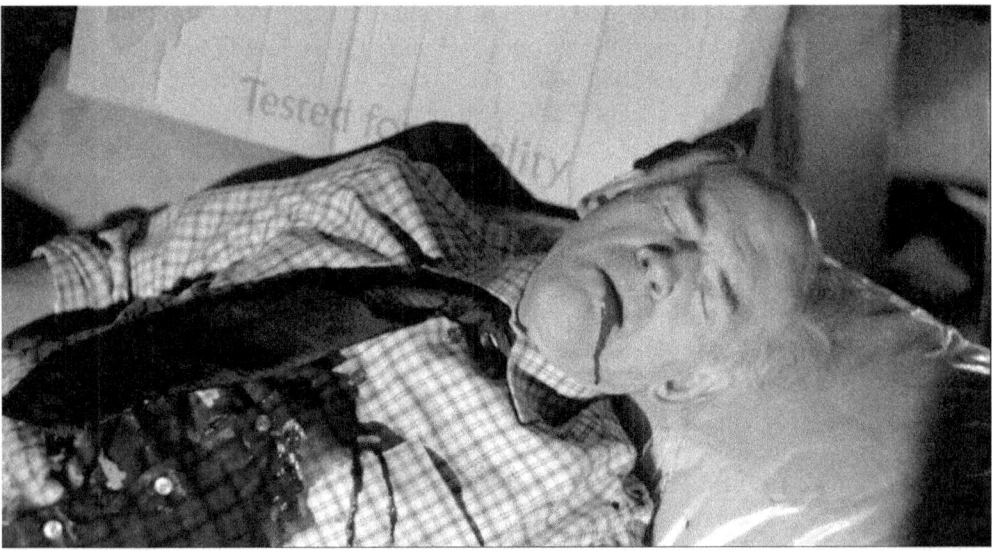

Veteran actor Michael Barrington comes to a grisly end in Ian Merrick's brilliant and harrowing *The Black Panther*. **Donald Neilson murdered four people during a series of violent robberies of sub–post offices in England from 1971 to 1974 before kidnapping and murdering teenager and heiress, Lesley Whittle (courtesy Ian Merrick).**

reminds me of another incident during the filming that I didn't know about. That car, we did the establishing shot during the first week of filming. Then we had one shot to finish and it kept getting put off and off. I said, "When are we going to do that other shot with the car?" I was told, "Don't worry, we will do it soon." You know what happened? They had gone and rented the car from the guy who owned it and took it back to him every night. Then the bloody car got stolen during the middle of the shoot. Eventually it turned up with the gearbox and engine stripped out and we had to pull the car with rope during that final scene! [Laughs.]

The press turned up on another occasion. They heard the film was being shot and about twenty of them turned up and that was a nasty scene. I told them to "fuck off." I told them that if they wanted a real story to make an appointment. They did eventually go.

ME: *What is interesting about the film is how you present Neilson's actions in an undramatic way. You simply present his crimes in a matter-of-fact way until his eventual arrest. Why did you choose this approach?*

IM: I felt that because there was very little dialogue, and that he was on his own all the time, so I wanted him to be very extroverted and have very exact movements. Donald Sumpter did the rest. That was his interpretation of the character and I was happy with that. One thing I believe is that if you have a good actor you let him act. That's how that came about. It was a very intense way of acting.

ME: *Sumpter's portrayal of Neilson is brilliant because he plays him as someone who sees himself as a criminal mastermind and an exceptional soldier yet ultimately he is a vile bully—especially towards his family—and his plans always go awry!*

IM: They did! He must have felt he was jinxed. He had a terrible internal fury going on because his whole life had been a disaster. I had a background which was working class/middle class and I met a lot of these people who are desperate who came out of the Second World War. Britain was a dark place. Neilson had an unhappy childhood and was bitter. He always felt he had been screwed over by the establishment. He got conscripted into the army and he was shipped out to Cyprus and Africa. This was exotic for him and he had a gun. This was before he began his crimes in England. I am sure they were torturing these terrorists in Cyprus when they caught them. He would have saw all of that and that would have given him a false sense of power. When he came back to England and was just dumped back on the streets it shook him up. The country was grim then. His bitterness grew.

ME: *He is unhinged in the film....*

IM: My view is that he definitely crossed the line and lost it. He did lose it. That last scene when he forgets to put his mask on when he goes down into the tunnel. When he did that it was another nail in his coffin. Whether he pushed her [Lesley Whittle] or whether she fell off by accident, I don't know.

ME: *You leave it ambiguous in the film, though you lean more towards the idea that he murdered her by pushing her off.*

IM: It is implied. You don't see him push her but you cut to her hanging and swinging. You see him looking over the edge with an awful look on his face before he rushes off.

ME: *There is a chilling scene earlier when he is going through his scrapbook after his first kill and he grins. You show him as a man who has no remorse for his crimes.*

IM: You mean the part when he is looking in his clippings book? Yes, we had to embellish that a bit. I think he collected photographs and he definitely hankered over his past. He did have photographs of his days in the military but I think I introduced the idea of the album as a way of keeping a log of his actions—and I am not sure if he actually did that. I thought if he kept clippings of his military days he would keep newspaper cuttings of his crimes.

ME: *We touched on this briefly earlier, but you allude to the incompetence of the police and the collusion with the press. Is it fair to say that the police's and media's handling of the case played a big role in Lesley Whittle's death?*

IM: Absolutely. She would have never died if the police had done their job properly or had the right experience. The offer of help from Scotland Yard was ignored and the West Midlands Police has always been seen as a corrupt force. What actually happened was that—and I couldn't say this in the film—someone in the police knew of the meeting and tipped off the press. A police officer tipped off the press and that's how the press turned up at the same time the brother of Lesley Whittle was waiting with the money. Obviously, Donald Neilson saw that because in the film I show the press turn up and the brother go berserk. They did turn up and they caused the first exchange to fall apart. Then the second time was when the brother had to deliver the ransom to the meeting point in a park but gets lost in his car. Instead, Neilson sees a lovers' car and he flashes a light, thinking it is the brother with the money, and they flash their lights back and drive off. The lovers thought it was a snooper. This is all a balls-up by the police because they should have roads closed off or someone to redirect the traffic. So that was a screw up. There was also a helicopter that came from somewhere and Neilson heard it and got spooked—newspapers and the press have confirmed this.

The police also said that they couldn't find any clues in the park. When it was all over, and they had found the body of Lesley Whittle, Scotland Yard did get involved and they went up to that park and on the first day there they found forty major pieces of evidence. They found the tape recorder, food supplies, stuff that was thrown away by Neilson. It was unbelievable. The police and the press were culpable. Big time.

ME: *Do you think that because you questioned the role of the media in the film that this played a part in the savage response the film received at the time?*

IM: Yes, and there are two things going on there. One, I was an upstart. Remember, Richard Attenborough did *10 Rillington Place*, in which he is seen garroting, gassing and raping this woman. It was gross. They knighted him for that. However, he was part of the establishment and I was not. I was an upstart. I remember going to the British Academy of Film for members and they had Brian Forbes there giving a speech about how terrible the British Film Industry was and how nothing was going to happen. I stood up in that meeting because I got fed up of hearing them all groaning and moaning and I told them to get off their butts and get a bit of money and make a film. "Whoa, whoa, who is this guy talking?" and "Here is the fella who likes the sound of his own voice" was the reaction. Anyway, when I went downstairs for refreshments, Brian Forbes was there pouring himself some coffee. I went over to him and said, "Brian, you can make a film for around £100,000." And he said, "I think you will need a bit more than that, dear boy." Two months later I was making the film. There is no question that I showed them up and they did not like that. I was the upstart and an outsider. The press also wanted to make me the bad guy instead of making them look like the bad guy. They were definitely culpable and so were the police. The police wanted to shut me down.

When we showed the film in Birmingham I remember that the police were there and the local city council officials turned up with the police. The screening finished and up popped the police from their seats. They were waiting to jump on me and arrest me for something. They were angry. The police had leaked the ransom point where the ransom was due to be paid. They leaked that to the press and the press were there. That's what threw Donald Neilson off. They thought I was going to say that. I merely implied that in the film. I implied they were lackadaisical and inefficient. They should have got Scotland Yard involved.

ME: You appeared on BBC TV's Newsnight *with Sue Lawley. What happened?*

IM: Sue Lawley got me on her show to talk about *The Black Panther* and she lied. She had never seen the film. She said she had, but she hadn't. She said it was "sick." She had been put up to it by the police. Actually, at that point, neither myself nor the distributor had allowed anyone to see the film, let alone the BBC! The audience had around 14 million viewers and it was a disaster. The *Newsnight* interview pretty much sealed mine and the film's fate. The distributors got alarmed and backed down and the 300-print release, which was ready to go and fully paid for, was canceled. I had been hanging around in England for a year without any money and waiting for this release. With the backlash from the press and local councils banning the film—which they did in Hull—I decided to return to America to pursue my filmmaking career. However, the government wrote me a letter saying that they didn't want me leaving the country until my finances had been fully investigated! They did not want me to leave the country. They said they were not issuing an order on me but they implied that if I did try to leave they would issue a stopping order. That is truth! I had to send in all these reports and what had happened and why the company went bankrupt. They wanted to investigate me! I don't know who put them up to that? The police? They were looking to give me great trouble and I was actually so broke that when I finally went back to America I slept in a friend's office for six months. My friend would bring me sandwiches and food and let me sleep on his coach. I don't know how I got out of that! It was grim. You have no idea what they did to me.

ME: The film was effectively banned then.

IM: Yes, it was. That's the right words, "effectively banned." I have press cutting demanding that the film be banned. I wish that someone would bring this up about how I was illegally treated and how the police were corrupt and how they stitched me up.

ME: They went for you, didn't they? It was a personal attack.

IM: Of course, and I had a phone call from the Post Office Police saying, "Do drop this, or else." They tried to threaten my life. They couldn't get me legally so what else does that mean? Were they going to beat me up or I'll be involved in an "accident"? This is the truth.

ME: I understand that the National Federation of Sub-Postmasters also took exception to the film and tried to ban it!

IM: Yes, because they were being bullied by the press and the police. Most likely the press. The press wanted the story that this is the vilest film ever made and it had to be banned and that I was telling lies and that I was trying to make the press look bad when in fact they had nothing to do with it. They have no idea how they damaged my life and my career.

ME: I think your film touched a few nerves.
   IM: I am sure of that.

ME: Can you give one example of a nerve that it touched?
   IM: Do you mean the apathy or the darkness of those psychopaths and that there are lots of those around?

ME: Yes, but I was thinking more about the police's incompetence and their corruption.
   IM: Yes, that was probably the biggest thing. There is a scene in the film with David Swift, who played the Detective Chief Superintendent, when the ransom is supposed to be happening and he is laying back in his chair with a lethargic look.

ME: He is very dismissive, isn't he?
   IM: Yes, then the brother comes in and says, "How the hell did this get out?" He tried to explain it away because they massively cocked it up.

ME: I think it is despicable how they went for you.
   IM: It is despicable the way they treated me. The British Academy of Film, I sent them a copy of *The Black Panther*, because as a member we are all allowed a members screen. That is every director's right. I sent the film to them and there was a lot of subterfuge. I thought I would hear from them in a couple of weeks and a month/six weeks went by and I had heard nothing. So I called them up and I got to speak to the secretary Johnny Goodman, and he is not really a film guy but they get these jobs, and he said, "Hasn't anyone written to you?," and I said, "No!" He said, "Nobody has told you?," and I said, "No!" He said, "Well, listen old boy, this is not a film that the members wish to see." A week before they had been showing this crap film about the Sex Pistols raping this girl and shitting in hats on the stage. That is the sort of film they do show and mine isn't. I was staggered by that. I did show in the film kids fighting on the street and how impersonal Donald Neilson was to the inner-city decay. Maybe that upset them! Though, I had a right to screen it! It still goes on in the UK. The BBC won't show it—I've tried umpteen times.

ME: It is a shame that the film was vilified and died because there is so much brilliance in the movie. I love the way that you contrast the beauty of rural England with shots of grim urban decay—a country in decline. Was that your intention?
   IM: Yes, you picked that up! Great. Yes, I wanted to show the idyllic of the country and the squalor of the cities. I wanted to show the migration of blacks to the UK and how this was seen as an irritant. Britain was a country in decay at the time. I wanted to show how the country had been destroyed with these monstrous concrete buildings.

ME: Did you experience any opposition from the victims' families?
   IM: No, I did talk to the brother but he didn't want to get involved. He just told us to go ahead and do it. He knew that something like this [a film] was likely to be done. It was a few years after the event. It's not as if we did it the next day. He wasn't angry or unreasonable. He understood but he didn't want to be involved. I did him a courtesy talking to him. I tried to waylay any fears so I didn't have any hassle or lawsuits from

them. If they had gone to a lawyer there is nothing they could have done anyway as I was making a film based on a real-life story. If I defamed them then they would have had a case. I knew I wasn't going to do that because there was nothing to defame them about.

ME: Did you find distribution in the U.S.?

IM: In America, they thought it was a nice film, though hard to distribute because it was "too British." I'd like for it to sell in America and I showed it to Netflix and they said it was "great." However, in terms of picking it up, they said it doesn't fit. It's not an important film in America. It is a respected film and it has received good reviews in the U.S.

ME: I thought Debbie Farrington was great as Lesley Whittle. How did she become attached to the film?

IM: In the early stages of coming back to England, I had bought a place in the South of France, and I thought I would commute to London and America. Other directors do it. That's another tragedy, I lost that place because I couldn't keep up the payments due to this film. Anyway, I was at Mother's house [in England] and I see this girl on TV playing this young girl. She was actually twenty-five when we made the film! In the film she plays Lesley Whittle who was seventeen at the time. I thought she was a good actress so I got in touch with her. I literally saw her on television six months before.

ME: Did she have any problems doing the full-frontal nudity?

IM: No, she knew that was part of what had to happen. At the time it might have been a little bit risky but nowadays you see that sort of thing all the time. Maybe I should have put a slip on her but we were doing the real thing and I thought it was authentic. It says a lot about what Neilson was like. He wasn't sexual. In one sense he had these good British ethics and he applied a lot of this to what he did. On the other hand he was cold and callous and didn't think anything of killing people because he had apparently shot and killed people when in Cyprus and Africa. His unit had been very active. Despite his callousness his other characteristics still crept in.

ME: The British Film Institute has really got behind the film.

IM: Yes, that blew me away and it is all thanks to a guy called Sam Dunn. They remastered the film and I got a brand new film! The BFI helped me get sales in France, Italy and Japan. It does sell.

ME: I believe the film is a classic of British cinema.

IM: It helped that I had full control during the making of the film. I had no distributor or producer breathing down my neck because I had raised the money myself. I raised the money independently and all I got was that people thought I was a crook! I raised the money for a film during the greatest depression the country had ever known! All in all, there was a lot of substance to the story, especially Neilson's military days. He did drive a jeep around and he did walk about in military outfits. It is a wonder he wasn't stopped beforehand. It is unbelievable that he was on the loose for so many years. Sadly, if I had had the chance to make another good film that was equally as important then it may have helped *The Black Panther*.[1] Sadly that never happened.

4

Angst

A Conversation Between
Director Gerald Kargl
and Marcus Stiglegger

A genre such as the thriller is virtually non-existent in Austrian cinema. Well known especially for their experimental productions, everyday topics and problematic dramas, Austrian films are comparable to the art films of New German Cinema or to the kind of German TV movies that share a similar "anti-cinematic" take on the medium. Therefore, it should come as no surprise that Gerald Kargl's psycho-thriller *Angst* (*Fear*, 1983) has rarely been distributed commercially on videotape. Even today this disturbing film—which follows the bloody course of a twice-convicted serial killer through the Austrian countryside—can hardly be seen.

Angst is based on an actual case of triple murder, the "Kniesek case," which is as famous in Austria as the Fritz Haarmann and Peter Kürten trials in Germany, or the Ed Gein case in America. Like these and other serial killers, Werner Kniesek from Salzburg—who killed three people out of pure lust in 1980—stands as a threatening symbol of senseless death and destruction for its own sake. In the film *Angst* some of the authentic facts are changed, the names of the people and cities are altered and certain events are modified. The most obvious and significant change is the director's decision to add the killer's voice-over, as he quotes passages from other serial killers' confessions, especially those of Peter Kürten, the so-called "Vampire of Düsseldorf." This strictly subjective one-person drama is shot with a strong use of high-angle shots and handheld camerawork, and the minimal narration shows similarities to Aristide Massaccesi's Italian stalk 'n' slash epic *Rosso Sangue* (*Absurd*, 1982). But in fact, Kargl manages to direct a European counterpart to John McNaughton's *Henry: Portrait of a Serial Killer* (1986): irritating, gory and absolutely hopeless.

Angst is exceptional in Austrian as well as in German cinema for at least two reasons: it is both a "true crime" semi-documentary, and a stylized "slasher film" resembling those from the Italian tradition. Yet it is very different as well. The film confronts the viewer with the most horrible details of the authentic case, and stands as the collaborative effort of first-time director Kargl and his writer-cameraman Zbigniew Rybczynski; the third "author" is composer Klaus Schulze (from the "Krautrock" group Tangerine Dream), whose cold yet haunting electronic rhythms add a great deal to the alienating atmosphere.

Angst uses real-time narration nearly all the way through; only a few ellipses appear

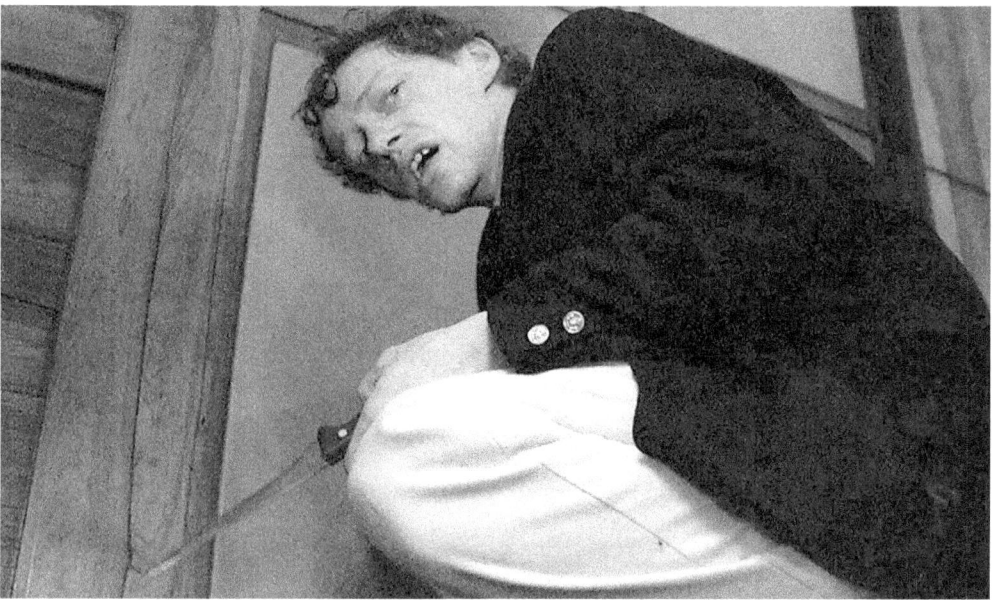

Erwin Leder as K., the psychopath in Gerald Kargl's disturbing horror thriller *Angst* (1983), based on mass murderer Werner Kniesek (courtesy Gerald Kargl).

in the second part, but most of the film is staged in detailed on-screen action, filmed with long tracking shots, sometimes even in planned sequences. Dialogue scenes are extremely rare, due to the concentration on a subjective, one-person drama. The film starts in a prison cell, establishing the killer (Erwin Leder) through an off-screen monologue in which he reflects about his past, his deeds, his needs, his sexual desires and his supposedly lost childhood. The film's irritating atmosphere is established via clear, often high-key, but always greyish visuals—only broken by some stylish chiaroscuro in the cell. When released from prison ten years later, the off-screen narration leaves the viewer with no illusions: the killer will be stalking his next victim soon. When he enters a small diner we are forced to "scan" the guests through the killer's eyes. Every human being is a potential victim. First he enters a taxi, directs the female driver into a forest and tries to strangle her. But he fails, as she has sensed something weird the whole time. His potential victim manages to kick him out of the car and escapes. The killer flees through the forest until he reaches a huge villa. He breaks into this supposedly empty house and meets—here the semi-documentary begins—a disabled and mentally retarded young man in a wheelchair (Rudolf Goetz). Soon the other occupants of the house arrive: a middle-aged woman (Silvia Rabenreither), and her adolescent daughter (Edith Rosset).

Accompanied by his own quietly spoken voice-over, the killer starts his bloody "work": the son is drowned in the bathtub, and the mother gets strangled in her bedroom. The daughter tries to escape, but the killer hunts her down in the basement garage and viciously stabs her with a bread knife. Here the most disturbing sequence of *Angst* runs its course: after massacring the young woman in a total frenzy, the killer rapes the corpse postmortem. All of this is shot in real-time. After this disturbing climax, the film returns to its low-key narrative, and shows us the killer's actions after the murders: having slept at the crime scene, he washes himself, stuffs the corpses in the trunk of the family's car, and—once again—visits the diner from earlier in the picture. While there, he behaves suspiciously. The police are on to him, because on his way he had caused an accident and fled in panic. Finally, they force him to open the trunk, a sequence filmed in long, circling tracking shots, symbolizing the circle of crime and punishment in which the killer is so consciously trapped.

What is so frightening about *Angst* is that the killer is characterized as a threat to every human being crossing his path. To be seen by him is to be his potential victim. He easily invades the residence of a bourgeois household—a place that is normally synonymous with warmth and safety. And he brings murder to a dispassionate middle-class society in which "death" would appear to be the only and last taboo. Interestingly, the disabled son seems to be "hidden" by his own family in this villa by the edge of the forest.

As noted earlier, *Angst*'s dramatic structure is reduced to only a very small amount of narration: we are simply shown the killer's murder spree on his one and only day of freedom. What might cause some empathy with this dangerous character—his own first-person narration—in fact functions to alienate the viewer even more. This because the voice-overs simply double on the verbal level the monstrous incidents shown to us in all their graphic horror. Through the use of this technique, the film creates a distance between audience and protagonist that never really subsides. The murder sequences may be visually shocking, but they are also deeply reflective. Kargl avoids providing any type of entertainment, conventional thrill or suspense. In fact, Kargl and Rybczynski seem to believe that entertainment through stalk 'n' slash splatter films is a sign of cynicism and should be avoided. As a result, they have tried to develop a directing method marked by intellectual distance.

This interview was conducted on August 29, 2003, in the Xenon Cinema Berlin. Thanks to Jörg Buttgereit.

Marcus Stiglegger: What was the inspirational impulse for the making of Angst?

Gerald Kargl: I was very interested in the psychology of this serial killer and

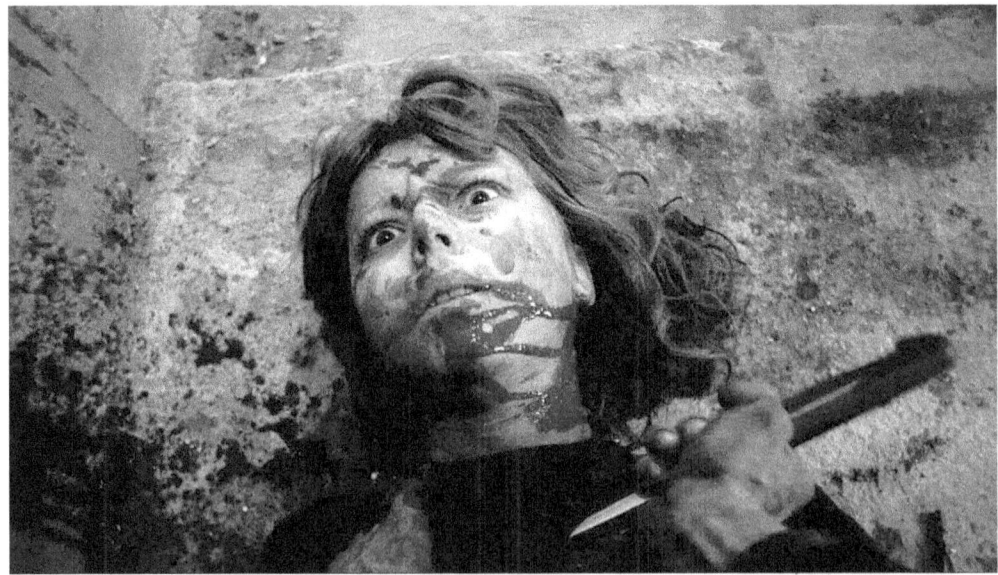

The grim handiwork of killer K. in *Angst* (courtesy Gerald Kargl).

wanted to provide a deep look inside his deranged psyche via mainly real-time narration and his inner voice, present here as the running off-commentary.

MS: What is your biographical background? How did you get into contact with filmmaking? What is your profession today?

GK: I already did short films in the seventies, but *Angst* was my first full-time feature. After this—which I produced completely on my own—I was happy to direct a lot of commercials. Finally, I was able to pay back all the money I lost. Later I did some educational films as well. And a new film project is in development—but this will be very different to *Angst*.

MS: What was the economic situation during the making of the film? What was the budget?

GK: The budget was around 400,000 euro, a sum which was completely provided by myself via debts. I was ruined for years after that....

MS: What is the position of this film within the context of Austrian national cinema at that time?

GK: There are very few films produced in Austria, and most of them are not very interesting. There is no genre cinema. *Angst* virtually appeared "out of nowhere" and was very untypical for its time and place....

MS: The camerawork in this film is very elaborate (e.g., the crane shot in the beginning or the handheld camerawork of Kniesek's POV). What were the technical conditions during the making of the film? Some words on the Director of Photography?

GK: Especially for this film the cameraman Zbyg invented some technical props. Most of the shots were done via a mirror system that enabled us to use very strange perspectives. But there were also a lot of limits because of this. He developed a rope system that was used for the very long and fast tracking shots in the woods. All this was very expensive and I am not sure if it was all necessary in the end, because the mirrors also stood in our way.

MS: In some scenes the camera is very close, strapped on the actor looking at his face. This effect is also used later to great effect in Darren Aronofsky's Pi.

GK: The camera was fixed on a ring which loosely swung around the actor. This produced the effect of him always staying in focus, isolating him from his surroundings. He lives in his own world.

MS: Some words on the casting? How did you find the main actors?

GK: Erwin Leder, our main actor, was at the time already well known from his performance in Wolfgang Petersen's *Das Boot*. He searched for a new and different role and was very obsessed by this extremely excessive character. In a way he enjoyed playing the "madman." He actually grew up in the psychiatric institute his father led. A youth amongst schizophrenic people seems to leave its marks. The other actors mainly were ambitious young performers—except the old man in the diner, who is played by our special equipment architect.

MS: How did the connection to composer Klaus Schulze come about?

GK: I knew Schulze's music solo and with Tangerine Dream and liked it. We got along very well when we met in Munich. I like the music versions in the film much more than the mixes on the soundtrack CD, which is probably more well known than the film itself. When I returned from a meeting in Munich I heard in the news that Kniesek had tried to escape. That was a strange coincidence.

MS: *What was the concept in shooting the on-screen violence in* Angst? *What were the limitations?*

GK: Principally we wanted to show everything and in the most realistic way possible. Unfortunately, the most excessive scenes would work much better if they were not shown in such bright detail. Today I would go for more ellipses and off-screen action. The really horrible things should happen in the audience's imagination.

MS: *Did you have problems with censorship concerning the violence?*

GK: The film was discussed in Austria in the context of the early video violence debate. But it got its cinema release without cuts. In France it was available as a VHS tape called *Schizophrenia* and became a cult movie. In Britain and Germany some labels were interested but it would have been banned for violent content. Therefore it never came out there…. In the USA the film was rated XXX, which marked it as "pornographical," therefore the distributor stepped back.

MS: *How was the critical and commercial reception of this film?*

GK: The film got some good critics, but it was no financial success at all. I lost nearly all my money then…. The later reception is better and the film has a good reputation now.

MS: *What is your own opinion on* Angst *seeing it again today?*

GK: I am not satisfied throughout. Especially the central violence is over the top and should not be shown that way. I would do it differently today.

5

Manson Family Movies
An Interview with Director John Aes-Nihil

The murders committed by the Manson family, under the instruction of their cult leader Charles Manson, still reverberate today in pop culture as an emblem of both the brutality and depravity of the Manson cult and the insanity, violence and notoriety of a case that not only rocked Hollywood, but the whole of the U.S. Literary books, songs and movies have been inspired by Manson and his crimes, to the point that even Quentin Tarantino is getting in on the act with *Once Upon a Time in… Hollywood* (2019), the title an obvious nod to the work of Sergio Leone. Countless films have tried to tackle the Manson murders with varying degrees of success (the better of which being *Helter Skelter* [director Tom Gries, 1976], *The Manson Family* [director Jim Van Bebber, 1997] and obscure sexploitation flicks such as Kentucky Jones's *The Manson Massacre* [1972]).

Yet one of the most unsettling of films based on the notorious killings is the rarely seen and obscure underground classic *Manson Family Movies* (1984), directed by John Aes-Nihil. Shot on 8mm, without dialogue, and with a cast of unprofessional actors—a deliberate ploy used by the director—the film is inspired by rumors that Charles Manson and his followers filmed their activities and went as far as to recreate them. With its primitive and grainy veneer, you could easily believe that the footage assembled by Aes-Nihil is at times the real deal, such is his attention to detail. To achieve this, Aes-Nihil took to filming scenes at the actual locations where the incidents transpired, and through overloading his film with sequences inspired by the activities the group indulged in (these sequences were inspired either by interviews with Manson's followers, newspapers or Aes-Nihil's own inside information). It is only Aes-Nihil's injection of comedic moments, and sequences of satire, that remind you that this film is purely fictional.

Shot for a mere $1,000, and primarily in the summer of 1974 (with other scenes being shot over the course of the next seven and eight years), the film recreates all the key parts known about the Manson family, starting with Charles Manson badly cutting the ear of Gary Hinman before he is stabbed by Bobby Beausoleil and forced to sign over his car to Manson. He is then left for dead. The film does not shy away from showing the gruesome killings committed by members of the Manson family or their penchant for indulging in drugs and orgies (group sex). With its guerrilla filmmaking aesthetic, and despite a few moments of shoddy acting, the film is a unique and brutal portrayal of Charles Manson and his followers. Mixing historic detail, hearsay and rumor, Aes-Nihil takes us on a wild journey into the heart of the Manson family, their antics, their commune, their hedonistic lifestyle and ultimately the brutality of their crimes, which culminates with the Tate murders.

Pre-dating the found footage horror sub-genre, kick started by *The Blair Witch Project* (1999), *Manson Family Movies* holds many of the motifs and cinematic devices associated with these films in that it is presented as if it were a discovered film or video recording and should be considered as one of the first examples of this kind of film. Where the film really succeeds is when the image on-screen feels as if we are watching real life. This purely authentic vibe comes down to Aes-Nihil's attention to detail and his deep understanding of the crimes of the Manson family. Aes-Nihil's knowledge of the case is astonishing and plaudits should be given for densely cramming the film with a magnitude of references that even the most ardent Mansonologist will have a hard time keeping up with.

Manson Family Movies is a strange, violent, weird celluloid manifestation that doesn't pander to the expected demands of commercial filmmaking or narrative storytelling. It is essentially a series of sequences, based on fact or hearsay, stitched together to create a strange, wordless feature. Owing much to the avant-garde, or the films of Kenneth Anger, this experimental and radical film revels in its non-traditional aesthetic and, as a result, Aes-Nihil has created one of the most authentic films on the Manson family, though less sympathetic audiences will find the film an ordeal to sit through. That said, wipe away its scummy and violent veneer and you actually have a film that oozes fact and rumor about the Manson crimes, though the director takes for granted that you are familiar with the story/background of the case. Those who are not will be left scratching their heads and will be left alienated by the material. Aes-Nihil makes no apologies for his film and presents Manson as a charismatic leader of the cult, yet seems to imply that the brutal killings were not ordered by him and that in some ways Manson has become the vilified monster. This is but one of the controversial strands of the movie but one of the elements that provide food for thought upon watching this grueling yet highly original piece of work. For sure it is a film that will divide audiences. You either dig it or hate it. Yet, it's a piece of work that is hard to ignore.

In December 2018 I had the pleasure of interviewing the director John Aes-Nihil about his work and how he came to shoot this strange but memorable film. I thank Mr. Aes-Nihil for all the work he put into this interview.

Matthew Edwards: *Your film* Manson Family Movies *is one of the most provocative and unsettling films based on the crimes of Charles Manson. What prompted you to make the film about the Manson murders? Was it a reaction to some of the content that was out there?*

John Aes-Nihil: Originally I was going to make a movie based on the antics of these 2 girls I knew who were around 16 and I was 19. They called themselves King Hawg or King MaMa and Son of Hawg or Prince Gwank. When they visited someone they would do stuff like shit in boots in the closet and lick everything and spit on everything and put soap in food on the stove. Then I was in NYC when *Pink Flamingos* (1972) was at the Elgin at midnight. I went to see the movie with the drummer from my band and I was shocked that someone else had made the movie I was considering. That winter, myself and the woman who played Pat and the guy who played Charlie and Pat's 7-year-old boy, went camping in the desert and on the way back we decided to make a

Manson movie and so drove all night thinking about who could play who. When I was in college in '69–'70 I was always arguing with people about if Charlie made those people kill for him or if they did it on their own volition, the latter which I believe. So when the case broke in December '69, a month after I was at Altamont, I became obsessed with it. Russ Meyer told me that the murder in *Beyond the Valley of the Dolls* (1970) was based on the Tate murders and parties in Tierra del Fuego of all places.

ME: How did you set about casting and shooting the film? Was it easy to pull together a cast and crew for what I imagine at the time in 1974 was still a controversial and emotive subject?

JA: Well the casting was the result of the woman who played Pat collecting people which I found rather annoying but then realized that we had a captive cast but not that captive. The reason that parts are played by as many as 4 different people and that men played women and women played men is that since no one was paid sometimes they would show up and sometimes not. I would shoot the scene no matter what, so we would just call people until we had a cast for the scene. This guy called Moka played Voyteck, Rosemary and Paul Watkins. He ran off to the Krishna Temple in Berkeley so we had to have Katie play Voyteck and she also played Sadie. The Cosmic Ray also played the Black Panther Spy. As for a crew, well that was me and at times Ray and the 7-year-old. The girl who played Squeaky looked exactly like her and knew Squeaky and Blue. Her apartment caught fire so she refused to be in the movie again so I had Audrey play Squeaky.

ME: Where did you find the actor who played Charles Manson? I felt he was surprisingly good in the role.

JA: The guy who played Charlie had been a Green Baret in Vietnam and was somewhat insane. He was the boyfriend of the woman who played Pat and who was the mother of the 7-year-old. He was 5'3" just as Charlie was. I wanted the guy who played Clem to play Charlie but Jacquetta (Pat) said he was way too tall and that Rick was perfect. Of course he looks Mexican, however he was also half German. He said he had a Mexican body and a German mind. As for finding him, he lived in a house that we all had in Oakland.

ME: I understand that the film took five years to complete. Was this due to budgetary reasons?

JA: It took a lot longer than that and was made with virtually no money. I think I was the only one who knew it would get finished.

ME: I sense the lengthy production of the film caused you one or two issues with the actors in the film. I ask because I note that the character Leslie is played by about six people and that the Tate murder scenes were shot over a number of years.

JA: I think a bit of the Tate murder was shot a year apart. Leslie was first played by this drag queen Brad who has disappeared. I'm not even sure who played her later.

ME: A facet of the film that is immediately apparent when watching Manson Family Movies *is the level of authenticity you achieved. By and large, you tried to shoot the film where the incidents actually occurred, like at the Tate House and Bella Drive (to mention but a few). You went to painstaking detail to get things accurate in the film, didn't you, and not just with the locations?*

JA: The craziest location shot was actually driving to Lake Isabella to get 3 minutes of footage for when Leno and Rosemary were driving from there to LA. We went to Barker Ranch in '79 the first time and the bus was still there. I tried to figure out what really happened, however I also did satires on what the media claimed happened like that scene where they are shooting up acetone with a horse syringe, which Blue objected to.

ME: *One of the most striking, and unsettling, aspects of your film is that your use of 8mm film stock adds a layer of authenticity to your film in that it feels like we are watching real footage shot by Manson and his followers. Taking aside some of the comedic/satirical parts that do occur in the film, your film at times feels markedly real as though we are watching the inner workings of Charles Manson and his followers. Was that your intention?*

JA: The premise was that the Manson family is rumored to have filmed their activities and even recreated the murders. As for the real Manson family movies, Ed Sanders stated that a famous New York artist bought them: Warhol. So for years I've discussed with John Waters if Warhol really did have them. John Waters said if you ask him he will say I don't know. So in '79 we moved to LA and rented a ranch in Chasworth to finish the movie. The guy Moka, who played 3 parts [in the movie], was with me walking down Hollywood Boulevard and we saw a sign that said Andy Warhol in front of a store so we went in and got in line to meet him. So I asked him, "Do you have the Manson family movies?," and he said, "I don't know." So if he did have them, Moka in NYC has them now.

ME: *Do you think he has them?*

JA: I'm not saying that Moka had the real Manson family movies as he was just an actor in my movie. Warhol is rumored to have had them, in that the Warhol Estate film collection went to Moka. That is where they are if they exist. The Warhol Estate was in court for many years, enabling the lawyers to get most of the money—see the book *Death & Disaster* for that sordid story. Ron Tavel told me that at first the Warhol Foundation had the rights to the movies and they hated the movies and would let no one do anything with them, i.e., they just sued people over them. Eventually Moka was allowed to store them, restore them and show them along with the Whitney and the Warhol museums, who are also allowed to show them. Speaking of which, Ken Anger exhibited my crime scene photos at said museum in his show there. I also acquired originals of the crime scene photos, some stamped by the coroner's office, and the morgue photos and what was actually the last photos ever taken of Sharon, Jay and Voyteck on August 5. The slides are even stamped August 1969. I found the exact date via a contact from the son of an actress who was there that day. Jay and Voyteck took pics of Sharon and each other. Roman had photographed Sharon for *Playboy* on the set of *The Fearless Vampire Killers* (1967), interior shots. I also got his original slides of his own set of these which were exterior shots of Sharon nude in the snow [these real-life crime scene photos of the Tate murders are shown as an extra on the *Cult Epics* DVD release and make for disturbing viewing].

ME: *Stylistically, how did you set about shooting the movie? Were the shots planned out or was there an improv feel to the filming process?*

JA: Well I never found someone to play Tex so I did and John Waters said that was the best depiction of a serial killer he had ever seen. The problem with that was that

I had to act, direct and shoot. This 7-year-old kid actually shot some of it in a way in that I would set up the shot and he would turn the camera on. One reason it turned out at all was that the camera was totally manual so for each shot someone had to measure the point from the film in the camera to the scene and set the feet, then do a light meter reading and set the aperture. There was always some improvisation going on. Like when the guy who had been playing Leslie didn't show up so we asked the older woman whose house we were shooting at to put on the wig and jacket the character had been wearing and do the scene. I knew that when I—as Tex—handed her the knife that she would do what Leslie had done for real and refuse the knife. Also the only reason the acting is any good is that since it was silent everyone had to act to convey anything. That scene with Rosemary and Leno on the couch. Jamie said that was amazing acting and that was a guy playing Rosemary and a girl, Judy, playing Leno.

ME: *The acid orgy scene is one of the most surreal moments in the film: when George (played by Palmo) is high on LSD and begins to actually lick the pussy of one of the actresses. That actor seemed game for anything in the film (Judy)! Talk us through the filming of that scene! It seems everyone was off their heads!*

JA: That is George Spahn. That guy's real name was Palmer French, a renowned book critic who lived up the street from us. A lot of the cast were collected by the woman who played Pat Krenwinkel and she would just move them into the house, which I often found annoying. However, when we came up with making a *Manson Family Movie* we had a very captive cast. Judy, many years later, when asked if she wanted to see it, said, "No way! I'm not like that anymore!"

ME: *The film has an edgy underground vibe to it and it is characterized by its guerrilla filmmaking aesthetic. Did your "on the fly" shooting approach get you in trouble with the authorities?*

JA: Of course, and that trouble is in the movie. In the fire orgy scene, which was shot at Point Reyes Beach, we found that if you want the desert you go to the beach and shoot away from the ocean and into the sand dunes, so those rangers asking for ID did that because they claimed the fire was illegal. During that scene I used the Manson song about showing ID as the soundtrack. The first time we were a block from where we lived in Oakland and were shooting a driveway of a house and someone called the cops saying we were staking out a house for a burglary and we told the cops that a group of 10 people with a movie camera were hardly doing that. Then there was this park up in the hills from where we lived with an abandoned log cabin which we were shooting a scene in and this black guy dressed like a pimp in a pink suit shows up and turns out he's an undercover narc disguised as a pimp to bust blacks smoking weed. So we filmed him and he's in that scene.

ME: *Towards the end of the film there is a scene when Manson imagines himself as a Christ-like figure and is seen carrying around a huge crucifix (which gets dumped in a trash can, if I recall correctly). Talk us through the filming of that scene, as I understand it a group of German tourists stumbled across you as you were shooting! What was their reaction?*

JA: We were shooting the end scene of the movie in a park farther up in the Oakland hills and there were these picnic areas carved out of the forest. So the guy playing Charlie, well, his girlfriend wanted him to do [that scene] nude, so he did it in green underwear. So we had these girls whipping him [Charlie] on the cross and these German tourists showed up and then just left. What that scene is based on is an article by the writer Wayne McGuire, who in '69/'70 wrote about Manson, Mel Lyman and so on. He wrote out this scene based on the convergence of C. S. Lewis and Nietzsche, which he said occurred in the Lewis book *That Hideous Strength*, the scene being a thousand-foot image of the Messiah appears and the face is constantly changing from Christ to Satan to Hitler and so forth and hordes of humanity run to it and pass right through it and fall into the abyss filled with rats and skeletons. I could not figure out how to pull that scene off.

ME: I thought Cosmic Ray's acting as the maid was hilarious! Talk a little about his role in the film?
JA: I talked to the Cosmic Ray a few hours ago about this. My idea was to have an Australian Aboriginal, which Ray is, play an American black stereotype knowing that the audience would just figure that Ray is black. I didn't really tell Ray this, he just figured that it should be played that way. In the part when he's going up the driveway to the Tate house, it was shot in the rain so I said just act like it's not raining. He improvised the part about being jealous of Sharon. The part where he is reading Nietzsche to Sharon was an in-joke based on a scene in Polanski's film *What?* (1972), in which a servant tried to read to this old man and gets beaten with the book. Ray was, in the beginning, an almost equal partner in the production and shot a lot of it also. However, he would do things and not tell me like running the film back via back winding and getting double exposures which was used once, but generally made for confusion and re-shots. He said he never ever imagined that the film would get finished or ultimately get commercially released.

ME: In the film you suggest that the Manson family had staked out the Tate house prior to the killings and that they didn't think Sharon Tate was going to be there. Is this based on fact?
JA: Yes, it is based on fact from several sources. William Garretson said that on August 8 he hitchhiked to Sunset Strip to get cigarettes and hitched back and got a ride from a black VW bus full of hippies and when they got to Cielo Drive he said, "I can get out here," and they said, "Oh we're going up the hill," and then they drove right into the Tate property. He was getting freaked out and got out of the van and ran to the guest house and turned around and saw that they had guns and they opened Jay's truck and took something and left.

ME: Wasn't William Garretson the caretaker to the Tate household?
JA: Yes, he was the caretaker of the property for owner Rudy Altabelli and Rudy hired him because Rudy thought he was hot. The murders were the sole work of Tex Watson, who committed them due to his penchant for corrupt drug deals in which he ripped his customers off. The one that started this process was when Tex took some of the girls to a black drug dealer's house on a drug caper and when Poppa gave Tex the money he left the girls there with Poppa and split with the money. Then Poppa called the Spahn Ranch phone and told Charlie he was gonna off the girls if he didn't get his money back. So Charlie had to go over there and had to shoot Poppa and take the girls back, however, Poppa was just wounded.

However, Tex and the girls decided that Poppa was a Black Panther and started that race war business behind that. A bit before that the family had lived with Gary Hinman in Topanga Canyon and that connection was Bobby, who was having a thing with Gary. Tex and Bobby bought MDA from Gary, which Gary made in his basement, and sold it to biker gangs. It proved to be *bad* as in it made one *sick* so the bikers were threatening to attack the Spahn Ranch. So Charlie told Bobby to go deal with it so Bobby and Sadie and Mary were driven to Gary's by Bruce and Bruce left them there. After a day of Gary insisting he had no money, Bobby called Charlie and him and Bruce went to Gary's and Charlie cut Gary's ear with a sword and left (which is shown in my film). Gary was still acting up so Bobby killed him and the 2 girls left and hitchhiked back to the ranch and Bobby had made Gary sign over his car so he drove off in it. He was so tired he slept in it, with the bloody clothes and a knife, and got arrested. Then the girls decided that they had to get Bobby out of jail so they came up with a copycat killing scheme. Meanwhile various members of the Manson group had been partying at the Cielo house when Terry had it and later when the Polanskis had it. Dennis Wilson picked up some Manson girls hitchhiking and took them to his estate and they told him of Charlie so they went to Spahn and Dennis loved the music so he started setting things up to put out records. He took Terry to the ranch and he was interested and one of the Wrecking Crew claims that he played on a session with Charlie set up by Terry, who had always denied that he did anything with Charlie. Charlie and Sadie went to visit Terry and met up with Rudy, Sharon and her photographer Hitomi. Rudy said to Charlie, "Terry moved out, go away." The Bug always maintained that Charlie thought Terry still lived there and that is why that house was chosen. According to Paul Krasner, Charlie and Sadie visited again and Voyteck and Abagail were there and invited them in and they did MDA and had an orgy, which was filmed and which Paul claims he saw. I put that in the movie by the way. Jay and Voyteck were trying to corner the MDA drug market and were working with these 3 Canadian drug dealers who supplied Mama Cass, etc. There was this complex and confusing drug deal involving Jay, Voyteck, Tex and a possible double agent, whom my drummer played. Voyteck bought MDA, which was fake, and so he went to Sunset Strip and brought him back to the house and everyone whipped him. Somehow Tex and Voyteck thought that each other had humiliated and/or ripped them off. Tex went back to the Ranch and told Charlie that those people at Terry's old house ripped him off. So this is what Charlie said to Tex: "If you're man enough to get your money back then go do it, if you're not then just shut up about it." So that's what got Charlie sentenced to death. So, Tex got some of the girls who were gung-ho to do this copycat killing to get Bobby out and off they went. They were also on speed and possibly some sort of LSD hence the Mania to the murders.

As for all these stories about Helter Skelter and a race war and vengeance for Charlie not getting a recording contract with Terry ... well it's all campfire talk. The killers keep it going trying to get out. A great deal of this "talk" came from Paul Watkins, who, near the end of his life, apparently said in an interview—that can't be found—that the Bug told him if he didn't go along with this Helter Skelter motive that Paul would be convicted of conspiracy to commit first degree murder, just like Charlie was. This brings up the band Desert Sun, which was Paul, his brother Brooks, his girlfriend Jane and this other guy. Brooks and Paul had done the soundtrack for Robert Hendrickson's film *Manson*, made at Spahn with whoever was not in prison in 1970. Clem and the girls also did a soundtrack called *Family Jams*. *Family Jams* was the price Robert had to pay to make the movie. The family told him that if he recorded *Family Jams* he could make the movie. That is the tape I found in the radio station archives and used on the soundtrack.

Now the point about Desert Sun goes back to a 1984 concert that Brooks and Jane did in Venice, which I attended. I had finished the *Manson* movie and was considering the soundtrack. Between sets I told Brooks I had done a somewhat comedic *Manson* movie and he said, "That's a good way to look at it." So I asked him if he wanted to contribute to the soundtrack and he said yes and that he had recorded some of Charlie's songs. He gave me a phone number, which did not work. I started talking to Nick Bougas about all this and that he was making a series of documentaries on Manson and serial killers in general for a studio in Burbank. He said he would look into contacting Brooks and he found that they both lived in Burbank so he went to meet him and bought some tapes of Brooks and Jane. However Brooks denied the entire conversation with me and totally denied that he ever recorded Charlie's songs. Eventually I talked to Brooks again, and he again denied it all. A few years back all these Desert Sun CDs turn up available online. Several people I know bought all 15 of them, including Don Murphy, who had been trying to make a pro Manson movie for many years. I got 6 of the CDs and found that they had recorded Charlie's songs so Brooks was lying and it rather proves that Paul had not turned on Charlie as he said in court.

ME: There is a scene in the film where, after the Tate murders, the killers dump their clothes in Benedict Canyon. Is it true that you tossed the clothes out at the actual location where the original clothes were left?

JA: As for the clothes dumping site we dumped the clothes in the movie at the exact site. In '69 there was a news crew who found the exact site and I figured it out based on that.

ME: What was the reaction to the film when you released it? How was it received critically?

JA: The film was shot from '74 to '79 and put on VHS in '84 and shown at EZTV in LA on the opening night of the Olympics to whoever showed up. John Waters was somewhat involved with it and did the first review. I met John Waters at the premiere of *Desperate Living* in NYC and was introduced to him by Jamie Remar, who was in *The Warriors*, etc., and who I met through the guy who played the double agent narc in the movie, was the drummer in my band and grew up with Jamie. I showed John stills and he said he wanted to see it. That winter we went to Barker Ranch to shoot and I sent John Waters a card from the area. We get back to Oakland and John calls and says he's in SF and wants to come over to see the film so I had to literally glue together a rough cut and so he saw it and photos were taken of that visit. In 2006 Cult Epics commercially released it and at that point I got to restore it. The 8mm film reels had not been projected since '84 when it was put on VHS. We projected it to make a master off of it and found that all the cuts held up perfectly; making that movie was the first time I ever did editing and was the first movie I ever made also. Over the years several video elements had been added so those were removed and the released version is 100 percent shot on film. Then we encountered a weird problem with the soundtrack as now all the music pieces were too short. Turned out that the place that put it onto VHS ran it at sound speed, however, it was a silent movie and all those years it was seen at the wrong speed. Then me and this guy had to make every piece of music longer. After Cult Epics released it, it got a number of reviews, some very negative as they compared it to "normal movies" made with money. It also got some great reviews like one from this guy in New Zealand called "Rape Man." Warhol's writer Ron Tavel reviewed all my movies, as did the underground filmmaker George Kuchar. Ken Anger did a one-line quote—"Looks like the real thing." He suggested that the best soundtrack would have been to use ambient noise.

ME: How did Cult Epics come to release the film?

JA: Nico B. of Cult Epics decided to put out my movie possibly on the recommendation of James Healey, who was putting out Anger's movies. Nico also had a gallery wherein we did a Sharon Tate exhibition and later a William S. Burroughs one, both called "Last Photos," in that I took the last photos of WSB at his home in Kansas months before his death.

ME: Did Charles Manson ever see the film?

JA: No, I don't see how he could have. Blue [Sandra Collins Good] saw it and didn't get the jokes and satire in it.

ME: The film features no dialogue, just music over the visuals and title cards. I felt this was very effective and the right way to go with the film as it would have been unlikely the Manson family would have recorded sound to accompany their "home movies." Was that your intention?

JA: It was shot on regular 8mm film, which cannot have a soundtrack applied to it, unlike Super 8mm film. It was shot that way in that I found an 8mm camera at a yard sale for $10 and shot the entire movie with it and I still have it. It was shot on out-of-date 8mm film bought from the local drug store for $1.50 a roll and processed there also. Later I found that regular 8mm sound equipment did exist for about 6 months and even found such a camera, however Kodak could not put sound on it anyway. Originally I used a lot of rock music and as a number of people have found the Pink Floyd album *Meddle* worked well as a soundtrack. When it was released I had to avoid music copyright issues so instead of Pink Floyd I used Bobby Beausoleil's music Modern Barbarian, which was never released, and then I found in a radio archive the *Family Jams* music from 1970 done by Clem and the girls. One piece we used was Patty Duke's version of "(Theme from) *The Valley of the Dolls*," which was taken from her 1967 album "Patty Duke sings songs from *The Valley of the Dolls* and other selections." This resulted in Andre Previn having my movie in his online credits.

ME: Looking back, are you proud of what you achieved on the film?

JA: Well sure. It was made for under $1,000 dollars and was commercially released.

6

Henry: Portrait of a Serial Killer
An Interview with Director John McNaughton

In this author's opinion, John McNaughton's *Henry: Portrait of a Serial Killer* is the benchmark for all films that have been made about real-life killers. A disturbing and sublime character study of a serial killer, the film is a harrowing, shocking, depressing, grueling and genuinely frightening journey into the mind of a psychopathic killer, made all the more convincing by Michael Rooker's seminal performance as the killer. Loosely chronicling the exploits of drifter and mass murderer Henry Lee Lucas, who was convicted of 11 counts of murder, the film follows Henry Lee Lucas as he randomly commits a series of brutal crimes before encouraging his roommate Otis (Ottis Toole) to become complicit in the murders.

Though a fictional retelling of Lucas's crimes, the film heavily plays on the idea that Henry also murdered Otis's niece Becky Powell, which is hinted at in the film during the depressing finale, along with the idea that the two became romantically involved prior to Henry killing her. This is considered fact, though the film does differ from historical events, instead venturing into fictional territory with the death of Otis. What is presented on-screen differs from the actual events in that Ottis Toole died in police custody on September 15, 1996, aged 46.

Despite the fictional/historical inaccuracies, the film is still an intelligent piece of cinema, and justifiably living up to its title of being an accurate portrayal of a serial killer. McNaughton attaches no glamour to Henry's character, or cinematic tropes to make him out to be a monster. McNaughton refuses to pander to these expectations and instead he realistically shows the man for what he truly is: a dirty, violent and scummy psychopath. Yet it is this attention to detail and realism wherein lies the brilliance of the film and the heightening of the horror of the picture, even though strictly speaking it is not a "horror film." It is a film that holds up a mirror to the audiences, reflecting back the depravities that mankind can plunge to. With this realistic approach to the crimes of Lucas, McNaughton was effectively challenging the mainstream's depiction of killers and murderers and on-screen violence.

For the majority of film audiences, such films had to present the killer as a monster and the film had to adhere to fantastical elements in order to detach the viewer from the on-screen violence. McNaughton objected to such an approach and deliberately tried to

Iconic image of Michael Rooker as infamous serial killer Henry Lee Lucas in *Henry: Portrait of a Serial Killer* (courtesy John McNaughton/MPI).

place the viewer at the center of the violence so that they would not be distanced from it. To achieve this, McNaughton attempted to press home the notion of violence as entertainment in the infamous home invasion scene, which saw Lucas and Otis filming their exploits. As this disturbing scene unfolds, we see the pair murdering the father, the mother and their small child. To make matters worse, we are forced to witness Otis sexually abusing the mother before and after her death, which he does so with excited glee. It is only at the end of this scene that the camera pans back to reveal Henry and Otis on the sofa rewatching their exploits. In the eerie silence, we, too, have become complicit in both the violence and their voyeurism.

In the UK, when the film was finally released in cinemas in 1991 by Electric Pictures, it was severely censored and recut by the British Board of Film Classification. Initially, 24 seconds of cuts were required, before further cuts were requested. The film was finally passed with 62 seconds' worth of cuts. Firstly, the shot of the prostitute with the broken shard of glass rammed into her face was cut entirely, constituting 38 seconds' worth of cuts. Secondly, the sexual violence in the home invasion scene caused the then head of the BBFC James Ferman to demand cuts, in particular the sight of Otis grabbing the mother's breasts and his wandering hands edging closer to her vaginal region. However, when the film came to be released on home video, the BBFC took a tougher stance as it was deemed the film still posed a threat to the vulnerable and society in general! To compound matters, Ferman demanded that the shot of Otis and Henry sitting on the sofa should be inserted halfway through the sequence, thus changing the context of the scene and destroying the point McNaughton was trying to make. Not content with meddling with McNaughton's film, Ferman now demanded more cuts, which saw the home invasion scene receiving cuts totaling 71 seconds and the intellectual point McNaughton was trying to make forever ruined. Farman's crusade as the moral guardian for what could be seen and not seen in living rooms in Britain did not end there, and he pulled out his scissors once again to cut four seconds from the murder of the TV salesman. Satisfied that the people of Britain could not be corrupted by the film, *Henry: Portrait of a Serial Killer* was granted an 18 certificate. Yet, Ferman's meddling ways saw him receive much deserved criticism for the way he re-edited the film, and soon moral guardians such as Ferman would pretty much become obsolete as Hollywood increased the gore/violence content in their films and the BBFC could no longer justify picking on the small guys when the Hollywood machine became as gratuitous as the exploitation

Original advertisement for John McNaughton's powerful *Henry: Portrait of a Serial Killer* (courtesy John McNaughton/MPI).

films that were supposedly corrupting the green and pleasant land. Couple that with the rise of DVDs and the easiness of getting alternative versions of films from Europe or America, and the BBFC began to loosen up a bit. In 2003, *Henry* was finally released uncut in the United Kingdom.

Henry: Portrait of a Serial Killer's ability to unnerve and revolt audiences more than thirty years later is a testimony to the power of the film. The film offers no solutions or motives for their actions. There is no resolution at the end of the film, other than Otis getting his just desserts. Lucas, on the other hand, is not shown justice or apprehended by the law. It is a film that refuses to pass judgment on our killers. They are presented matter-of-factly, authentically; their cold-bloodedness numbing the audience as they fail to digest and comprehend their crimes. Depressingly, as the film concludes, Lucas is free to continue his crimes.

In August 2018 I had the honor of interviewing the director John McNaughton about his seminal film and the lasting impact the film has had on audiences. I thank him for speaking to me about one of the most important cinematic works in the last forty years.

Matthew Edwards: Henry: Portrait of a Serial Killer *is considered one of the most disturbing and terrifying films of all time. Why do you think the film has remained so potent after all these years?*

John McNaughton: I think it's because the film is so disturbing and unnerving. I think with the films that I have tried to make many of them hold up really well because both myself and my collaborators always avoided the superficial and went for the depth of human behavior. This always remains the same and if you base your stories on human behavior then they stay—unless you have them wearing extremely silly fashions from the moment that will age badly. With *Henry: Portrait of a Serial Killer* it has been watched and seen continuously for thirty-two years. When I was making *Henry* I kind of tore up the rule book but that's because I feel art is transgressive, well the art that I like and admire I like to think of it as transgressive. [Laughs.]

ME: *There is a timelessness about* Henry *in a way because the film could be set now....*
JM: You're right. You might have to change the cars, but that's about it.

ME: *Much has been talked about the history behind the production of the film, in that the film came about after a documentary you were geared up to make for MPI—on the Chicago wrestling scene—fell through. What prompted you and MPI to make a true-crime horror film, and what was it about Henry Lee Lucas's crimes that inspired you to base the film around him?*

JM: Waleed B. Ali—who is sadly deceased for some years now, he died of cancer—and his brother Malik—who is still alive and runs MPI; they are still making money off *Henry*, and I'm still not getting any of it even though it states so in the contract—asked me to a meeting to make a wrestling documentary. However, Waleed decided not to make the documentary because once the owners of the archival footage we were going to use found out that Waleed had some money they doubled the price. Waleed was insulted by that and told them to buzz off. So, when I came to his office I was expecting to outline the terms of our deal to make this wrestling documentary and get a down payment so I could start. However, he told me they weren't going to do that. Instead he told me he'd rather make a film: a horror film. He was very specific about that because they were selling very well on video, especially B-horror titles. The rights for those films were increasing in price and at that time they were buying some portions of the rights, but they weren't getting worldwide rights for all media perpetuity. They were getting this territory and that territory. The prices were going up and up, so they wanted to make a horror film that they owned all the rights to for all perpetuity. So, he offered me $100,000 to make a horror film. Before I walked out of the building I had the subject matter. When I walked out of Waleed's office I had no idea what the specific subject would be but as I was walking down the hallway, as I was heading out of the building, I stopped into another office which was occupied by an old childhood friend of mine and he was a collector and connoisseur of the arcane, the strange, the weird and the crazy! He had an office filled with all of this stuff that he had gleaned, and I walked in there dazed because Waleed had just offered me $100,000 to make a horror film. I had no idea that this would happen to me and this was the great desire of my life that I would get the chance to make a film. So, my friend asked me what I would make it about and I said, "I have no idea." And he just reached up, grabbed a VHS cassette and put it in the machine and it was a news magazine show *20/20* and they had a segment on Henry Lee Lucas. They had pictures of Henry and pictures of Ottis—his real name had a double "t" not one "t" as in Otis, which is one thing that we changed to make it a little less awkward—but no pictures of Becky. That program told his story, and Henry told some of his story himself, because he was interviewed, and it was very clear to me that this was the subject for a horror film. So that's how that came to be.

ME: Did you do much research for the film and Lucas's crimes?
   JM: Yes, we did. We did all we could, but you must remember that there was no internet. So, we used magazine and newspaper articles and the *20/20* TV show, which gave a summation of the real story, or at least what was considered the accepted story. We read all the articles that we could dig up with various versions of Henry's story to help us create ours.

ME: You said that you were working with very little money to make the film. You were working close to the bone, weren't you? How difficult was that for you?
   JM: No, it was easy! [Laughs.] In many ways I prefer it. It is much better than working with millions of dollars. I was spoilt because there was no one looking over my shoulder and I thought that was the way it would always be, and it certainly was the last time I worked like that, aside from a documentary I made about the artist George Condo, because we were self-financing, and we could drink wine while we were shooting. [Laughs.] I had never made a film before. Having $100,000 was a lot of money at the time, considering, as Malik told me many years later, that he was very much against making the film. He was the purse strings of the business and he and Waleed made a good pair. Waleed was the visionary and would spend every dime unless Malik restrained him. Malik was dead set against making the film because you have to understand that $100,000 in those days was more than my house cost. So, to me it was a lot of money that they were risking on a movie.

ME: You said you had never directed a film before, so how did you approach directing the film from a stylistic point of view?
   JM: Well, I had studied not so much film but still photography and I was very conversant with cameras and lenses and photography. Also, I went to art school and

when I was a boy my mother used to make my clothes. She was incredibly gifted, so I knew enough about fine arts to know what good production design would look like and enough about creating clothing to be able to judge wardrobe. I have known many, many people in my life and to me when I have characters I think who do I know who is like this? How do they behave? How do they speak? I also felt it was important to give all my collaborators a lot of room, if they are good. I think one of my great talents is recognizing talent in others. If you pick the right people and hire the right actors you can phone in the direction. So we had the right actors and you give them a lot space. I think I can judge when a performance is true or when a performance is false. That is another strength. One of the mistakes I have seen younger directors make is to think they are geniuses and they micromanage their collaborators which just causes frustration and they don't give you their best. They just wait for you to tell them exactly what you want, which usually isn't as good as what they would give you if you let them.

So I worked with really good people on *Henry*. My production designer had worked in the theater for years and years and he had worked in close collaboration with Pat Harp, who sadly died a few years ago. She did costumes in the theater in Chicago, and the two of them had done hundreds of plays together. It was also so nice because they worked so well together and the sets and costume were never at odds. My cinematographer Charlie Lieberman had shot a lot of big-budgeted commercials. As for the actors, I just picked the right ones. That was partly good fortune.

ME: Michael Rooker delivered an award-winning performance in the role of Henry Lee Lucas. How did you come to cast him in the film?

JM: [Laughs.] Michael came from Alabama originally and his family was poor. Interestingly, when he was a kid he was a great athlete at high school who played football. But he was a poor kid and dyslexic. In order to overcome this he participated in the school play and eventually he realized that this was his passion and in those days there was the Goodman School of Drama, a great dramatic arts school which has since been absorbed by DePaul University. He got a reading for a scholarship and he got it! I have no idea what he read, but he could have never afforded to go to the school without it. So he went through the Goodman School of Drama for four years and studied acting and was well trained. He was working painting houses when we found him. [Laughs.] He had acted in one small role in a film that came to town and he was up for a role at Steppenwolf, which is a prestigious theater company here in Chicago. It was founded by Laurie Metcalf, Terry Kenny, Jeff Perry and Gary Sinise. That was very prestigious and we weren't! However, we offered him the lead. He came to us through our make-up artist Jeffery Lyle Segal, who had worked with him in a play. We were having a hard time. We had found Otis (Tom Towles), because we took a lot of people from Stuart Gordon's company, The Organic Theater. That's where Stuart started in Chicago. Stuart's second collaborator was Richard Fire and both Richard and I wrote *Henry*. The Organic Theater had recently broken up and they were all looking for work. There was permanent company of about eight to ten people, which included Dennis Farina, and many of them went on to glory, so we were lucky that we found Tom Towles, who had been working as part of The Organic Theater Company, and cast him as Otis, and we cast Tracy Arnold, who had only recently started working for them. She wasn't one of the original members but she was a fresh face and we cast her.

We kept looking and looking for Henry and we weren't finding the right person, until Jeff Segal said, "Well I know this guy that I have worked with and I think he will be really good." It just so happened that Richard Fire and I toward the end of the process were putting together the crew and writing the script at his apartment and Richard said, "This guy is a jerk," blah, blah, blah [referring to Michael Rooker]. I just said, "What have we got to lose? Let's at least see the guy and if we don't like him, we don't like him." So the guy that was suggested was Michael. The minute I laid eyes on Michael I just knew he was perfect!

ME: When Michael was offered the part did you discuss with him what you wanted him to bring to the screen or did he bring some elements in himself to the role? You talked about collaboration earlier and how you allow others room to bring their own ideas to the production.

JM: Michael grew up not too dissimilarly to Henry Lee Lucas: poor, white, semi-rural town like Jasper, Alabama. One time Michael said something that I remember as very funny. I said, "Michael, where did you get this? Where would you get the inspiration for this?" "Oh, I had an uncle who was just like this guy!" [Laughs.]

ME: I also think the relationship between Michael and Tom on the screen really shines and comes through, doesn't it?

JM: They were a pair, that's for sure!

ME: They portrayed their characters extremely well. You really see that misogynistic side to them, especially that of Tom's character Otis.

JM: Well interestingly, part of Tom's training was that of a theater actor, and a wonderful one at that. It wasn't until he got to the movies, which was the second half of his career, that he really specialized in playing low-lives, criminals and scoundrels. [Laughs.] He was an amazing stage actor and when he was young he was very fit, big and handsome. He didn't play those types of roles, until he got to the movies. But, he has also trained at Second City. People come from all over the world to go through their improv training. That's where improv started, at the Second City in Chicago. I always thought at heart that Tom's performance is a comic performance. He is playing a buffoon.

ME: One of the tragic elements of the film is Becky, Otis's sister. In the film we see this young woman who has become so used to abnormal behavior that she doesn't pick up on the violent traits of Henry and Otis, and ultimately her naivety results in both sexual abuse and finally her own violent murder.

JM: That sounds like a perfect description for today's America and Trump! Again, Tracy created a lot of that character because there was very little about Becky's character. There was a real Becky and most likely Henry killed her. He stabbed her to death. So according to the little that came up, she was barely literate. She was not nearly as sympathetic.

Tracy is originally from Texas and Henry Lee Lucas supposedly murdered someone from the town she was from. Tracy created that character, to a large degree. It was her creation.

ME: Aesthetically, the film has a grimy feel to it and I feel that adds to the horror on the screen, making it more powerful and uncompromising. Throughout the entire film there is always a simmering violence bubbling under the surface waiting to explode. Was that your intention?

JM: Yes! [Laughs.] People always call *Henry: Portrait of a Serial Killer* a horror film or a slasher film. I dare you to tell me where the slashing comes from!

ME: I wouldn't say it was a slasher film.

JM: The character Henry was equated with a Freddy Krueger. Yes, I watched horror films as a kid but I was more interested insomuch that came out of New York in the American theater in the post-war years, such as the Stanislavski method and other great method actors who came out the Lee Strasberg studio and the films that they made like *On the Waterfront* (1954). These films were very gritty and very actorly. They were socially conscious. They were social realism, which was probably much more appealing to me as a kid than straight up horror films. I also liked the British kitchen sink school. I saw so many of those films on television, like *Look Back in Anger* (1959). I saw all the great, small, gritty little films coming out, and often these films originated as plays. These films had great actors and writers and not a lot of money. They were probably more influential on *Henry* than most people realize. That period and style, and acting, had a big influence on *Henry*, much more so than *The Giant Behemoth* (1959) that came out in Britain at the same time or you name any B-horror that came out in America. Those movies were fun but they weren't serious. *Henry: Portrait of a Serial Killer* is a serious film.

ME: Hence why it has lasted the test of time. Stylistically, the opening murders are very well done. They remind me of still photographs. We seem to be catching a glimpse of the aftermath of Henry's crimes with the harrowing audio playing over it. What was your thinking behind those opening death scenes?

JM: I didn't want to make an exploitation film. I hate to say it but I wanted to make an art film. Modern Art in the post-war era in America is a mash-up of high and low and you take from here and you take from there. So yes, we took from the exploitation genre and we took from the horror genre, but we also took from the British kitchen sink style and the post-war American method acting style. I studied still photography so that opening was partly inspired by that. So yes, I was trying to make a film that could be called horror but that was just to please my financiers. It was more of a character study about people who do horrific things. In reality, it is unlike any other horror film. Both Richard Fire and I made the decision to redefine the horror film. If the idea of a horror film is to horrify an audience, then rubber monsters and ghosts and spaceships from another planet are not really scary. When you leave the theater it is over. It is all fantasy based. There is some level of the supernatural and the unreal. Let's take that away. Let's deny ourselves fantasy. Let's admit to ourselves that the most horrific things that we can imagine have been done by human beings. One just has to look at World War II. The greatest horror lies in the darkness of the human capability.

ME: Had Henry *been a straight horror film or exploitation film you would have shown those murders at the beginning of the film ...*

JM: Yes.

ME: ... in gratuitous fashion. But you didn't do that. You deliberately shied away from that path. In fact, that opening was more horrifying. Seeing those corpses, with the audio playing over it, has a greater impact on the viewer, I believe.

JM: When you want to set up a horrific occurrence I think the best way is to do a 1, 2, 3, 4, 5, 6, here is the shots and make it very clear what is going to happen. You have the bad person pick up a butcher's knife, the victim's eyes go wide, the knife comes up in the air, etc. You follow the shots step by step and you realize this person is going to get their head chopped off and yells! You make that clear to the audience that this is going to happen, then as the old cliché goes, you see the knife coming down and the perpetrator getting a splash of blood in the face. You don't show the event. You let each viewer be clear as to what will happen and let them complete it in their own mind. That way it becomes more horrific.

So when we made *Henry*, we knew it was a film about a person who kills a number of people so you can't just start out with victim number nine. Also, audio, especially when you don't have much money, is a great tool. If you are too graphic it is too literal, unless you are going for something like *Cannibal Holocaust* (1980), where your goal is to see how vile you can be.

I am very proud to say that *Henry: Portrait of a Serial Killer* has never inspired anyone to imitate what was on-screen. You know, the old argument about films inspiring viewers to commit similar acts. Well as filmmakers we bare no responsibility if someone goes out and imitates our films and kills somebody. It has nothing to do with us and that person is bad and they would have done it anyway. I watch a show called *Copycat Killers* and three guys were inspired by *Reservoir Dogs* (1992) and these idiots murdered and tried to cut an ear off a 15-year-old boy [the case in question concerns the torture and murder of Michael Moss in Litherland, Nr Liverpool, UK, by Allan Bentley, Mark McKeefrey and Graham Neary, who was subjected to appalling violence. After brutally attacking him, Bentley tried to cut off Moss's ear with a broken bottle in a re-enactment of the infamous scene in *Reservoir Dogs*]. They didn't have a sharp knife so they used a sharp bottle. As they pointed out in the show, it is really hard to cut someone's ear off. They didn't succeed. They made a big mess of the poor kid's ear and then they killed him. There are certain natural-born killers. There are confessed murderers who said they watched *Natural Born Killers* (1994) over and over again. So the idea that there is no connection to me is a cheap place to hide. There is. Now, you can't be held personally responsible because some idiot was stupid enough to copy your film and they might have committed a crime anyway, perhaps even probably so, but there are too many instances of people being specifically inspired. I remember as a kid we used to watch the movie of the week on network television. I forget the movie, but there is this homeless guy and they douse him in gasoline and set him on fire. The next day in New York somebody did that. So please don't tell me that there is no connection. But I am proud to say that we de-glorified the violence in *Henry*. We made it so repulsive that to date—and I am knocking on wood—no one has ever referenced *Henry* as an inspiration for their violence.

ME: *There is imagery in* Henry *that lingers long after the credits have rolled, most notably the home invasion scene. Did you get a lot of flak at the time for that scene?*

JM: Oh yeah! That's what caused the British Board of Film censors [the British Board of Film Classification (BBFC)] to ban it. Then they cut it and they cut it in a way that anyone with an IQ over 50 realized that it only made it worse!

ME: *It was James Ferman, head of the BBFC, he re-edited your film!*

JM: He re-edited it and made it exactly what we were trying not to do. It made it fun violence. The intent of that scene was to pin the blame on the exploitation of violence on ourselves as filmmakers but just by the way we wound up shooting it, it also implicates the audience as consumers of violence because when you see the home invasion at the very end you realize that you haven't really been there and you have been watching the videotape. You are sitting on the sofa right next to them, watching that scene. How are you better? But they recut it so that implication was lost! The responsibility was removed and glorification was its replacement.

ME: The BBFC at the time cut a huge chunk out of the home invasion scene. As I said, James Ferman was responsible for that....
  JM: Yes, I remember hearing his name a lot.

ME: He ruined that scene and the message you were trying to convey.
  JM: Well, the way the movie industry, especially Hollywood with films like *Rambo*, uses violence is to entertain and to gratify the urge of violence that lies within us all. We did one scene in our film in that manner to set up the home invasion scene later. That earlier scene was when Ray Atherton, the big heavyset guy who gets a TV whacked over his head, is stabbed and strangled. The character Fence insults Henry and Otis repeatedly and the audience knows what these guys are capable of. Of course, he doesn't. Finally, Fence is such a nasty character that the intent was that you wanted Henry to get him! "Don't take that shit from this guy, kill him!" Which they did. It was played for laughs. Then the home invasion follows! Which wasn't played for laughs.

ME: The UK distributor at the time, Electric Pictures, also precut the film before submitting it to the BBFC.
  JM: I never saw what they had done to the film, nor did I have any interest. What could I do? Except be unhappy? A producer friend of mine was fond of saying, "No solution, no problem." It took me a while to figure it out but it is quite profound! There was nothing I could do about it. Eventually they came around. Actually, the film was rereleased in the U.S. two years ago and it came back with the same rating.

ME: The film is now uncut here in the UK. One of the scenes that was precut was the image of the prostitute on the toilet.
  JM: I didn't know that.

ME: What is interesting is how audiences today react to the home invasion scene, especially as we live in a world that has so much access to violent imagery on the news on their televisions/internet, etc. What has been your experience? I still find it shocking.
  JM: I showed that scene at Second City where I teach. There are not many directors living in Chicago who have worked at the studio level in Hollywood. As I have no real background in comedy they call my course *Special Topics in Comedy*. [Laughs.] In the first class I show them *Henry: Portrait of a Serial Killer*. I tell them that this was a movie made in this city by people with not a lot more experience than the guys in the class. The students in my morning class—I have one class in the morning and another in the afternoon—were very millennial and politically correct. Before the film I had to give them a warning because they are all such fragile flowers these days. I said listen, there is some rough stuff in it and the movie has a reputation, etc., etc., so be prepared. There is one particularly bad scene and I will warn them when it is coming. So, the lights went down and before the movie starts three young women get up and walk out. I never saw them again! They never came back! [Laughs.] To me, if you were going to stay until you saw something offensive, then left and then came back during the break and called me

a sonofabitch, or how dare I, then I would be fine! But to let ideology overwhelm your thought process and not even see the scene ... then you are a fool and I was pleased they didn't come back to my class.

ME: *Michael Rooker videotaped that footage in the scene, is that correct?*
JM: Yes, he was actually shooting that.

ME: *How did you direct him?*
JM: We blocked it out for him. There was one crew member there and the cinematographer and me, along with the actors. That was it.

ME: *Lisa Temple was the mother in that scene.*
JM: Yes, she was very interesting. She was from Kansas. She and her husband had studied musical theater and they had come to Chicago to get on the stage. They had no interest in horror. But for any young actor any part is precious to them. You don't know how much time I spent with Lisa. She was a very nice person and I said, "Listen, this is going to be a really rough and really horrific." She said, "I am professional, I've studied the script," but I said, "Yes, but you really have to understand how bad this is going to be. Be prepared." So, she did the scene and we shot it twice. The second time, after I had called cut, I turned to the room and said, "None of us are going to heaven after this." [Laughs.] Lisa claims she hurt her neck. I remember her sitting on the floor with her back on the wall in a daze. We took her to the emergency room but it is my opinion to this day that it wasn't her neck but she was traumatized by the events. But I still get emails from her and she says she always says it was one of the great experiences of her life, blah, blah, blah. It remained a highpoint in her career.

ME: *After the film was made it went into cinematic limbo for a while.*
JM: Well, MPI really didn't like the film at all but I will give them this caveat: We only had $100,000 and we didn't have money to make a print. It was going straight to video as that was MPI's business. So when I first showed them we showed a rough cut and there I learned a lesson that I should never have forgotten but I always get my arm twisted and that is that you never show your benefactors, the studio executives or your agents a picture until it is ready. We showed them that cut and all the color drained out of their faces because they have their money and career invested in the film. What happened was because we had very little money to cut the film we didn't have digital editing systems—we cut the film manually. Elena Maganini, the editor, cut the film and we had a first cut which ran 2 hours and twenty minutes, though the eventual film was 83 minutes. We had no way of showing the final cut to them at that point because you weren't going to time the negative and make a print, at that point. We were always going to show it to them in some kind of rough form. In those days you cut films on a machine called a flatbed that ran spools of film and you chopped them. It had a little crappy black-and-white video screen that flickered. So to show them what their $100,000 had bought, we took the very video camera from the movie because the one that got thrown out of the window and smashed was bought from a Sony distributor and it was already damaged. Those video cameras were $900 dollars in those days which was roughly 1 percent of our budget, so we weren't going to destroy it. Instead we bought a dummy for about 100 bucks and threw that out of the window. So we had the original video camera so we shot the movie off that flicker screen and we aimed the speaker at the video camera's microphone! [Laughs.] There was no sound mix. It was

merely a two-and-a-half-hour black-and-white flickering video facsimile of the movie. It was awful! And that was basically the end of my relationship with them. They let us finish the film of course but I learned never show the film in that kind of rough state because they form a first impression that sticks. If you look at what happened when we did finish the film and put it out into the world, it got on *Time* magazine's ten best films of the year and on Roger Ebert's ten best films of the year and it was reviewed positively everywhere. However, in those guys' minds [MPI] it was still a piece of shit that they didn't think they could sell.

ME: *Chuck Parello played a part in the marketing of the film, didn't he?*
JM: Chuck was working for MPI doing publicity. I believe that's how I met him. I was kind of estranged from MPI. As soon as I delivered the film I pretty much split from MPI and we really didn't speak or have anything to do with one another. Chuck was not working for them during the making of *Henry*, but while the film was sitting there doing nothing, Chuck came to work for them and watched it and he liked it. And so, I would work with Chuck and in those days they were a video distribution company and they had one of the first duplication houses to open in Chicago. They did very high quality work. The first generation of VHS copies of *Henry* that went out were really first rate. Then they found someone who could do it 10 cents cheaper per unit so they switched and the quality went down dramatically. The point being, there was no shortage of videocassettes of *Henry*, so Chuck would order up a batch and send it out to various film critics and kept pushing it and pushing it until it finally saw the light of day.

ME: *Overtime it built up a cult following and ironically MPI went on to make a sequel which was directed by Chuck.*
JM: Well that's an interesting story. Chuck had a different script about insurance fraud. He was one person with a script like one out of five million with their little script that they wanted to get produced but no one was interested. However, he was working for MPI and they could produce a film and they wanted nothing more than to produce a sequel to *Henry* because at that time they had made plenty of money with it. So, Chuck was flexible enough to fold his script into a *Henry* sequel. I can't remember exactly what happens but the characters are pulling some kind of scam in the film. So he got a movie made which is better than having a script in your pocket!

ME: *I thought he did a good job on the sequel.*
JM: Actually, they wouldn't do a deal with Michael and they wouldn't even speak to me. I wasn't involved at all. They sat and spoke to Michael but they offered him a crap deal which was basically insulting.

ME: *What did you think of the sequel?*
JM: If you take into consideration that it was Chuck's story and he turned it into a sequel so it was bound to have some rough spots, but I felt there was some good actors in there and good cinematography by Michael Kohnhorst, so all told I think he did a really good job. Neil Giuntoli will never beat Michael Rooker, but he was a wonderful actor and I cast him in *The Borrower* (1991) … if you could control him! [Laughs.]

ME: *Lastly, are you proud of what you achieved with the film and its legacy?*
JM: Yes, I think the film has a sense of classism and it has continued to be released for over thirty years. Today you would have to be careful making the film in showing

someone killing too many women! We were very careful back then; we thought if he is going to kill a woman we have to show him killing a man. We can't just have him going around slaughtering a lot of women because to gratify that urge is not why we are here, though that was primarily what business Henry Lee Lucas was in. He had issues with his mother and nothing goes deeper than that, as Freud was happy to point out.

7

Jack the Ripper
An Interview with Director David Wickes

David Wickes's *Jack the Ripper* (1988) was a British televisual two-part drama based on the world's most infamous serial killer produced to mark the 100th anniversary of his slayings. Divided into two ninety-minute episodes, which played over consecutive evenings during its original broadcast, the film featured a star-studded cast and lavish sets while boastfully claiming that the series would finally reveal the culprit of the murders, based on newly found documentation at the time. While the identity of Ripper is still hotly debated with Ripper scholars, academics, the media and Ripperologists, there is no denying the fact that Wickes created a truly memorable piece of television, whether or not you agree with the film's ultimate findings or with the series' suggestion that Ripper may have had an accomplice.

Upon release, the Wickes mini-series drew in huge TV audiences, and critical acclaim. Starring Michael Caine as Chief Inspector Frederick Abberline and Lewis Collins as Sergeant George Godley, this epic whodunit follows their investigation into the brutal murders occurring in Whitechapel and the hysteria that is whipped up in the community as fear grips the local populace, partly fueled by the tabloids. As Wickes throws in multiple suspects, which include American actor Richard Mansfield, police surgeon Dr. Henry Llewellyn, Robert Lees, Prince Albert Victor and Sir William Gull, to name but a few, the series follows the now controversial theory proposed by Thomas E. A. Stowell, and later Stephen Knight in his book *Jack the Ripper: The Final Solution* (1976), on who committed the Ripper crimes.

Ultimately, all this matters not a jot as the series is historically faithful to both the characters of the time period and Wickes's attention to Victorian London is impressive, especially its depiction of flea-pit back alleys and grimy, smoky pubs inhabited by people from the lowest rungs and fringes of London society. Furthermore, Wickes's attention to Abberline's private life is given more dramatic scope, especially his alcoholism and dependency on the bottle, but this never detracts from the story. Where the film scores highly is in the presentation of victims. Wickes refuses to present them as stereotypical sex workers who pay the price for their perceived immoral trade. Instead, Wickes defines each victim as real characters and, resultantly, their deaths elicit a sense of pity and sympathy for them by the audience. Wickes refuses to show their deaths, only their corpses, and the film is devoid of any explicit or graphic violence yet it remains the definitive visual telling of Jack the Ripper's crimes. This is no doubt helped by the wonderful performances given by the cast, most notably Michael Caine and Jane Seymour, and Wickes's assured direction.

The following interview was arranged with director David Wickes to not only talk about his seminal 1988 cinematic/televisual rendition of Jack the Ripper's life but to also talk about his earlier work tackling the Ripper's crimes in the rarely seen 1973 BBC series *Jack the Ripper*, of which Wickes directed two episodes. I thank David Wickes for agreeing to be interviewed as part of this collection and sharing his memories on making a firm fan favorite and cult series that is still fondly remembered, and highly acclaimed, on both sides of the Atlantic.

Matthew Edwards: The murders of Jack the Ripper have been the source of inspiration for many films, television series and books over the last one-hundred and twenty years. Looking at your own filmography, you have tackled the case of Jack the Ripper twice, first with the highly acclaimed 1973 BBC drama Jack the Ripper, *where you directed two episodes (episode 3, "Butchery," and episode 6, "The Highest in the Land"). How did you get involved in this series?*

Promotional poster of David Wickes's *Jack the Ripper* (1988), starring Michael Caine and Jane Seymour (courtesy David Wickes).

David Wickes: I had worked with BBC staff producer Leonard Lewis on the very successful police series *Softly, Softly*. Len and I became good friends and, one day, he showed me a letter from Elwyn Jones (creator of *Softly*) in which Elwyn suggested ways of exploiting the fame of his two main characters Barlow (Stratford Johns) and Watt (Frank Windsor).

The ideas in the letter included having Barlow and Watt investigate unsolved real crimes that were still on the police books and having them criticize "unsound" court verdicts from the past. Neither of these ideas inspired Len. I agreed with him. Nonetheless, we lunched with Elwyn and at the end of a somber meal in the Balzac in Shepherd's Bush, Elwyn suddenly perked up and said, "Why don't Barlow and Watt solve the Ripper murders?"

Len jumped at the idea and immediately submitted it to the mysterious BBC machinery known in those days as the "Offers" process. No one down at my level could fathom how "Offers" worked. Only the most senior layers of BBC officialdom were privy to matters of such importance. One effect of this was that it took forever to get a decision from up high.

Freelance directors need to earn a living, so I went off to do other things. But several months later, Len called to say that he had been given a green light and was I still interested?

ME: What are your memories working on the episodes and how did the themes presented in that series shape your own televisual drama Jack the Ripper?

DW: The scripting stage was tedious, not least because we had to read at least six or eight books on the subject (there are upwards of 40 Ripper books now) and each one seems to come to a different and sometimes absurd conclusion. Most of the authors claim to have discovered some secret conspiracy known only to them.

Unsurprisingly, when the series was announced, an army of self-styled Ripperologists came out of the woodwork. Poor Elwyn's mailbag was full of "absolute proof" that Ripper was a woman or gay or Jewish or a pimp or a vicar from Market Rasen.

At one point, TV personality and author Daniel Farson argued with Len and me for hours, trying to convince us that Ripper was a deranged cricketer called Drewitt. When we asked him why Prime Minister Lord Salisbury would have insisted on the files being kept secret for 100 years if all he wanted to do was protect an unknown cricketer, Dan became quite angry—a sure sign that his conclusion was rubbish, said Len afterwards.

Still, the rehearsals, the shooting and the editing were fun. Alan Stratford Johns and Frank Windsor were good to work with, and Elwyn's scripts were nicely crafted. As a bonus, I met quite a few interesting people. Among the most fascinating of these was the artist Joseph "Hobo" Sickert, who claimed to be the illegitimate son of the court painter Walter Sickert. Hobo's theory was that Prince Albert Victor, the second-in-line to the throne, had secretly married a working-class girl and that the powers that be sent Walter Sickert to kill a bunch of prostitutes who knew about the marriage. (It was British snobbery wot done it, guv'nor.) The problem here is that Hobo later admitted that he made the whole thing up. But that didn't stop a well-known American author from using Hobo's invented story in not one but *two* "authoritative" Ripper books.

ME: You returned to the Ripper murders for the centenary television drama Jack the Ripper *in 1988. Were you attached to the project from the get-go? I ask because originally the mini-series saw actor Barry Foster play detective Frederick Abberline.*

DW: After the BBC series, I spent most of the next decade moving back and forth between Hollywood and London, making shows like *The Professionals* and *The Sweeney* here and *Philip Marlowe* over there. I also made a number of cinema movies, but, deep in the back of my mind, I always felt that the Ripper story was worthy of a bigger canvas than the BBC had given it. The BBC series had its attractions but it relied on conversations in offices, bits of period reconstruction and visits to much-changed murder sites. Granted, it went down well with UK audiences in the 1970s but it was hardly an international blockbuster.

My old friend and mentor Lloyd Shirley, the head of drama at Thames and the founder of Euston Films, had been bugging me for some time to bring him a show. I had recently finished the second series of *Marlowe* (for Home Box Office in America) and had taken on a young graduate called Sue Davies for two weeks' work experience at Twickenham Studios. We were busy in development at the time and my business partner wanted her out from under our feet, so I told Sue to do a précis on one of the Ripper books.

That was the start of a marathon assignment that we extended over and over again. In the end, Sue researched, theorized and delved into Ripperology for four whole years. Every time we thought of letting her go, she would produce another snippet of information or another connection or another anomaly which made us more intrigued. She analyzed the Public Record Office files, the Scotland Yard files, the Home Office files, the coroner's records, the Cabinet papers, Hansard, newspaper microfiches at the London papers, ditto at several of the New York and San Francisco newspapers, and she wrote an accurate précis of at least six Ripper books. She also made friends wherever she went and persuaded several of them to let her copy their research. Towards the end of the four years, our production offices at Twickenham were piled high with photocopies and we had spent a small fortune. Best of all, two factors came together at the same time: first, the centenary was approaching, and second, Sue unearthed some truly startling evidence that pointed to Gull.

That's when I called Lloyd Shirley at Thames. I wrote a pitch document, prepared a speech and socked it to the Thames board. Unlike the BBC, they decided in a week. But there was a snag: my proposed budget was too rich for them. Yes, they would do it, but it would have to be based at their Teddington Studios, shot on tape and be three hours long, not four. Three hours of ITV prime time nationwide doesn't land in your lap every day, so I said yes.

ME: *So, like the Caine version, the Foster version was originally funded by Thames Television as well?*

DW: I had worked with Barry Foster on *Van der Valk* and I had cast him as the villain in the EMI feature film *Sweeney*! So I knew his capabilities and I felt sure he would play Abberline well. I interviewed a few writers and decided on Derek Marlowe who had done a couple of *Adventures of Sherlock Holmes* episodes, so I knew he could cope with Victoriana.

ME: *Did Michael Caine's interest in the project result in production halting on the original version and the securement of American investment? How did Barry Foster feel about this?*

DW: No, the American interest had nothing to do with Michael—he came on board a little later. The way it happened was very Hollywood. A cinema movie of mine (*Silver Dream Racer*) had done quite well in the USA and the two Marlowe series had earned high ratings for HBO, so I was what my American agent called "hot" at that time. He knew that I wanted to do *Dr. Jekyll and Mr. Hyde* and he suggested it to Leslie Moonves (then CEO of Lorimar, now chairman of CBS). When I said I would not be available until I had finished *Ripper*, apparently Leslie said to the agent something on the lines of "Jack the Ripper? Why isn't he doing it for us?" So in the middle of the night, I got a call from my agent saying that Lorimar had the clout to get 4 hours of coast-to-coast prime time on CBS—why was I playing around with Thames?

Long story short, my friends at Thames (Lloyd Shirley, Richard Dunn, David Elstein) were very keen on getting their first co-production with CBS, one of the three biggest free-to-air broadcasting networks in the world (the other two are NBC and ABC).

So the negotiations began … 4 hours not 3, much higher budget, A-list cast, major-movie crew talent, big built sets … you name it, they wanted it.

While all this was going on, I was still shooting on tape with Barry Foster. To be honest, I didn't think the deal would get done, and neither did Barry. Then, about halfway through the shoot, Lloyd beckoned me off the set and told me to wrap. The cast would be paid off, he said, the Thames crew would be assigned to another show—and would I please fly to LA with him next week?

How did Barry take it? Same as the crew—badly. All of them had put their backs into the show and were loving it. Then suddenly blackout. I organized a wake, which turned into a tearful booze-up.

A couple of days later, Lloyd told me that Michael Caine was in London and would I please have lunch with him before he went home to Beverly Hills? So we lunched at Michael's own restaurant Langan's in the company of his agent, the "Silver Fox" Dennis Sellinger. Michael is not just a good actor, he is also a first-rate human being and we got on like a house on fire. Yes, he'd play Abberline if the script was good enough. Like the big-name agent that he was, Dennis added that it would also depend on the fee. As it happened, I knew what was in the new budget, so I was certain Michael was in the bag.

To understand what a coup this was, you have to remember that Michael was a major movie star, not a TV actor—and once you get a big name in the lead, you need to cast strong supports—hence Jane Seymour, Susan George, Armand Assante and so on.

Fortunately, it all paid off. Michael won the Golden Globe for his role as Abberline. There were three more Golden Globe nominations, including Best Mini-Series or Movie for Television. There were record ratings for CBS in America and for Thames in the UK, plus record overseas sales for Thames International. I'm told the show has been dubbed into four different languages.

ME: How did you and Derek Marlowe set about writing the script and did focusing on the investigation by Detective Frederick Abberline make the most narrative sense? Like From Hell *(2001), which seems to borrow elements of your film, you imply that*

Jack the Ripper stalks the streets of Whitechapel (courtesy David Wickes).

Abberline was a man plagued with his own vices and demons (in this case, alcoholism). This added an interesting element into the drama.

DW: In 1888, the investigation of the Ripper murders was Scotland Yard's biggest operation by far. The whole country and several others (including America), were agog at the serial brutality. As a result, the police were under enormous pressure. There's your drama. Also, Sue Davies had unearthed some evidence to suggest that the real-life Frederick Abberline liked a drink. A man under pressure who is fond of a dram? Bingo, there's your character.

ME: *I thought you captured the feel and look of Victorian Britain brilliantly in the series, especially the flea-pit back alleys and the grimy pubs. How did you set about achieving the look of Victorian Britain? I believe it is one of the best-looking and authentic Jack the Ripper productions to date.*

DW: There are very few parts of London that have not changed since 1888. Getting the look right was incredibly difficult—an Art Department nightmare. Our production designer John Blezard and his crew worked their socks off to "re-periodize" many of the exterior locations. Most of the interiors were sound-stage sets at Pinewood.

ME: *Talk us through the wonderful Jekyll-and-Hyde transformation scenes in the theater. I thought it was one of the most memorable set-pieces in the movie and raises interesting questions in the drama of the nature of schizophrenia or that the Ripper could have been someone with a fractured/duel psychosis, conditions that were not accepted in the medical profession at the time. I thought that was cleverly realized.*

DW: Nowadays, computer-generated imagery is everywhere. Augmented reality and virtual reality are everywhere else. Early versions of effects-tech were, of course, available in 1988 when the show was made, but I chose to avoid them. Even some present-day techniques aren't convincing, let alone scary.

So we shot what are called "floor effects," meaning something that happens in real time on the set. This involved layers of prosthetic skin with tiny inflatable balloons under them—requiring hours in the make-up chair and lots of rehearsal time. Armand Assante (in the role of the American actor Richard Mansfield) knew that the real-life Mansfield had "transformed" himself on the London stage, terrifying audiences and causing the press to demand that the Lord Chamberlain should ban the schizophrenic-like performance at a time when a madman was loose on the streets killing prostitutes. Armand was a real trouper. He went through the prosthetics ordeal without complaint, and his acting was pretty convincing.

ME: *Interestingly, in the mini-series you do not show any of the murders explicitly on-screen. We either see their corpses or the camera cuts away at the point of the attack. As this was a major televisual drama, intended for prime-time audiences in Britain and America, was there a need for a degree of restraint when showing the killings?*

DW: Neither CBS nor Thames was specific about restraint, even though both companies had codes covering violence and gore. The lack of blood and dismemberment must be laid at my door. I was, and remain, convinced that fear of the unknown and terror of the unseen are far more powerful than overt slashings and gushes of blood. What has been called the pornography of violence is, in my view, just that—pornography, not drama.

ME: *Equally, all the victims were portrayed with a great deal of respect and empathy in the series. You don't fall into the trap of presenting them as stereotypical Victorian whores but as defined characters that the audience feels pity and sympathy for. Was this a conscious decision of yours?*

DW: Yes, it was. These poor women weren't evil; they were plying a trade. Puritans may decry the oldest profession but for the five Ripper victims it was a necessity born of poverty.

ME: *I thought the chemistry between Michael Caine and Lewis Collins worked well. Were you pleased with their performances and that of Jane Seymour?*

DW: Yes, is the short answer. I had worked with Lew on *The Professionals* and I wanted Abberline to have a down-to-earth sergeant who could handle a fight. The real-life Sergeant Godly was nicknamed "Upright" Godly … and Lew was just that—a good man to have in a tight spot. Jane played Emma Prentice pretty convincingly, in my opinion. She portrayed her like a cool socialite who, while never admitting it, was fascinated by "the other half" of society—hence the affair with Abberline.

ME: *Audiences have responded very well to the film, and to this day the series receives, and rightly so, great acclaim and plaudits. Yet, how have Ripperologists reacted to the film, especially the controversy of stating that Sir William Gull was Jack the Ripper and that the murders were carried out to protect the scandalous secret of Prince Albert Victor's illegal marriage?*

DW: Our conclusion was that Gull was a schizophrenic, a man of two opposing halves and that the polar opposite of his "doctor self" was a "killer self" who murdered the prostitutes. Gull had had a stroke about two years before the killings and his behavior had become unpredictable. On one occasion, he is said to have shocked a dinner party by producing a human heart from his pocket and offering it to the guests for dessert.

There are other anecdotes, some just as outrageous, which may or may not be accurate, but the difference between our conclusion and that of Stephen Knight (for example) was that Gull, in his capacity of Physician-in-Ordinary to Queen Victoria, had a strong connection to royalty at a time when royalty was deeply unpopular. There were street riots in London and elsewhere (Lusk, etc.) demanding the abolition of the monarchy.

With the whole country aghast at the Ripper murders, the last thing Lord Salisbury's government wanted was a massive scandal connecting the murders to Buckingham Palace—hence the cover-up and the embargo on the Cabinet Papers for an unprecedented 100 years. As mentioned above, that wouldn't have been done to protect a cricketer with a down on whores, or a Jewish immigrant tailor, or most of the other "proven" Rippers.

ME: *One of the interesting aspects of the film is that you present the fact that coach driver Charles Netley was also involved in the Ripper killings because of the distance between the double murder sites. Do you still stand by that viewpoint? Also, you imply at the end of the film that his death was suspicious and not simply an "accident."*

DW: Sue's research showed that, on the night of the double murder, Ripper could not have walked from one murder site to the next between the time when the first body was found and the time when the second body was found. However, he could have covered the distance with a coach and horses. Netley had worked for the Royal Mews and he had also driven Gull on several occasions. Netley seems to have been quite healthy, yet he died young. Suspicious? Who knows? We believed it was worth mentioning.

ME: Looking back, are you proud of both versions of the Jack the Ripper story that you were involved in?

DW: Proud of both? Yes, I think so. The two shows were very different, of course. In some ways, they were each other's opposite. One was a modern-day investigation by two fictional detectives. The other was an historical investigation by two real-life detectives played by modern-day actors. The BBC series was a low-budget studio production with some film inserts. The CBS show was a 35mm movie with some sound stage interiors.

8

Citizen X

An Interview with
Director Chris Gerolmo
(with Johanna Edwards)

Considered one of Russia's worst serial killers, Andrei Chikatilo, who murdered at least 52 women and children during a reign of terror that lasted between 1978 and 1990, is no stranger to having his sadistic handiwork dramatized on film. The Malcolm McDowell vehicle *Evilenko* (2004), partly based on his crimes, was a good attempt at portraying the Chikatilo story, while the big-budgeted *Child 44* (2015), starring Tom Hardy and Gary Oldman, underwhelmed, focusing too heavily on its commercial endeavors as to adequately explore the psychosis or crimes of Chikatilo accurately. More of interest, and the best cinematic adaption to date, came during the mid-nineties courtesy of HBO. A televisual work that has sadly sunken into obscurity, despite a stellar cast featuring Stephen Rea, Donald Sutherland, Max Von Sydow, Jeffrey DeMunn, Joss Ackland and Imelda Staunton, the film *Citizen X* received numerous plaudits upon its release and a bevy of awards, including an Emmy Award and Golden Globe Award for best supporting actor (Donald Sutherland) before disappearing.

Directed by Chris Gerolmo, Citizen X is a grim exploration of Andrei Chikatilo's crimes against a backdrop of a crumbling Soviet Union. Stephen Rea plays Lt. Viktor Burakov, a Russian pathologist who is assigned to track down a depraved murderer who preys on his victims at railway stations before dispatching them in the nearby woods. As Burakov hunts for the murderer, his efforts to apprehend the killer are continually hampered by bureaucratic obstacles, incompetence, propaganda and the Soviet hierarchy, who believe that a decadent "Western phenomenon" such as a serial killer could not exist in the USSR. To compound matters, Burakov's cynical superior, Col. Mikhail Fetisov (played superbly by Donald Sutherland), is just as skeptical. Toeing the party line that the killings are not the work of a serial killer, Fetisov is initially revealed as a man who is keen on working the Soviet System for his own advantage and own personal gain. Meanwhile, Chikatilo is allowed to continue his crime spree as he lures his victims into his predatory grip—his killings shown fleetingly in the film, a wise move by Chris Gerolmo (though the first kill is particularly disturbing). Despite being at loggerheads, the relationship between Burakov and Fetisov thaws, and just as Gorbachev (Glasnost) heralds a new era of economic and social reforms, Fetisov's cold bureaucratic exterior begins to crumble. Swayed by a newfound mutual respect for one another, both parties unite to catch the Rostov Ripper, with the help of Dr.

Alexandr Bukhanovsky (Max Von Sydow), who breaks Russian protocol to help capture the elusive killer.

Director Gerolmo elicits strong performances from his star-studded cast and none more so than Jeffrey DeMunn as Andrei Chikatilo. DeMunn is terrifying as the killer, yet both Gerolmo and DeMunn bring a humanist element to the killer, who, despite his horrific crimes, invokes a sense of empathy without ever condoning or undermining the magnitude of his crimes. The film presents Chikatilo as a man constantly humiliated by his wife and subjected to constant ridicule/oppression in his workplace by his coworkers. This humiliation paved the way for him—a man whose masculinity and respect has been stripped away from him—to lash out at society by committing his hideous killing spree as a means of gaining power and control over his defenseless victims (in this case, mainly young children).

What marks *Citizen X* as an excellent film is that it ultimately shows that with determination, diligence and rigor, even against a stifling Communist machine, the truth will triumph. Despite the grim subject matter, the film is a taut, intelligent masterpiece that rightly fails to glorify the tragic murders of Chikatilo's victims yet it is not scared to examine the damaged psychosis of the killer and what factors contributed to him committing such vile and wicked acts. *Citizen X*'s masterstroke is that it examines how Soviet bureaucracy and Communist ideology allowed for killers such as Chikatilo to evade capture for so long. Equally, it is neither a film told from the viewpoint of the killer nor a conventional police procedural drama, as frequently seen in films of this ilk. *Citizen X* cleverly combines both of these strands and merges it with a look at the dying embers of the Soviet State and how the fall of the Soviet Union ultimately paved the

HBO's original DVD artwork for Chris Gerolmo's excellent serial killer film *Citizen X*, 1995 (courtesy Matthew Edwards).

way for Chikatilo to be caught and brought to justice. Director Gerolmo cleverly shows that the real story is less about Chikatilo's crimes and more about how the State, in this case the USSR, enabled him to get away with his crimes for so long. Therein is where the true horror lies.

In 2018, we had the pleasure of interviewing director Chris Gerolmo about this important work, one that still resonates with audiences to this day. We thank Chris Gerolmo for the generous amount of time he put into this interview.

Matthew Edwards: Citizen X *is based on the true story of Russian serial killer Andrei Chikatilo, who was convicted of 52 murders. What prompted you to make a film about one of Russia's most notorious serial killers?*

Chris Gerolmo: The opportunity arose because I got an essay from a Laura Bickford, who I knew from college and was a producer in town, who had been given it from some other kids who went to the same college we went to—Matthew and Robert Stone—and when Chikatilo was finally arrested I think they read about the case in the *New York Times* and flew to Moscow and then on to Rostov and secured the rights. They wrote a thirty-page essay about the case and they gave it to all the producers they knew, including Laura—who went on to produce *Traffic* (2000) and *Ché* (2008)—and she gave it to me and asked me whether I would be interested in writing such a movie. I read the essay and immediately said, "No, thanks." It was too distressing and ugly a subject for me and then I read it again three weeks later and I said, "You know, this is not just a serial killer or detective story it is also about this huge sea of change in the history of culture after the Soviet Union." I said that you could actually make a really good movie about that. So that's when I decided to go ahead and say "Yes" to the project if I can direct it. So we went around and pitched it in town and at HBO they said "Yes" and wanted to give it a try. So that is how the film came together. HBO greenlighted the movie based on a first draft, which had never happened at HBO before that. They were taking a chance on a first-time director, as well. I think that was very courageous of them, I have to say.

ME: *What prompted HBO to greenlight the film straightaway? There must have been something in your script that attracted them.*

CG: I think there were two things that stood out to them, though I am guessing about some of this as they didn't tell me why. I think it was that idea that the film was what we call in Hollywood an "elevated genre story." It is a story about a serial killer and that the good guys get him in the end but it was elevated because it was also about the collapse of the Soviet Union, bureaucracy, the strength of the people and all the elements that brought the Soviet Union down. I think they were impressed by that. Also, there is this story of two men who appear to be quite different. One is a manipulator and an operator and the other is a passionate and committed man and they kind of exchange selves by the end of the film. They become a lot like each other. One learns passion while the other learns manipulation. HBO felt this was a good story and that they should do it.

A lot of first drafts come in not that well organized. My script wasn't perfect, but it had some really strong ideas in it. I am saying nice things about it and I am not doing that to wave my own flag but I've just rewatched it for the first time in many years and I found it very moving. That's why people greenlight movies at this level—not big commercial movies—because they have a feeling when they read the script.

ME: *The book* The Killer Department *by Robert Cullen, did that have any influence? Some places cite that as a text that helped inspire the film.*

CG: Robert Cullen was writing his book at the same time I was writing the screenplay. He was a smart guy and very well connected. I think he had been the bureau chief for either *Time* or *Newsweek* in Moscow. He knew all the people involved and got to talk to everybody. That was great, but it hadn't been written yet. It was one of two times in my career that I have adapted a book that didn't at that point exist. The Stone brothers and Cullen had got different sets of rights and they were rights that we used to legally base our story on. It had less to do what was in the book but more to do with the legal questions.

ME: *How did you draw the strands together? Did you add fictional elements into the script?*

CG: I am going to tell the truth, when I adapt reality I try to get as familiar with all the incidents that occurred so that eventually I can come up with a story that is often made up. While the story is made up the incidents all occurred. The people were there but they didn't do what was in the story. Both of the lead characters in this story had different roles in real life as opposed to the movie. They didn't become best friends and they didn't exchange characteristics or learn from each other. They just worked together over the course of many years and they helped each other. Essentially, I used all the facts that I could possibly use and made up the story. I made up the strength of Burakov's wife (Imelda Staunton). Burakov did actually have a breakdown and had to go to a sanatorium for six weeks. They also actually arrested Chikatilo and had to let him go. All those events occurred but the story was fictional. It is a template that has been used many times in Hollywood before, the buddy story where there are two guys who can't stand each other at the beginning and come to understand each other over the course of the story.

ME: *Once HBO greenlit the film, you managed to secure a wonderful cast for the film. How did you set about casting for* Citizen X?

CG: Damn do I know! Joyce Nettles was the English casting lady and she didn't cast the stars but casted everyone else. They were fantastic! Laura Bickford got to both Stephen Rea and Donald Sutherland first. Neither of them were on my list. I didn't even really know who Stephen Rea was at that time. When I heard about him I watched *The Crying Game* (1992). When I was writing the story I was thinking more on the lines of a Harvey Keitel, someone a lot tougher than Stephen. However, the choice of Stephen—who is a very sensitive and soulful guy—turned out to be fantastic for the movie, however I can't take any credit for that. Donald Sutherland was a super, super veteran and he had already been in eighty-four movies at that time.

ME: *Also, you had Max von Sydow....*

CG: When I heard the name Max von Sydow in conversation I said, "Sure, let's try him!" Luckily enough he said, "Yes," and I don't know why [Laughs.] I would love to believe it was because he thought it was such an interesting character to play but I don't know. He was fantastic and a super pro. He was really nice and everyone thought it was special having him on set.

ME: *One of the key strengths is the fabulous acting from not only the stars but also the supporting cast, like Imelda Staunton.*

CG: Imelda came from Joyce Nettles. I think Jeffrey DeMunn was on his way to becoming a star in theater in New York but it hadn't really worked out for him. We knew him as a really talented actor and he won a couple of awards for his acting in *Citizen X*. I thought he was great. He was the one who made me stop and care a little bit about Chikatilo. Until then I had found it very hard to give a shit about this guy.

ME: *That's interesting, because despite his awful crimes you do attempt to humanize him a little in the film. You don't portray him as a monster. We see him as a family man with a normal job. I think in order to understand him we must first recognize that he was human.*

CG: I would say it was in large part Jeffrey DeMunn who made me understand that he was a person. He really wanted to inhabit and understand the guy. That helped me understand him.

Actually, I did in fact meet Chikatilo. Having this real confrontation with this real guy was very powerful to me. I recall I had met him before I wrote the story. Laura and I went to Russia with her interpreter and we went to Rostov. We spent a few days with Burakov—the real guy—and one morning he came to our hotel and said, "OK, let's go." He took us to the prison where Chikatilo was being held, which was thirty or forty miles outside of Rostov. It was a two-hundred-year-old stone prison and we knocked on the door. Burakov said, "I'm Burakov and we are visiting Chikatilo." They said, "OK," and went to get the warden. We met the warden. At this time you have to understand that Burakov was as famous as Popeye Doyle. Everyone in the legal system knew who he was so when he showed up at the prison they let us in. If we had asked and gone down the bureaucratic channels to meet Chikatilo then I don't think it would ever have happened. Burakov didn't do that. We had a twenty-minute meeting with the warden who was at a loss of how to deal with this demand. Finally, he disqualified one of our group from coming in—our interpreter—because he found out he could speak Russian. It was fine, it just

Brutal serial killer Andrei Chikatilo is played brilliantly by Jeffrey DeMunn (courtesy Chris Gerolmo/HBO).

helped cover the warden's ass a little bit from his superiors in case anything had gone wrong. In any case, we walked down to Chikatilo and it was more like a dungeon than a prison. It had clanging metal gates everywhere. We went through about ten different corridors and it made us get more and more nervous as we went along. By the time we got to the cell, Laura was so spooked that she couldn't go in. She waited by the doorway. She had been so courageous to get that far! The rest of us went inside this tiny little cell with two beds inside of it and they brought in Chikatilo and sat him on one of the beds. I was almost knee to knee with him. There was about a foot between our knees. I think he was still handcuffed. Both lenses in his glasses were broken. They obviously weren't attending to his every need there. We spent about an hour interviewing him and he kept saying how Soviet Communism had made him do it and now that the Soviet Union had fallen apart that he should be let go. I guess this was his rap for Westerners.

The other thing is he remembered every single person he killed. He remembered their names, what he talked about with them, he remembered where he took them and where he killed them. In every other way they didn't really exist to him. You could tell by the way he talked that to him they were just names and stories about what he did to them. I have to admit that during that hour I conceived an intense desire to punch him in the face! I don't hit people but man did I want to hit him! I was looking at the guards—there were around six of them so it was very crowded in the cell—and I was thinking if I could hit him once I could break his jaw and no one would care. The guards would probably say, "Oh dear, he fell over." Of course I didn't, but by the end of it I was really revved up and I was hopping mad outside the prison with Laura. I remember saying, "Why the fuck did I decide to do this? It was horrible. I can't stand this guy. I came 12,000 miles to talk to this asshole." I just couldn't believe it. It took me a couple of weeks to calm down and realize that the story was only partially about him but also about Burakov and Fetisov. It was also about the dedication of these other guys. But as I said, Jeffrey made me understand what Chikatilo was going through, but I don't agree that if you have problems getting an erection that you get to kill people. I'm really sorry about that but that doesn't give you a reason to kill people.

The fact is in the end Chikatilo killed people because he liked it. The first girl he killed, as I understand the story, is a girl he knew from his school teaching. He managed to persuade her to come to a little hut on the outskirts of town and he tried to touch her and she freaked out and he remembers that he started hitting her. He realized that he was hitting her with a knife and he ejaculated. So it was that experience that made him keep doing it.

ME: *He seemed to have no remorse for what he had done.*

CG: No, he didn't. From a contemporary Western definition he was sane and was fit to stand trial because he knew it was wrong and went to great lengths to hide what he did for ten to twelve years. It is clear that he knew the difference between right and wrong but at some level he didn't care. It didn't matter to him. His victims didn't matter to him as they were just vehicles for his release, his satisfaction.

Johanna Edwards: *When you came to shoot the film you chose not to make it in Russia but in Hungary. Why was that? Was it for budgetary reasons?*

CG: We shot in Hungary and yes it was for budgetary reasons. Another reason was that we were scared that the Russian authorities would come to the set on Monday morning and demand 50,000 Rubles or we won't release your equipment. It was a pretty wild time in Russia at that time. Whereas, in Budapest, they had a stable filmmaking community and a lot of American movies set in Eastern Europe were shot in Budapest at that time. We had gone to Southern Russia on that trip to meet Chikatilo and we had looked around and it was very interesting because we noticed it was very Russian but it also had a strong Mediterranean influence, like the colors of the doors, for example. People's houses had red or yellow or green or blue doors, unlike the Stalinist image that they had. In Budapest they have the same kind of thing, far out colors of doors, but also a really, really rundown town and it looked a lot like Southern Russia.

ME: Talk us through the production. Was it a fairly easy shoot in Hungary? Did you encounter any problems or was it a straightforward shoot?

CG: I felt it was pretty straightforward. I was a beginner but I think it went well. One of the ideas I had had as a young director was reasons relating to the Stalinist fantasy of a world where there was no serial killer and that the Soviet Union was perfect, so I wanted shoot everything straight on. I wanted everything to be perfectly symmetrical. Two round windows on a building would be shot perfectly. All the doorways I shoot straight at. You never look at them from an angle. That used to freak out the DP and his assistant and we would have half-hour-long arguments about it. They felt things were more beautiful at an angle whereas I didn't think that had anything to do with anything.

It was basically straightforward, apart from one exception. Stephen Rea and Donald Sutherland didn't get along. Both are terrific guys in my opinion. Stephen is a soulful, honorable and great guy. He was forty-five and had been in many theatrical productions, many of which he directed before he became a star. He was a normal person. He was extremely respectful with directors and he never asked to change a line in the screenplay. Never. For that reason—and he was number one on the cast sheet—no one else did. If Stephen was going to do it as written then everyone else was going to do that, too. Even to the point Josh Ackland came up to me and asked if he could change a line in the script. I asked him which line and asked to change the word "job" to the word "post"

Stephen Rea as Lt. Viktor Burakov in *Citizen X* **(courtesy Chris Gerolmo).**

because most people get "posted" in Russia. I said, "Fine." That was for a scene that was not going to be shot for two days. So he came up to me to ask about changing one word. That is outstanding but that was because of Stephen. The most important people on the set—and he was more important than I was—dictate the way things operate. Donald followed that lead, too, and did it as written, as Stephen did. But in the end they didn't get along. It got bad enough that one day well into the production—day thirty out of thirty-six—we were going to shoot this important scene at the end of the second act when Burakov (Stephen) walks into the room and Fetisov (Donald) is there, and he has just been to Moscow and appointed General and Stephen's character Burakov has been appointed a Colonel, and Fetisov tells Burakov all these fantastic things about him and that the FBI admires him, etc. Burakov gets all the credit he has never had before or deserved and starts to cry. That particular day we knew it was going to be a big acting day and of course it started out totally poorly. Stephen walked in, in the first moment of the first shot, and then stopped it and said, "He didn't even turn around when I walked in." Donald explained he was going to turn around when he heard him speak but Stephen said "You would have heard the door when I opened it." Donald replied, "That doesn't have anything to do with anything, I was going to turn when you speak." It then became a half-an-hour fight. Finally I said, "That's it. The day is not starting the way I want it to, so I am leaving." I left and went and stood in the middle of the courtyard of the building where we were shooting. I waited by myself for ten minutes until Stephen came down and said, "All right, I'll do it his way, for Christ sake. It's pissing me off." I said to Stephen, "None of this matters. I will choose in the editing suite when Donald turns. It had nothing to do with what we are doing today. If I want him to turn at the sound of the door then I will do that and if I want him to turn at the sound of your first line then I will do that because you are not in the same shot so it doesn't matter." He was all right with that and went away. Ten minutes later Donald came down and said the same thing. I explained the same thing to him and we went back to work. We wasted forty-five minutes but we went back to work.

Then of course this scene was about Stephen's character crying. He gets all this acknowledgment that he has never known he is getting and it moves him so much that he cries. We shot Stephen out first. We shot about fifteen takes of Stephen crying at three lens sizes—wide, medium and close. He had about five times to get what he was doing right. He cried legitimately from the emotion of the scene twelve times out of the fifteen. Then he was running out of gas and needed a little bit of help prop wise to help him cry for the last few takes. Then we turned around and shot Donald. He proceeded to cry sixteen times in a row. Sixteen takes! Only he wasn't supposed to cry! But he was damned if he wasn't going to demonstrate that he was better at crying and could do it more often than Stephen, and he did. I went over to Donald and each time said, "It is really, really real but you don't have to cry. He is going to cry." He would nod and do it again. We got one take of him not crying and we were done. It was like a little crying competition. It was really silly but fantastic to be a part of. The scene is really moving to me and I ran into Quentin Tarantino at a party thrown in Hollywood around ten–fifteen years after this was made. We were introduced, and I told him how much I admired his movies and he heard that I had made *Citizen X* and he went, "Oh, shit," and quoted four or five lines from that scene. I was knocked out, man. He really liked the movie and that moment was really moving. Great, it worked. It was a pain in the ass but it worked.

JE: *I thought you captured the sense of the Eastern Bloc well, especially the greyness and the conformity of Soviet Russia. I thought your production design was exceptional.*

CG: I think so, too. Our location choosing was really great. We scoured Budapest for all those wonderful looking doors, walls and alleyways, and we put up our picture of Lenin on this fantastic street. They did a great job. The DP contributed enormously to the way it looked, too. The other thing about trying to do the Soviet Bloc right was trying to not only getting the drabness right but also the bureaucracy. The stultifying bureaucracy. That was one of the things I completely made up in the story, the committee that meets all the time. It was illustrated for Westerners as to how the system worked. It was difficult to get anything done and I remember being there in the first week or two and Radu Amzulescu, the terrific Romanian actor, the guy with the black hat—he was fantastic—he asked me at one point, "How did you know how this all worked?! How did you know how it was under Communism?" I said, "What are you talking about? I work in Hollywood. We have these types of committees at every step in Hollywood! People don't know what you are doing or why you are good at what you are doing or why you are in charge of what you are doing!" That's how I related to it. In some ways it is very much about getting the credit for being as good as you are and that is really the story of Burakov. Working your ass off until you end up in the insane asylum. Then suddenly someone finally recognizes you.

JE: *How much research went into the socio-economic climate of the time? I felt you captured that perfectly from the start. It was visually well portrayed.*

CG: Yes, it was. I think it was definitely a movie about working people. There was one kind of aristocratic guy in Donald Sutherland while almost everyone else was of working class, Soviet style. I think we got to cast faces people were unfamiliar with. If we had cast this in Hollywood it would have been a lot harder to find, and use, the faces we found. Some of the people who answer the door who talk about their children that died, they look incredible. The one guy with the smashed nose is unbelievable. They would never bring you that guy as an extra in Hollywood. Everyone is good looking, you know! We were there and we were free to do whatever we wanted. I told all the local casting people that I wanted real people when you can get them. It is very politically incorrect to call people "retarded" but they do in this movie—as this was a long time ago—and the kid who puts the coin on the train track to be smashed, he was really developmentally unstable. He lived in a group home and he came and worked with us that day and he loved being in the movie. He looks a little odd but I thought it was fantastic to have people like him in the film. We have a lot of famous actors in the film but the regular people were very regular.

JE: *We have talked about the socio-economic climate of the time but what I think is interesting is how the climate of the time, and the bureaucracy, fed into and hindered the investigation.*

CG: Once the Soviet Union fell I think they caught Chikatilo within a year. Had they been allowed to do whatever came into their heads then they could have solved this case many years before but they just weren't allowed to do what they knew they needed to do. They certainly weren't allowed to ask for Western help, which is too bad as we have about twenty-five more serial killers here in America [Laughs.] Though we are much better at catching them!

JE: Equally, would you say the system itself allowed Chikatilo to get away with it?

CG: Absolutely. He was a very canny guy and very smart about organizing his life. He started out as a teacher but he got the boot. Actually, the first time he touched a girl he got fired sideways and got another job teaching. The second time he touched a girl he got fired but he got a job working at a factory where basically his job was to go on the road with a trunk full of vodka and rubles and bribe the suppliers at other factories to get the stuff he needed to keep his factory on the schedule they were supposed to get it there. That's just the way the Russian system worked at that time. You had to grease everybody's palms or they just wouldn't do what they said they would do. So his job was to drive around with rubles and vodka in the car. He had a very loose schedule and he picked that job because he could kill people. It gave him the freedom to do it. So he was very canny about using the system and the system really, really did fail in this situation. You can't pretend everything is OK in the case of a serial killer like this and get away with it.

ME: But they did pretend everything was OK, or certainly buried their head in the sand as shown by the scene in Citizen X *when they scoff that there couldn't possibly be a serial killer operating in the Soviet Union. That was their attitude, wasn't it?*

CG: Yes it was. I think that was specifically acknowledged, at one point. It was something that didn't happen in the Soviet Union.

ME: It was a Western problem.

CG: Yes, a decadent Western problem. A Western phenomenon.

JE: Equally, you capture the frustration of Stephen Rea's character and how one unguarded comment could potentially damage your career, or indeed, worse.

CG: There was a climate of suspicion and the paranoia of the Soviet system was very real in this case and we used a little bit in the movie. If you said the wrong thing that was enough for somebody who didn't want you around to get rid of you. This whole idea of committing the culture to fantasy by saying, "There is no sexual crimes in Russia, and that's that." That's scary. It is scary when the people in charge are committed to a fantasy because it can be so costly to regular people.

JE: Another aspect of the film that was achieved well was how you chart the political change in the film. I felt you got the message across well—the era of Glasnost, Lenin posters ripped down.

CG: I just rewatched the film and I remember now how many scenes there were and how much material we were trying to manage in a very short amount of time. There were ten or twelve years in this story and the whole world changed; there were fifty-two murders and so we were trying to use all these storytelling techniques to compress the story. For instance, the first murder that we watch is the fourteen-year-old girl. You really watch that. You watch the whole thing. By the fifth murder, you see one slow-motion shot of a kid's head falling down and that stands for another murder. So we tried to compress the story as much as we could and so when we got to the times when we were trying to tell the story of everything changing in Russia we had to compress it down to these exchanges between Burakov and Fetisov. We couldn't pretend to cover the whole change in a huge nation. We had to make it a tiny little event here that changed everything for these two guys. We tried to put one thing in to stand for a lot of other things.

ME: You touched on the death scenes, just then. I thought they were stylishly done. As you just mentioned, the first death is quite graphic—where you see the girl getting stabbed repeatedly—later on the deaths are merely represented with the victim's head falling back in slow motion. How did you approach the filming of those scenes? Was there any pressure from HBO not to be too graphic?

CG: No, not really. I had already seen *Raging Bull* and *Raging Bull* uses the same compression-related story techniques. The first boxing match that you see is quite long and there is a riot at the end. The tenth boxing match is one slow-motion shot of a gloved fist moving through the frame. So that's what was inspiring to me. I thought I would get all the kids who die in the movie—which was around ten of them—and we took them all to the woods one afternoon and we went through and filmed slow motion shots of each of them falling sideways and falling forwards. Then we rigged a little lean-to with two mattresses divided by about 5 inches under which the DP could lie so the kids could fall towards the camera in slow motion. We shot all the kids doing the same thing. Actually, it turned out to be a demonstration of what real movie acting is because the little fourteen-year-old girl who was killed in the first scene—she was the best actor of the bunch and she had starred in two features beforehand—was an actor. The others were just kids. What I mean by a demonstration of movie acting is when a regular kid has to fall toward the camera with his eyes closed, like he is dreaming that he is falling, they will fall perfectly until they are about twelve inches away from the mattress then they start grimacing to get ready for the blow. Everybody does that, except the little movie star. She could just fall and fall, even on the second or third take, she could fall all the way and not react to hitting the mattress until she hit it. She would commit to the moment so much that she was just falling. Watching these dallies for forty-five minutes and like, "Oh, that's what movie acting is!" People who can commit to that moment even though they know they will get hit. That's far out, man.

ME: On completion of the film, was it originally shown on HBO?

CG: It was. It was an HBO production and shown on HBO Films, I think. HBO was a different entity than they have now. I think it was released theatrically in some countries, though I am not wholly sure. I know it was released theatrically in Egypt because I won an award for best screenplay at the Egyptian Film Awards.

ME: How was the film received generally, when released in America?

CG: It was a big hit for HBO. Their job was to do shows that would get nominated for awards. That's what they wanted and that is what they strive to do. They are a subscription service. The film won many awards, including a Golden Globe, an Emmy and two CableACE Awards, and won others around the world and was nominated for many more. Donald Sutherland had been in eighty-four movies before this and never been nominated for any awards. When he got nominated for the Golden Globe I bet him $50 that he would win. He said, "Forget it, it will never happen." When we were at the dinner the supporting actor award is one of the first to be given and when he won he went to collect his award, and he was quite nervous, and he made a speech, then he came over to my table and put a crisp new fifty-dollar bill on the table. He had gone out of his way to go to the bank to get a fifty! So he was prepared!

9

Henry: Portrait of a Serial Killer, Part II, *Ed Gein* and *The Hillside Strangler*

An Interview with
Director Chuck Parello

If you watched any number of serial killer flicks from the late nineties to the early 2000s, then it is highly probable that Chuck Parello was the director. With three well-known features to his credit, Parello first burst onto the screen with the honorable follow-up to John McNaughton's classic thriller *Henry: Portrait of a Serial Killer*, *Henry Portrait of a Serial Killer, Part II: Mask of Sanity* (1996). Following this, Parello directed the excellent biopic of murderer and grave-robber *Ed Gein* (2000), with Steve Railsback giving a memorable performance as the killer. Parello then directed the violently sleazy *The Hillside Strangler* (2004), which pushed the envelope of on-screen depravity to the limits of a commercial flick and simultaneously created a cult, scummy classic of crime cinema, no less helped by two award-winning performances from the film's leads, Thomas C. Howell and Nicholas Turturro.

In August 2017, I had the pleasure of conducting a career-spanning interview with Chuck Parello, discussing in depth all of his "killer" works and his contribution to the serial killer genre. I thank him for all the effort and time he put into this interview.

Matthew Edwards: Henry: Portrait of a Serial Killer *is widely considered a classic of the horror genre. What prompted you to make a sequel? I understand at the time you were working as a running director on John McNaughton's production company. Did this association with McNaughton, and having worked with MPI, help bring the project to fruition?*

Chuck Parello: I first met director John McNaughton in 1986 when he came into the offices of a trade publication I was working at in Chicago that chronicled the film and video production scene in the Windy City. John had recently completed a film called *Henry: Portrait of a Serial Killer*, which was about to premiere at the Chicago International Film Festival, and he thought someone at the publication might like to write about it.

As I have always been interested in serial killers, I ended up taking John's VHS tape of *Henry* home with me and watching it. And boy was I surprised by how great it was! I was expecting some low-budget piece of crap and here was this freaky, scary, completely unforgettable masterpiece. So I called John and arranged an interview. We met and talked a lot and I wrote an article about his great film.

I eventually got a publicist job at MPI Home Video (now MPI Media Group), the home video distribution company that put up the production budget for *Henry*. When I first started working at MPI, *Henry* was languishing on a shelf after being branded with a commercially prohibitive "X" rating by the Motion Picture Association of America because of its "disturbing moral content." So I started showing the film around to journalist friends and eventually got it a theatrical booking as a midnight movie in Chicago. The reviews were good and *Henry* started building up a cult following. So eventually the film was given a small theatrical release and awarded with reams of press and stellar reviews.

Since *Henry* was getting so much great press, John McNaughton's career suddenly took off. Martin Scorsese saw *Henry* and loved it, so he offered John a gig directing the film *Mad Dog and Glory*, which eventually ended up starring Robert De Niro, Bill Murray and Uma Thurman. John and his producing partner Steve Jones gave me a job on *Mad Dog and Glory* as their assistant and I ended up working for them for almost four years. While I was working for John and Steve, I was also looking for opportunities to branch out on my own.

So I went back to my old bosses at MPI and proposed my putting together a follow-up to *Henry* for them. And I was surprised and completely delighted when they actually said yes! I was originally just going to write the screenplay for *Henry 2*, but then both John McNaughton and Michael Rooker passed on reprising their roles for the sequel, so I was elected to be the director, too!

ME: How did you approach the writing of the screenplay? What themes were you looking to explore and was the arsonist element based partly on Ottis Toole's own background?

CP: Henry is such a great bad guy character that it was a real challenge to dream up what exciting adventures came next for him. Early in my writing process I toyed with the very realistic scenario of having Henry eventually being captured and locked up on death row, but then that felt static and a little anti-climatic to me. I wanted Henry to be out in the universe, running free with his nasty habits still very much intact.

The arson angle came from a news story I read about in downstate Illinois in which this ring of criminals who were starting huge arson fires for profit eventually graduated into killing people to protect their criminal enterprises. For me the premise fit Henry's story perfectly because it was outrageous, yet still frighteningly believable. I felt the arson angle was something that audiences wouldn't be expecting, plus I knew it would look very cool on film. I'm not sure if Ottis Toole ever was an arsonist, but I did read that a lot of serial killers first experiment with setting fires before graduating to murdering people.

ME: How did you come to cast Neil Giuntoli in the role as Henry?

CP: I met Neil through John McNaughton and Steve Jones. Neil had played the role of Scully in McNaughton's science fiction horror comedy *The Borrower* (1989). (A great film if you haven't seen it!) and he also worked on a TV project of John's. After Michael Rooker passed on *Henry 2*, somebody suggested that Neil play Henry as he always seems to get cast as rapists and killers in movies and on television anyway, and

Neil Giuntoil as Henry Lee Lucas in *Henry: Portrait of a Serial Killer, Part II: Mask of Sanity* (courtesy Chuck Parello).

he even slightly resembles Michael Rooker. I knew Neil was a great actor and could do great things with the part, so he ended up getting the job.

ME: *I felt Giuntoli's portrayal of Henry captured in some ways the essence of the character so brilliantly defined by Michael Rooker in the original and in certain scenes, especially during the end when Louisa shoots herself, he brings a human quality to his character. Were you pleased with his performance?*

  CP: I was pleased with Neil's performance, I can't imagine any other actor who could have done what he did better. He really did bring a deep humanity to the part, which I was not expecting to be there. And when he turned on his evil spigot, things really got terrifying! It was interesting that Neil had never even seen the original *Henry* film; he's squeamish about movie violence believe it or not! So he was free to make the part his own without seeming like he was simply mimicking the great Michael Rooker.

ME: *I understand the film was shot in Chicago, yet the film is not set in any discernible part of the U.S. In essence, what we see in the film could be any part of suburban America and feeds into the legend that Lucas's crime spree was spread across all the country. Was that a deliberate choice of yours to move the narrative out of Chicago, if not the filming?*

  CP: It was my feeling that Henry would have been smart enough to leave Chicago after all of his homicidal activities in the first film. So I set the next film in an environment which was a little more rural. However, the people who were putting up the money for the film (MPI) had their offices in the south suburbs of Chicago and that was where our production offices were located so that was about as rural a setting as our budget would allow. It was a deliberate choice to move the filming outside of Chicago to reflect Lucas's cross country crime spree, but it would have been nice to move it really far out of Chicago where it wasn't so freezing cold!

ME: In essence, I thought you captured the spirit of the original film in Henry: Portrait of a Serial Killer, Part II: Mask of Sanity. *Stylistically, how did you approach the filming of the film?*

CP: Thank you for saying that. That is one consistent comment I get about my sequel, that it captures the spirit of the original film. I guess I really just connected to the warped worldview of the sociopathic characters in the original, that that film really spoke to me as someone who loves true crime and who can find humor in the bleakest, most uncomfortable places. I guess hanging around with the creators of the original film for a number of years must have rubbed off on me, too!

Stylistically I wanted a film that was beautifully composed and shot, but I didn't want any of my style choices to draw attention to themselves or to detract from the story line. I was aiming for a classic, unfussy style that showcased the dark and gritty world these characters inhabited. All in all, I feel like I succeeded in my approach thanks to the amazing cinematography by Michael Kohnhurst (love his night scenes) and the practical locations we found in the south suburbs of Chicago and in Joliet, Illinois.

ME: Talk us through the production of the film. Did you encounter any problems during the making of the picture? Did shooting on location provide any logistical problems?

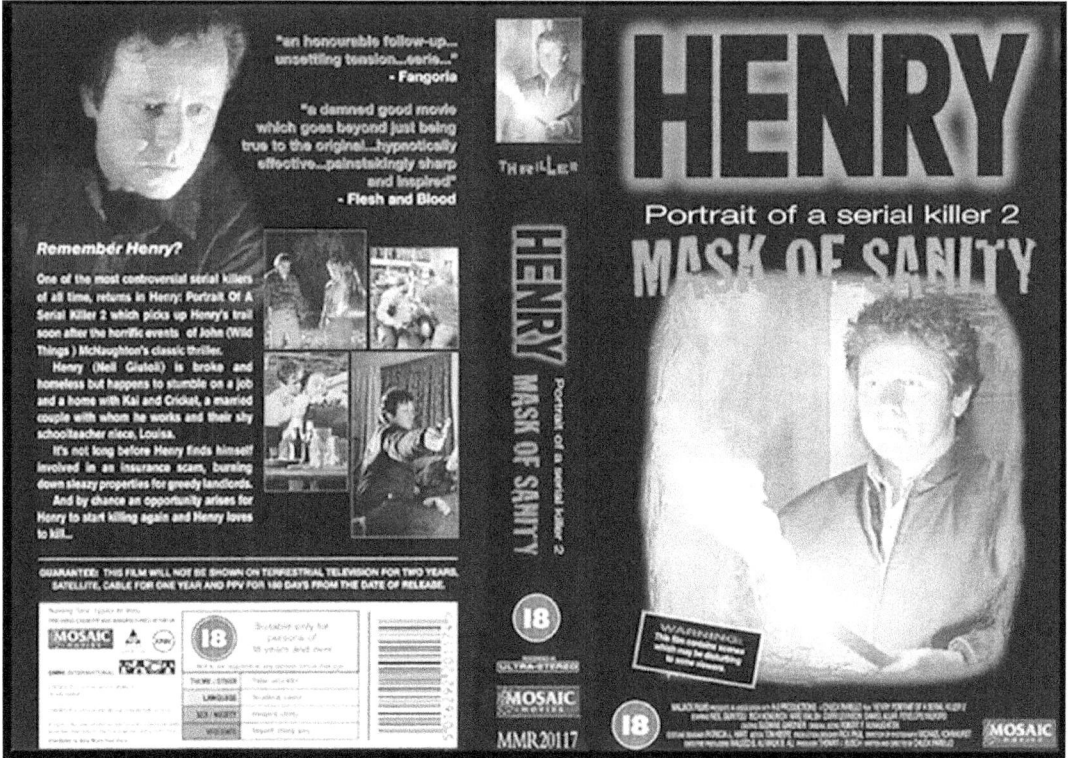

Mosaic Movies DVD artwork of *Henry: Portrait of a Serial Killer, Part II: Mask of Sanity.*

CP: It took a while to finally get the production going as MPI and everybody involved really wanted to make something special. Everybody seemed to agree that I had done a great job writing the script, but then came the equally important part of making it all come to life.

One of my main concerns was for the safety of the cast and crew, what with the potentially dangerous arson and murder scenes we were filming. But everybody was such a pro that there were no problems. And shooting on location did not provide too many logistical problems as we were mainly filming in deserted places without crowds around to distract us.

ME: One of the interesting elements of the film is that you again show the power of Henry to drag others into his perverse world and become complicit in the killings. In the original film, Otis comes to enjoy the killings (especially during the home invasion scene), while in your film Kai tries to resist yet he cannot escape the vortex he has been sucked into (in contrast, Kai is sickened by their actions when they murder the couple). Did you feel that was a key facet that needed to be explored in the film?

CP: For me, it was much more realistic that somebody would react with disgust when murder rears its ugly head. Murder and killings are so often portrayed in films like they are no big deal, and the devastating after-effects of homicidal behavior are rarely even brought up. I wanted to show how tough it would be for somebody to be pulled into something so horrendous. To me, that read as extremely realistic, and extremely scary. I think what makes the *Henry* movies so memorable is that they deal with the real emotions and real horror behind serial murder, so I was very interested in continuing that thread when I wrote and directed my sequel.

ME: The death scenes are graphic, gory and brutally realized in the film. They have the feel of a slasher film, as opposed to the documentary/snuff feel of the original. How did you approach the filming of the cinematic deaths on-screen?

CP: I approached the death scenes as realistically as I could. I wanted the victims to seem like real people who were unfortunately in the wrong place at the wrong time, and for there to be strong motivations for Henry and Kai to commit the murders. I was blessed to have a superb special effects team on the film who really made the blood spurt in spectacular fashion. But this also meant that I had a long battle with the Motion Picture Association of America, who kept threatening to brand *Henry 2* with the same commercially prohibitive "X" rating that they bestowed on the original film if I did not tone down the graphic gore and violence.

ME: I particularly enjoyed the decapitation scene. Talk us through the filming of that memorable scene!

CP: The decapitation scene was a particularly brutal one to pull off, especially for the actor who gets his head cut off while tied to a bed (Richard Henzel). Credit the effectiveness of that scene to special effects whiz Art Anthony, who built a very realistic-looking fake head. Art had the actor put his head under a pillow and put the fake head on top of the pillow. Then he had blood hoses going off as Henry worked his blade. Poor Richard said he nearly drowned in all of that fake blood!

ME: I thought you handled the burning/explosion sequences well in the film. How did you handle them and were they dangerous to film? (In the finale, I understand that you burned down a real house that was located in a suburban neighborhood.)

CP: The burning and explosion scenes were mainly done as inserts at a training center for firemen. So even though there were fire trucks and hoses everywhere, I was terrified that one of the fires must rage out of control in the windy conditions we were filming in and go after the crew or one of my actors. Luckily there were no bad incidents though. And yes, the finale did involve an explosion in a suburban home. There had to be a couple hundred people standing around watching when the explosion went off—it was so rad!

ME: How was the film received critically on release?

CP: Reviewers generally liked the film. They said it was chilling and well crafted and that the performances by everybody in the cast were sublime. However, there were also reviewers who weren't about to give this film a chance, who saw it as a crass rip-off of the original. And I totally understand that kind of thinking as I probably would have had the same knee-jerk reaction if I found out there was going to be what I perceived to be a whoring follow-up to a film I loved and worshiped.

But we really did our best with *Henry 2* and tried to live up to the spirit of the stupendous original. It gives me great satisfaction when I read articles in which *Henry 2* is reassessed in glowing terms as I think it holds up well and is still a damn good, damn scary picture to watch. *Henry 2* could have been utter junk, but I think it really has some value because it was made by a team of people who really cared about what they were putting together. All in all, I know I must have done something right with making *Henry 2* as it got me more directing work, and I still get fan mail about the picture from all over the world all of these years later.

ME: After Henry: Portrait of a Serial Killer, Part II, *you directed* Ed Gein. *How did that opportunity come about?*

CP: They were actually marketing *Henry: Portrait of a Serial Killer, Part II* at the Cannes Film Festival and I believe that Hamish McAlpine, who was the president at Tartan Films, was at a party with director John McNaughton, who directed the original *Henry: Portrait of a Serial Killer*. Hamish started ribbing John saying that we were ripping his idea off with *Henry: Portrait of a Serial Killer, Part II* and asked him what he thought of that. John said, "That's Chuck's film and he did a really good job with it." Hamish was flabbergasted as he assumed that John would be all over it and say mean stuff about it. The fact that he stuck up for the film and he said it was a good film kind of stuck in Hamish's mind. Then Hamish saw *Henry: Portrait of a Serial Killer, Part II* and he really liked it. He was a big fan of the original film and *Henry: Portrait of a Serial Killer, Part II* so when the opportunity of *Ed Gein* came along Hamish said he needed someone who can do something similar to those films. So I got the phone call.

ME: I never knew Tartan Films went into film production until researching this book.

CP: *Ed Gein* was their first production. Hamish had long wanted to be a film producer. He was kicking around in LA. Someone had a script for *Ed Gein* and he said "let's do this," as he knew how popular the material is, especially in the UK where films about serial killers are extremely popular. So it went from there.

ME: What was producer Hamish McAlpine like? Some say he has a bit of a reputation.

CP: He's a total character! [Laughs.] He is a force of nature to be reckoned with. I don't know what he is up to now. I have heard various things about him. I heard he was trying to re-set up his company and get his production slate going again. I do believe he ran into a lot of issues—which I am not at liberty to talk about—but I do believe his company and film library was sold off. I don't know why. He always had extremely good taste in films and he always took chances with material that other people wouldn't touch with a ten-foot pole! I definitely respect him for that. I have heard various rumors here. The relationship with him was a fruitful one and we did a couple of films together and they were both successful.

ME: What attracted you to Stephen Johnston's script?

CP: The script itself was good because it was a pretty honest retelling of the Ed Gein story. It didn't embellish it and turn it into some kind of goofy horror film. I did some research into the Ed Gein story and I saw that there were many different levels to it. I felt if you could present it as something realistic, as something that really happened, it was going to be pretty disturbing and that there would be no need to embellish it because what went on was so horrific. You had this creepy guy who was digging up graves and killed two women out of some far-fetched loyalty to his mother. Presenting that in a matter-of-fact fashion, I knew that it would resonate with audiences. I could see why all those other films had used fictionalized versions of the story but this was going to be the first time it was going to be told the way it actually happened. I think it works well and I often get fan mail from people saying it is one of their favorite films.

ME: The Ed Gein story has been the inspiration for a slew of movies, including Psycho *and* The Texas Chain Saw Massacre, *but what I liked about your film is that you purposely tried to portray a true account of him and his crimes. Was this your intention?*

CP: The budgetary considerations dictated that because it was done on an extremely low budget and we didn't have the money to have all the bells and whistles and fifteen million victims! [Laughs.] It was done on a shoestring budget but reading the accounts of what went on I realized it didn't need that much embellishment and that people wouldn't be bored with what actually went on. I see movies to this day that take the Ed Gein story and the victims are always twenty-something, beautiful blondes who can't wait to take their clothes off! In my mind, it was much more disturbing to show the victims as they actually were, middle-aged women. I took out the sexual element of it because I don't believe Ed Gein was doing what he did for a sexual outlet, he was doing it because of some kind of misguided love for his mother. He wanted his mother back. I don't think there was a rapist kind of thing going on there, but I may be wrong. I have heard rumors of necrophilia with some of the bodies that he dug up. Maybe, maybe not. His religious upbringing would prohibit something like that. I believe what was driving him was his loneliness and missing his mother which for me is much more profound than some guy who just wanted to stick his dick in old ladies! [Laughs.] I am sure there was a degree of sexual excitement because that's a lot of work to dig up a body and bring it home! But whether or not he crossed the line into necrophilia no one will ever know.

ME: Was it difficult to recreate the period working on a low budget horror film? Personally, I think you pulled that off.

CP: It was miraculous that when it was finished it looked like a regular film because there wasn't much money for anything at all. We were very lucky to be in Los Angeles, which has all the best production designers and best costumers to pick from. We had very talented people sign on board just because they wanted to work with me and they liked the script. They were working for rates that were a fraction of what they usually get but they came on board and they were really dedicated and we had a great cinematographer who knew how to keep the lights dark when the set or effects didn't look great [Laughs.] We did well to keep the imagination alive. There were times during the shoot when we threw up our hands and said "What are we doing here?" because there was no money to do anything. We were just so lucky that we got such a dedicated cast and crew. Everyone was just looking to make something that wasn't just junk and a film that would still be relevant ten, fifteen, twenty or thirty years after we made it. I think we succeeded.

ME: I agree, I think the film is excellent.
 CP: I attribute some of that to the cinematographer Vanja Cernjul, who is Croatian. He has gone on to have a very prolific career. He took what he had and made it look magic. The lighting, shadows and backgrounds … it is a beautiful yet creepy film to look at.

ME: You set the scene well with the use of old newsreels showing Ed Gein and locals speaking to local reporters. Did you feel this was important to get across to the viewer that this was based on a true story?
 CP: That was a last-minute addition, the newsreel footage of the old men speaking to the reporters. We started to look around in the archival footage and I saw those interviews, and the Plainfield sign, and I thought it would be a great intro to suck you into the story. I also wanted to underline that this stuff really happened. We were averse to putting "based on a true story" at the beginning of the movie as every film based on a true story does that! So this was a way of letting people know right off the bat that this was something that really happened. Not everyone who watches this movie is going to know that Ed Gein was a real person and that he did the things that he did. So I think when they see the intro they get that it actually happened.

I still find it incredible that the Ed Gein story is still so much in the public consciousness. The internet is awash with so much stuff on him. Bands write music about him, filmmakers make films about him, which is strange because the crimes of Ed Gein were horrific but he only killed two, possibly three people. He has been bested by psychos ten times over who have done worse stuff. In 1957, when he was caught, it was "oh my God, this is horrific" and no one had heard of anything so debased and horrid before. But you just have to open a newsfeed today to find folk doing way worse stuff and in more imaginative ways [Laughs.]

ME: Perhaps films like Psycho *and* Texas Chain Saw Massacre *have helped build up that mythology around him over the years.*
 CP: When we first started showing *Ed Gein* to people they were surprised that he only killed two people. Some of the comments were based on films that Ed Gein inspired. Some people asked, "Where is the chain saw?" [Laughs.] Also, "Where is the part where he dug up his mother?" That was coming from *Psycho*. Actually there are true aspects of the Ed Gein story that I didn't want to include because they were used in *The Silence of the Lambs*. There is a scene in that film where he is stitching together his skin suit so I didn't want anything that was "oh my God, he is stealing from *The Silence of the Lambs*" when Ed got there first. So the audience does bring a certain amount of baggage to the story through the films they have seen inspired by Ed Gein's crimes. I recently read a lot about Robert Bloch, who is the author of the book *Psycho,* and it is interest-

ing because he didn't live that far from Plainfield, Wisconsin. He wrote an inspired-by version of the Ed Gein story and it became Ed Gein's story. A lot of people thought Ed Gein ran a hotel, thinking that this was Norman Bates. *Psycho* is a fictitious riff on the Ed Gein story, it wasn't the real thing.

ME: Steve Railsback is a revelation in the film as Ed. How did you come to cast him in the film?

CP: Steve was actually somebody else's idea. Somebody else suggested him. I didn't know his body of work that well but I knew he had played Charles Manson in the original *Helter Skelter* movie, a performance that people are still talking about thirty years later. I knew he had an impressive body of work behind him, having been in films like *The Stunt Man* by Richard Rush. But I didn't know that much about him. Then I had a meeting with him and I saw immediately that he was Ed Gein. He looked like him. [Laughs.] He had the same small stature and he has this nervous laugh which was perfect for the role. I was like, "Sign the contract, please!" It worked out tremendously! He is Ed Gein.

It was interesting during the process of revising the script. Steve was so dedicated to the project that he would call me at three o'clock in the morning with ideas that he would have. He gets really involved and worked up about things when he is passionate about a character. I was like, "Oh my God, who am I talking to? Charles Manson or Ed Gein?" But he is a sweet guy and we muddled through. It was amazing to see him transform into Ed during the filming. Some of the comments we got were like, "He was so like Ed Gein that it was scary." And it is true. He did a great job and without him the film wouldn't have been the success that it was. I know there have been a few rip-off versions of my film, and I haven't seen them, but I think they took these detours that

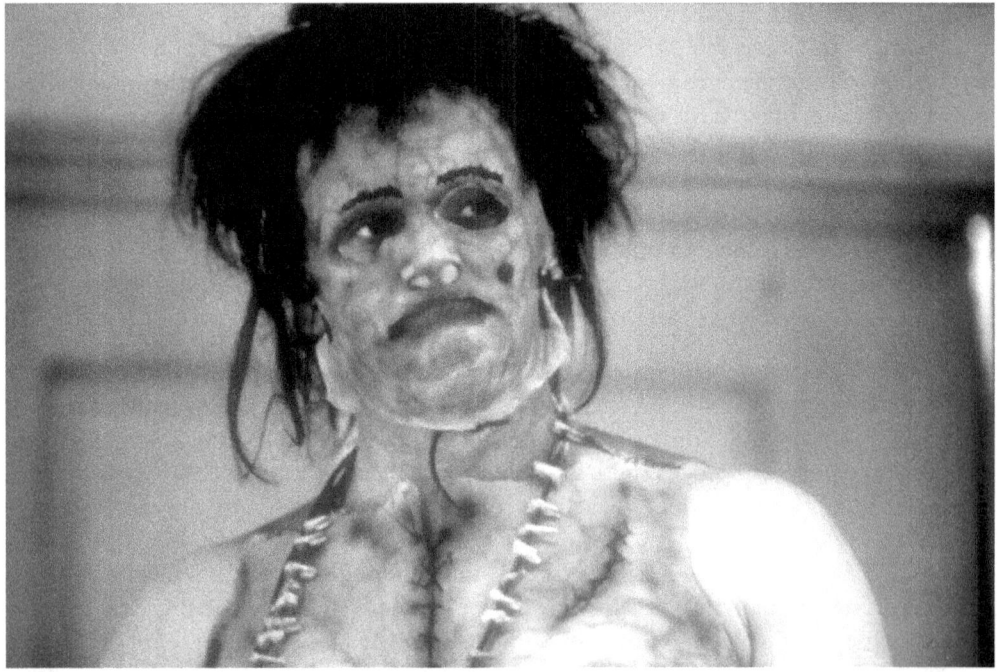

Ed Gein (Steve Railsback) partakes in a spot of dressing up (courtesy Chuck Parello).

I deliberately avoided—the victims were hot young women and the body count was upped. They took something that was successful and turned it into something more commercial. That is all well and good, and I am sure they made money, but to me that's not what I set out to do. I set out to make a film that was going to be around for a long time afterwards and a film that people could relate with. There is a relatability there with Steve Railsback's performance and the other wonderful performances in the film, including the late, great Carrie Snodgrass.

ME: Yes, she was. I thought Carrie Snodgress was superb in the film as the domineering mother. How did she become attached to the film?
    CP: She was terrific and so dedicated and obsessive about what she was doing. You wonder what was going on in her head and when you saw what she was doing playing the mother she was so creepy and scary. I met Carrie when she was in John McNaughton's film *Wild Things*. I knew she was a legendary actress and I went up to her after the screening of the film and I said I loved her performance in the film. In the film she plays a woman who runs an alligator camp. At that screening, she was a little perturbed by what she saw on the screen because one of the scenes she had been in had been cut! [Laughs.] So she was like, "Yeah, yeah, thanks." She was getting ready to ask John why her big scene had been cut! When I met her a few months later I reminded her of our first meeting and she said, "I remember you!" [Laughs.] We actually both became great friends. She was terrific. I was so devastated when she died and with the manner of her death. It was so tragic. She really was a legendary lady.

ME: I think Steve also captures the disturbed mental psychosis of Ed Gein brilliantly and of a man dangling on the precipice of insanity. In my view, the film implies that for all his monstrous deeds Ed Gein is in some ways a product of his violent upbringing from his abusive father and domineering mother. I feel you elicit a great deal of sympathy for Ed Gein.
    CP: I don't know if I ever went into this thinking this is a sympathetic character but I think that was Steve Railsback's decision. He said if this person is horrible and evil the whole time then the audience will not want to follow his story. Steve played Ed as such a sad and haunted figure that you do feel sorry for him. You feel that this is somebody you want to protect in a way. Which is kind of crazy, given the crimes he was up to!

ME: In the film, the parents come across as the monsters. It is his parents that have shaped him to what he has become.
    CP: Other people have had way worse upbringings than Ed Gein and did not go on to do the things that he did. We all make our own choices. He had a roof over his head and they fed him. No one brutalized him too intensively. He did have a mommy fixation. The difference between the Norman Bates character and Ed Gein is that Ed adored his mother. He would never have done anything to harm her. She was his dedicated carer for a number of years. Whereas in *Psycho* you get the feeling that Norman Bates hated his mother. There was a lot of hate there. Perhaps there was some resentment on Ed's part but for the most part he really did love that woman and thought she could do no wrong, which was sort of misguided in that this stunted his growth. I wasn't there when he was growing up but there was a reason why he didn't lead a normal life. He never married, moved out of the house or did anything normal people do as he was so under the wing of his mother. He loved her so much and when she wasn't there he didn't know

what to do with himself. He got lost in his dark dreams and fantasies and then into a whole heap of trouble. [Laughs.]

ME: Comparing Henry: Portrait of Serial Killer, Part II *and* The Hillside Strangler, *you reined in the explicit violence. Instead there is an element of black humor in the film, like when Ed Gein is trying on the different noses and the scene when he is dancing in the flayed skin. Both have a rich strain of morbid humor attached. Was that intentional?*

CP: Yes, it was. Some reviews said that the film had all this unintentional humor in it. It was always meant to be in the film. Humor makes films like this more palatable and I know audiences who enjoy these type of films were laughing. I am a bit of a sicko film fan myself and I find gallows humor gets you through stuff. I could have shot the film without any humor in there at all but I think a dash of funny stuff here and there added to the picture. It was funny when I watched people's reaction to the film and some funny part would come up and they didn't know whether to laugh or not. The thing is Ed Gein's story was so weird and strange that it inspired dark humor from the get-go. There were jokes that school kids used to crack called Geiners and dark jokes about him. Steve Railsback is a really funny guy, too. I thought the humor helped and that the irony added to the horror. The parts when you laugh you suddenly question. Why am I laughing? For me, that makes it even more uncomfortable.

ME: I really like the way you shot that scene when he is dancing in the flayed skin, with that pale blue lighting. It was very eerie and unworldly.

CP: That is funny, because that is the scene everyone remembers the most. Someone pointed out that what happens in the scene, which only lasts forty seconds or so, is basically a guy walks out onto his front lawn and starts twirling around before going back inside. There is so much in that scene, Ed has so much freedom and he is breaking free and living his dream. Remember at the very end of that scene he snickers before he goes back into the house and at one point in the editing we thought about cutting that part from the film because we thought it cut into the horror aspect of it. People fought against that cut, and I am glad they did because it was a nice moment. With *Ed Gein* we were trying to strike a balance between humor and horror.

ME: I think you succeeded.
CP: Thank you.

ME: How was the film received upon release?
CP: It was interesting because it won the best picture and actor award at the Sitges Film Festival. Europe was really crazy for the film; they wrote big long think pieces about it. It opened in cinemas in the UK and I did a week of interviews for it. Then it opened in a few theaters in the United States and both Steve and I attended a screening. We were worried there would be only two people in the theater and low and behold it was packed and the audience loved it. It made money on the direct video market in the U.S. but they didn't treat it with as much reverence as they did in Europe. Europeans tend to take horror films much more seriously than they do in the United States. It is interesting that European writers seem to know a lot more about American culture than Americans do. I used to work as a publicist and I worked on getting *Henry: Portrait of a Serial Killer* off the shelf where it was sitting with an "X" rating. I noticed that people in Europe and Asia knew a lot more about the film than Americans did. It became legendary overseas before Americans caught onto it.

I'm from Chicago and I was a teenager when John Wayne Gacy was arrested. He killed thirty-five boys and buried them in his crawl space. I will never forget that period because I was the same age as some of those boys that he murdered. Back then we didn't have the internet, but all the details of what happened were written about in the newspaper. People couldn't believe how someone could be so savage. It is so mind-boggling that this creepy guy was doing this. I totally get the fascination with serial killers/real killers. Some of them get way too much publicity, like Charles Manson. I don't know how many more Charles Manson movies I want to watch. [Laughs.]

ME: You followed up Ed Gein *with* The Hillside Strangler. *Do you have an interest in true crime or was that the type of films you were being offered at the time?*

CP: Hamish and I did *Ed Gein*, which was a tremendous success, and he wanted to do *Ted Bundy* right after that. *Ted Bundy* I was interested in doing but it was such a huge story, and it had been done before, so I felt it would be very problematic making that film on a tiny budget. I was initially supposed to direct the film but I got offered to do a werewolf movie in Spain with Brian Yuzna's company, which never actually happened. So I sat *Ted Bundy* out and that movie came and went. There are people who like Matthew Bright's version of the Bundy story and I am not discounting it or anything like that, but then I believe Hamish and Matthew got into *The Hillside Strangler* for various reasons and Matthew was originally slated to direct the film. Hamish and Matthew had a disagreement and the next thing I know is that I get a call asking me to direct the film. I said it sounded interesting and I started to read up on the case, which I sort of knew about. I remember when I was very young that it was in the papers but I lived in Chicago and the killings occurred in Los Angeles, so I didn't know all that much. But when I first started reading about the crimes I couldn't believe they seriously wanted to make a movie about this [laughs], but the more I got into the psychology of Angelo Buono (Nicholas Turturro) and Kenneth Bianchi (C. Thomas Howell) the more I was hooked. Their crimes were so horrible.

ME: You co-wrote the script with Stephen Johnston, didn't you?

CP: With *Ed Gein* I really revised the script and I don't know if Stephen liked what I did or not. It is different when making low-budget films. It is easy for a screenwriter to say this is what is going to happen but it really takes someone who has made a film, or been on set before, to realize when you have zero resources and zero time what you can actually do. So I had to revise parts of the *Ed Gein* script. With *The Hillside Strangler*, Matthew Bright wrote a version of the script which was pretty much a catalogue of the crimes. He just took all their crimes and strung them together. Then they gave it to Stephen who fleshed it out and then they gave it to me and I sweated over every word a thousand times. I did do quite a lot of work on *The Hillside Strangler* script. It was a tough one because the violence is so extreme to me it felt that if there wasn't a motivating factor to keep watching then you would want to turn it off as it would have been a film about these two creepy guys.

ME: The relationship between the two is key to the film. Also the film is more exploitive and violent than Ed Gein, *but that is the nature of the story.*

CP: That was partly due to Hamish's input. He wanted to show everything. I didn't have any problem with that but the issue was there is a line you are crossing because you didn't want to be to horribly exploitative as it is real people with families who are still out there. So I agreed to have the violence in it but I wanted a reason for their motivation behind it, otherwise you will just want to turn it off. Some violence freaks don't have a problem with that but I knew I would get a lot of flak from moralistic critics.

ME: *This was a real-life case and as per the nature of the story you had to weigh up whether you show the sexual violence or not.*

CP: I think at the time Hamish had just released *Irreversible* [Gaspar Noé's film was released in the UK on Hamish McAlpine's distribution label Tartan Video to much controversy and furor due to the film's explicit sexual violence, most notably the opening rape scene]. There was a French wave of ultra-violent films and I do believe that Hamish had that kind of experience in mind. I said, "Wait, those are fiction. Those are made up. It is quite another thing when you are talking about real people." The stir I thought it might cause never really happened because I think audiences are so inured to movie violence now. Audiences are like, "OK, next killing please." When we showed *The Hillside Strangler* for the first time in LA I would say about thirty percent of the audience went running for the exit and by that time I had seen it so many times so I was used to the violence or shown it to people who weren't bothered by the violent content. I must say, parts of the film are pretty tough to watch.

ME: *You set up the relationship between the two killers well. It is only halfway through the film when the murders start kicking in. The film is grueling and hard to take but it is also shows what they were doing. I don't think you were being deliberately exploitive but that you were trying to capture the monstrous crimes these sickos committed.*

CP: Yes, the experience of the perpetrators is the most interesting aspect, especially when working on a low budget. We can't really show what the law enforcement

C. Thomas Howell (*left*) and Nicholas Turturro give memorable performances in Chuck Parello's violent flick *The Hillside Strangler* (courtesy Chuck Parello).

is up to. You notice that a lot of these true-crime films these days will be centered on the investigation into the crime as opposed to the perpetrator themselves. When you are working on a low budget film that is hard to do because it is hard to portray the law enforcement accurately when you don't have any money. I also think the lesson learned from *Henry: Portrait of a Serial Killer* was to stick to the perpetrator the whole time.

ME: I think that way you can get into the psychosis of the killer, which you do well in The Hillside Strangler. *Both killers are vile, especially Angelo.*
    CP: Little is known about what they actually did. Bianchi has come out and said that Angelo did this and that but he is such a colossal liar that you don't know what is truth and what is fiction. What I thought was very telling about those two was that they never really discussed what they were up to and they kind of had code words for when they would go out and hunt but they both must have mutually enjoyed what was going on. They must have because it is a lot of work to kill women in the way that they did! They could have done a lot of different things with their time and that's what they chose to do. There was nobody cracking a whip telling them to go out and do those crimes. They did it because they wanted to and because they enjoyed it. I thought it was interesting that they had this underground way of speaking about it and they didn't really say we did this because of this. Angelo was like a caveman, anyway—a man of few words—where Bianchi was a blabbermouth. I think there was an underlining homosexual attractiveness, too. Buono saw Bianchi as a younger, good-looking guy and Buono would stick his thing in anything. His son even said at one point he thought his dad was trying to bed him! So I think they had this underlined homosexual thing going on—usually if you have sex with a girl you don't invite another guy into your bedroom with you! [Laughs.] I don't want someone in there with me! They were so base and horrible that the most horrendous things became normal to them. I think they thought they were invincible for a while and that no one would catch them and that they could get away with these killings. They loved the fact that they were scaring the shit out of the whole of Los Angeles. Everyone was talking about them and for them that was great power. Very scary stuff.

ME: Like Ed Gein, *for the film to be a success you needed two good central performances from your actors when playing the sadistic killers, which you got. How did you come to cast C. Thomas Howell and Nicholas Turturro in the film?*
    CP: C. Thomas Howell became involved because we were looking around for someone to play Bianchi and a lot of names were bandied about. Hamish seemed to gravitate toward actors who had drug problems [laughs], which is not what you want when making a movie as they may not show up on set. In the end, I think C. Thomas Howell's manager suggested him and we thought that was a name from the past. I didn't know much about his work but I knew he had been in some big films. I didn't know he was as good as he was. So we went to meet with him—and I thought it was just a meeting—and Hamish was like, "We are thrilled that you are going to take this part on!" I was like "What?," because Hamish was being very picky about everyone else. I was like, "This is news to me," and C. Thomas Howell said, "Doesn't Chuck have something to say about this?" Obviously not! Actually, I am so glad that he did the part because he was just sublime. It just goes to show that when you are working with someone who is a pro and someone who has been acting for as long as he has then there are a lot of benefits

there. You are not working with a head case. He slipped so easily into that slimy character and his performance is so, so scary. It was a real departure from being this heroic guy who comes in and saves the day. All of a sudden he was this slimy, scary, rapist-pervert! So that worked out well.

Nicholas Turturro was actually someone else's idea. A friend of mine suggested him. Just looking at him, and his body of work, I knew that would be a good match. We offered the film to him and at the time he was like, "OK, a movie part." Then he finally realized he was going to do it so he read the script and the next thing I know Nicholas is having second thoughts about it. So I had to get on the phone with him and explain to him that it is a part you can chew up and spit out and that he could go in with savage relish and no one will look at anything else when you are on-screen. It is the perfect bad guy part. I did my best sales job. I said he would be like Edward G. Robinson. You will be like one of the great old bad guys. Then when on set, you would never had known he had any apprehension about doing the part. He went charging at it with such glee. He looked at the women afterwards and said, "Are you okay?" The women miraculously were never intimidated or had any problems with what went on. I would be so worried after a take because it was so convincing. I kept asking the women if they were all right, to which they replied they were fine. For example, the woman who has the bag placed over her head, I was dreading shooting that scene. When coming to the scene when she gets killed, the actress was like, "Wow, this is the best part of it all! I can't wait. I love stuff like this." I was like, "Oh, I love your attitude."

ME: How on earth do you cast for those parts?

CP: Yes, though I was worried about the woman who has the bag placed over her head. No sane person would take that on. Then we ended up with a really, really good actress agreeing to do the part called Brandin Rackley. She is a gorgeous lady, sexy as hell. She is a terrific actress but people wouldn't give her a shot because she was so sexy. She had it all and she could act, too. Sadly, people weren't hiring her for serious parts. She is a veracious blond with a killer body. I was thinking we would have to hire a porno star or something, who couldn't care less what they had to go through. Then someone said, "Brandin will do it."

ME: Did you have to hire any porno actresses for the film? I ask because I sense the actress at the beginning of the film looks like a porno starlet and seemed at ease doing the double penetration scene!

CP: Yes, she was recommended by Ron Jeremy. That part was a problem, because there was the double penetration scene. There was one sexy woman who was a career actress who was crazy enough to agree to it. She said, "Yeah that sounds great." Then she read the script and called back and said, "I am not doing that." She didn't mind doing the double penetration but when she read about what the characters were like she was like, "Urgh, no!" Then Ron Jeremy recommended this young actress called Kylie Rachel and she agreed to the part. Actually, her acting wasn't too bad. She was definitely a porno star! I remember in-between takes the wardrobe person tried to put a robe on her and she refused! She liked being nude all the time! She agreed to do it about twelve hours before we were due to shoot it. She agreed to be the meat in the Bianchi–Buono sandwich! She was all smiles as well. It was her first non-porno role.

ME: Stylistically, how did you approach this film compared to Ed Gein?

CP: Well *The Hillside Strangler* was shot in the seventies when this whole sexual revolution was taking place. Again we were limited to what we could do. I used the same costumer from *Ed Gein* and a great cinematographer called John Pirozzi. It was very problematic when shooting because every time we were filming the character Bianchi and driving out on the street we couldn't close off traffic or have a million period cars. We would be filming a really great take and then a SUV would come whizzing by in the background or a bus with artwork from a new film/TV show. It did make me think if anyone would recognize that this is a period piece. We were going to all this trouble because the film is set in 1977–1978.

ME: I thought the film did reflect the era. For me, the film captures a real scummy vibe and seediness to LA. Almost behind the glamor you expose a real dark underbelly which allowed the killers to do what they wanted.

CP: It is all cleaned up now but for a long time it was a total cesspool with porno movie theaters and strip joints. There were hookers everywhere. Hookers are on the internet now. There are still streetwalkers but they used to be lining Sunset Boulevard. It was all just a red-light district with sex, sin and partying. Porno movie theaters were prevalent. It was the same as New York with its 42nd street. Sex sells and sin, sin, sin. Now it is like Disneyland since it's all been cleaned up. It is family friendly. That's not necessarily a bad thing as I have been in a couple of those porno theaters and they were gross! Prostitutes were plying their wares in the foyer of the theater. There were cats moping around in the aisles because they were hunting rats!

ME: Did you encounter any problems during the making of the film?

CP: It was tough. It is never easy when you have no money. The cast and crew were all great and everyone worked hard. At times the stuff we were shooting was so harrowing that I thought we had just killed somebody. [Laughs.] Overall, it was tough. We had a short shoot with no buffer. We were supposed to be shooting in a mountainous region but we couldn't do that so we shot some scenes in a parking lot! Everyone was game and gung-ho. The ladies were terrific and C. Thomas and Nick were great. It was also the first time I worked with Lin Shaye. I knew she was a famous actress because of the film *There's Something About Mary*, but boy, the scene with her and her son with their verbal fireworks when she gets a napkin shoved in her mouth? Boy, those two went at it so convincingly and they loved it! To them that was the pinnacle of success in their careers. Lin said that was the strongest scene she had ever been in and she had been in more than a hundred and fifty movies.

ME: There are many strong scenes in the film and they are convincingly realized.

CP: They had to be if you wanted to get an inclination of the characters behind them. It is what it is and the performances are just terrific. In particular, I think C. Thomas Howell deserves a lot of credit because every take was perfect. He had no problems slipping into character. It was like another skin to him and he is just so much fun to watch. You didn't see the effort. An actor like Steve Railsback was so worried about everything but with C. Thomas he would show up and do it perfectly every time. I'd love to work with him again.

ME: How was the film received critically and commercially?

CP: I knew there would be a backlash to the film from mainstream critics, which is good because that makes more people want to see it. I definitely got a good critical re-

The Hillside Strangler **is based on the true crimes of Kenneth A. Bianchi and Angelo Buono. They would lure their victims into their car where they were sexually abused, tortured and murdered by methods such as injection (as pictured), electric shock or carbon monoxide poisoning. This image shows just one of the disturbing murders in the film (courtesy Chuck Parello).**

sponse from people who gave the film a chance. In Europe it was treated with a lot more respect than in the United States. The film did what it was supposed to do and it stays with you, which is a testament to the film's power. Again, it made money for Hamish and I am proud of the film. Low and behold I get fan mail about the film from people who say it is the best thing since sliced bread! [Laughs.] One guy wrote to say he has seen the movie three thousand times! It is very popular and that is partly down to extreme violence of the film. It is a film that horror fans watch over and over again because there are so many real, powerful scenes in the movie. There is a fascination with films with this kind of material which is never going to go away ... especially in the UK.

ME: Are you proud of your serial killer trilogy of films?

CP: Interestingly, with *Henry: Portrait of a Serial Killer, Part II* I knew making a sequel to the original was an uphill battle because to some people it is one of the best movies ever made. To do a follow-up without Michael Rooker and John McNaughton was sacrilegious. Yet, the film turned out really well and people who have seen it and liked it watch it a lot. I knew it was a good film after all the work and effort I put into it but there was this backlash from people who hadn't even seen it. Yet, they didn't know my background, that I worked with John and Michael. Actually, Michael Rooker was offered the opportunity to direct *Henry: Portrait of a Serial Killer, Part II* first. His demands were so absurd that it didn't work out. Had Michael been involved then I would have been nowhere near it. He would have brought his own people in and written his own script. I asked John McNaughton to do it and he wasn't interested. So it wasn't as if we didn't try to get them both involved in the sequel but there was such a weird backlash to *Henry: Portrait of a Serial Killer, Part II* that it was easy to lose track that it was a damn good movie. Then crazy Hamish came along and liked the film and asked me to do this all again. For a while, I tried not to continue this trajectory of weird serial killer films but you know that's what people want from me and I do them well. I would like to do a regular horror film one day but I must say that serial killer films have a tremendous sticking power.

10

Dahmer
An Interview with Director David Jacobson

The crimes of serial killer Jeffrey Dahmer have been the inspiration for a number of low-budget feature films since his arrest on July 22, 1991, and subsequent death in prison on November 28, 1994. Ranging from short films such as Adam Nelson's *Jeffrey* (2016) to risible fare such as *Dahmer vs. Gacy* (2010), where the FBI try to create the ultimate killer by mixing DNA for Dahmer and Gacy, Dahmer biopics have tended to be a mixed bag. Rich Ambler's *Raising Jeffrey Dahmer* (2006) underwhelmed, while Marc Meyers's adaption of the graphic novel *My Friend Dahmer* (2017) was a brilliant exploration of Dahmer's adolescent years and his transition into one of the world's most infamous serial killers. Sitting alongside Meyers's work is David Jacobson's brilliant biopic of Jeffrey Dahmer, starring Jeremy Renner, and his search for young males he can lure into his apartment and turn them into zombie sex slaves before finally killing them.

The film opens with Dahmer working the night shift on the assembly line at a chocolate factory. Although slightly aloof to his coworkers, Dahmer is presented as any regular blue-collar worker. Yet Jacobson shifts the action to him prowling around a mall looking for his next victim, Khamtay (Dion Basco), who he persuades to come back to his apartment on the pretense of taking nude pictures of him, before drugging him. As Dahmer slowly tortures his prey, drilling into his head and keeping him in his apartment, Khamtay awakes next to the body of one of Dahmer's victims and in a semi-comatose state flees the apartment. Returning from a late-night convenience store, Dahmer spots Khamtay with two concerned passers-by whereby Dahmer tries to drag him back to his domain. His plan is momentarily thwarted when a pair of Milwaukee cops arrive on the scene. Interrogating Dahmer in his apartment, Dahmer convinces the officers that they are "together" and that his friend is merely drunk, at once highlighting how he was able to get away with his crimes. While suspicious of Dahmer, the cops buy his story, partly due to their own general uneasiness brought on by their own bigotry and prejudices toward homosexuality. With the cops gone, Dahmer strangles Khamtay to the point of death before reviving him (for now!). A late-night phone call from Dahmer's grandma to help dispose of a crow in her kitchen induces the first of many flashbacks that help paint Dahmer's descent from socially awkward adolescent into an inhuman monster.

These flashbacks hint towards Dahmer's growing interest in fetishism and sexual abuse until his ultimate progression into murder. In one disturbing scene we see Dahmer at odds with his father, who argues about a mannequin that he is hiding in his cupboard. As they argue about the mannequin, because it is freaking out Dahmer's grandma, his father notices an old wooden box that once belonged to him. Dahmer's father (Bruce Davison) asks Dahmer for the key, as he wishes to look for a ring from an old girlfriend that may be stored inside. Dahmer refuses. As the two argue, displaying the fractured relationship between father and son, we soon learn why Dahmer is reluctant to open the box: inside lies the severed head of one of his victims. It is only through his quick thinking that Dahmer prevents his father from discovering his murderous pastime.

Later in the film, we see Dahmer picking up a new victim (Rodney, played by Artel Kayaru) in a knife shop, whereby a trip to a gay bar triggers flashbacks of Dahmer drugging and raping a number of young men. With strobe lighting and stylized editing, we see Dahmer's twisted torso and open black mouth against a blood-red background morph into a strange, abstract composition that recalls the work of English artist Francis Bacon, such as *Three Studies for a Crucifixion*, all to the tune of *More, More, More* by Andrea True Connection. Jacobson's portrayal of the gay community is one of vibrancy and normalcy: just young kids enjoying a good time like anyone else. This is a masterstroke by Jacobson as he refuses to demonize the gay community or present it negatively, which, in stark contrast, the press and law enforcement often did at the time of the killings. As we flash back from the present to the past, we witness the disintegration of Dahmer's family unit and how it triggered his first kill—Lance Bell (Matt Newton)—before, back in the present, we see Dahmer continuing his crimes when he attempts to garrote Rodney before Rodney flees.

Jacobson presents a world of late-night gay bars, glowing red neon and a murderous predator who lured his unsuspecting victims either willingly back to his apartment or through spiking their drinks. Jacobson's Dahmer is a pathological psychopath who patrolled the gay bars of Milwaukee looking for men he could seduce and control, torture and kill, at his own whim. In the film, Dahmer is not only seen as detached from

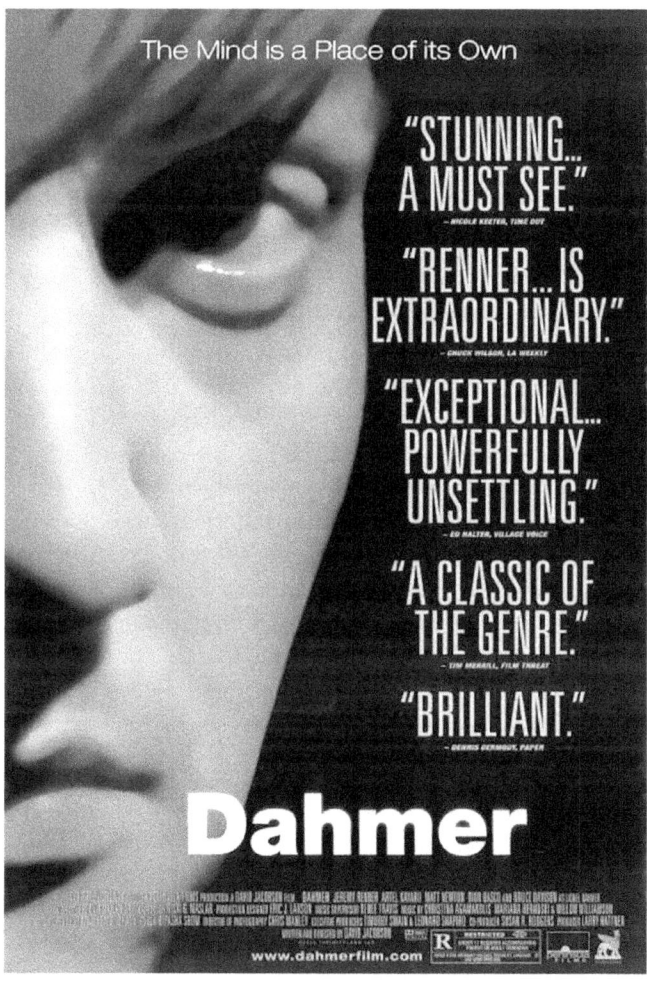

Promotional poster for David Jacobson's *Dahmer*, the unsettling exploration of the life of Jeffrey Dahmer, played by Jeremy Renner (courtesy David Jacobson).

his family but also from society and reality. Yet Jacobson humanizes Dahmer and shows that through his charm and awkward shyness he was able to build up the trust in his victims to the extent that they never perceived him to be a dangerous psychopath. Jacobson shows brilliantly that behind his aloof, shy, socially awkward demeanor lay a cunning and highly organized killer. A man on a self-serving quest to create his own sex zombies. To achieve this, Renner's performance as Dahmer is exceptional, capturing his contrasting and complex persona effectively while still humanizing him. While some viewers will find it hard to relate to the humanization of Dahmer in the film, to do so is to miss the point as it is that humanization which makes the film so frightening and memorable. Jacobson doesn't make excuses for Dahmer nor does he defend him. Jacobson offers no solutions as to Dahmer's descent into mass murder or fall into easy psychological motivations to justify Dahmer's actions. In the end we are merely shown that all Dahmer's vices and flaws are inherently human. Therein lies the horror.

In September 2017 I had the pleasure of interviewing director David Jacobson about his outstanding film and about the crimes of Jeffrey Dahmer. I thank him for the generous amount of time he put into the interview.

Matthew Edwards: *The early noughties saw a number of films being made based on real-life serial killers. How did you come to make a film based on the life of Jeffrey Dahmer?*

David Jacobson: I wasn't really out there trying to do true crime or a film on serial killers or horror or anything. My angle was something similar to my first film, *Criminal* (1994), which was a black-and-white film. I like to make interesting films and I was inspired by European cinema. So *Dahmer* came about because I was listening to a radio program and they were interviewing Dahmer's father, who had just published his book about being a father of a serial killer. So I bought a copy and I read it and I was blown away, especially when he described that he was an upper middle class guy, a scientist with a PhD who was part of a regular suburban family; he didn't know where this horror came from. I was astonished as his background was very much like my own. My dad had a PhD in science, and like Dahmer I came from a broken family. My parents were divorced. The emotional world that Dahmer grew up in was not that far from my own. That's what really got me into it. I thought, "Oh my God, he's a serial killer but there is something sort of understandable to me." Of course, there are a lot of things he did that aren't comprehensible but still enough that I wanted to tell this story about him. In a sense, ultimately, I wanted to show that someone like Dahmer isn't completely distant from humans. In some ways, there is a little bit of him in all of us.

ME: *That's interesting you say that because I feel you do humanize Dahmer, which makes the film more horrifying, in my opinion. You shy away from presenting Dahmer as a comic-book villain or someone like Michael Myers from* Halloween *(1978).*

DJ: Exactly, I definitely didn't want to do that. [Humanizing him] came from the initial feeling I got from his story. It got stronger and stronger. One of the things that came out of it for me was the whole idea of empathy and trying to understand what other people are feeling and how important that is. My conclusion was exactly what Dahmer didn't do. He clearly didn't have much empathy for his victims otherwise how could he have done the things he did to them? So it became a big revelation to me and since writing *Dahmer* I have always tried to understand the characters that you are portraying, even the despicable things that they do. I was also always interested in the moral ambiguity in movies and the characters who you couldn't say were good or you couldn't say were bad. Those are the most interesting characters, like Travis Bickle in *Taxi Driver* (1976) or films such as *Touch of Evil* (1958). Those are the films/characters that intrigued me. Even in *Psycho* (1960), which is one of my favorite movies, you definitely feel for Norman Bates.

ME: That's right, and in Dahmer *you do present a tortured soul. In terms of writing the screenplay how did you set about piecing together Dahmer's life into a movie?*

DJ: That was weird. I read the father's book and then I read three other books. This was in 1998. That's when I first started writing the script. It took a while, about a year or so to get it drafted. I then didn't make it for another year or so, so I did more changes. When I initially wrote the screenplay, I read a number of books and the one by British author Brian Masters—*The Shrine of Jeffrey Dahmer*—was the best by far. So I was reading all these books and ultimately I went to Milwaukee where the crimes took place and where he was tried. And when there I read the court transcripts and there was a one-hundred-and-twenty-page confession by Dahmer which he gave to the police, which was pretty much unredacted. I read that and that was very revealing about why he killed and what he thought he was doing. The very first plan was to narrow down the movie to one night where he is with the character Rodney. I wrote that first—I wrote all those scenes. Then I shied away from that rigorousness and I felt there were so many other incredible things about his story so I started to add other elements to that. A lot of work and thought went into the structure of the film. I didn't want to do one story with Rodney and just do these random flashbacks. I wanted to try and make the flashbacks a little more interesting. I liked the idea of the movie ending with a flashback. The whole structure of the film developed from that.

ME: I felt the narrative structure of the film was an interesting element of the film. I enjoyed the way the film flips between different time frames and it seems to represent Dahmer's fragmented psychosis and how places trigger memories in his brain of his past, his family and his previous kills.

DJ: Yes, they do but then again I tried to do it so it wasn't just little flashbacks to a main story. I wanted it to feel like the weaving of these different moments in his life.

ME: The way you edited the film it came across to me that we are peering into Dahmer's fractured mind and psychosis blurring into one. For example, when he is standing outside the club with Rodney and that triggers his memories of drugging and raping men in there.

DJ: Yes, that's right. I definitely wanted the moments going back and forth. I wanted him having something going through his head and cutting back into the past and seeing how far that past would take us in a meaningful way. The script wasn't exactly like that and this was done more during the editing. The ultimate structure of the movie changed in the editing suite.

ME: It sounds like the film changed from what you had envisioned when you wrote it.

DJ: Yes, not in a crazy way but the main thing was working on these transitions between the past and present and making them work. This was one of the big things I had to work on—cutting back and forth from the present to the past—and how to make it most effective. There were some scenes that didn't work. The film was shot in a short and concise period of time.

ME: *I understand that you shot the film in around 23 days. Is that correct?*

DJ: Yes, and some of the shooting came later. The initial shoot was around eighteen days and then we tacked on a few extra days. The film was shot in Los Angeles and then we tacked on a few days in Milwaukee, shooting exteriors. We wanted to give the film a sense of place. We had to bring Jeremy Renner there, the lead actor. We also had an extra couple of days shooting the special effects gore shots. [Laughs.]

ME: *Can you clarify a point regarding the script? Were you commissioned to write the script for* Dahmer *or did you write it independently?*

DJ: I totally wrote it on my own. I had made the low-budget film *Criminal* as my thesis film for Temple University, which went quite well for that kind of movie. Then I was in New York, trying to make a living, and the funny story is that while I was writing *Dahmer* I was editing promos for cartoons on Nickelodeon. [Laughs.] I thought that was funny. I'd be writing these Dahmer scenes in the morning and then go and edit Rugrats videos! Then I wrote a couple of scripts after *Criminal* trying to get to the next step in the professional world. I made the early mistake of writing big-budget and bizarre movies that would never get made, even today, unless I was a huge star. So I wrote the *Dahmer* script on impulse, something that I could make cheaply. That was partly my motivation for writing it. This was a great idea to work on as I could make it relatively cheaply but then low and behold I started sending the script around to a lot of places and it was universally rejected. Sometimes it was rejected angrily and morally: "Why would you want to make a movie about this subject?" That was kind of unnecessary when they rejected it. In this business, it is not about the ideas or narrative it is always about who is doing it. If you haven't done anything you can guarantee you will get a rejection.

After a while, I had earned some money and I had a bit of money given to me from a relative as inheritance, so I had about $125,000 dollars. I said I was going to make the film with this money and I found this producer called Larry Rattner. He was a real character! The reason I knew Larry—and to his credit—he helped *Criminal* get distributed through the channel you saw it on. [*Criminal* was released in the UK on Screen Edge Video, who specialized in ultra-low-budget films, and their proud motto was "Nothing Like Hollywood." They released *Cannibal: The Musical*, prior to Trey Parker's and Matt Stone's success with *South Park*, and a whole slew of interesting films before they descended into cheaply made horror flicks. They are still active now but specialize in punk/live rock recordings, though they still have a few titles available from their original catalogue.] He helped me get *Criminal* carried by that label.

I was living in New York at the time and I told Larry I wanted to make this movie and that I didn't have much money. He said he could probably get me some money for it, too. He advised me to come to LA and try and put it together. In the end, he didn't really come up with any more money, though I found a little more cash. We ended up shooting the film for $200,000.

ME: *Did Blockbuster Video get involved or inject any cash? They were certainly involved when making* Gacy.

DJ: They didn't come on board until it was completely done. Basically, it was my money. In a way, it was great because I had total control over the film and I haven't had that ever since. So it was all about me pushing it and getting it made and started. When it came to editing, I did a full edit and the producers—Larry and Susan Rodgers—did a good job of making the budget go as far as it could. They did contribute in a good way, in that respect. They made our budget stretch and helped us shoot on 35mm. Larry had a friend who had an editing company and we could use their editing system. We got to a picture lock and then we started showing it to distributors and buyers. At that point we had no more cash to finish it. We needed an extra $250,000 to finish it. We could have done it cheaper but that's what we ended up spending. We showed it to distributors, and most passed on it, and then Blockbuster came to one of our screenings and their main buyer really liked it. One of the fortuitous things for us was that the *Ed Gein* movie with Steve Railsback had just come out right before we showed our film. Again, it wasn't planned, and that film had done really well for Blockbuster. They had made a lot of money from rentals from that film. So for them this was the next one and they offered us—at the time—a hefty sum for the North American video rights, which was an exciting moment for me. It was around $950,000.

ME: *Wow!*

DJ: Yeah! Before that happened the film had been rejected at Sundance and another festival. I thought the film would never see the light of day and I had lost all this money. I was smart enough to realize that if you put money into an independent film you might not get it back. Still it was exciting to be one of the success stories where I made money. When we got that money—and it was great that I had the power to make the decisions—I knew that Blockbuster would try and sell it as an exploitation movie. I always wanted to make the film with a little bit more going on than that. That's what I thought I was making! [Laughs.] So, I took some of the money I got from Blockbuster and I did my own theatrical release. That was a great thing to have done, otherwise it would have gone straight to video. Again, Blockbuster was the equivalent of Netflix now, at that time. To be fair, Blockbuster did really push the film when it came out, however, having that theatrical release was great for me and introducing the film to people who I thought I was making it for. We didn't spend too much. We got a PR person and we booked it into a cinema chain called Landmark Cinemas. They had cinemas in all the big cities. The film did really well in its first week and they took it over and they put it in all their cinemas and paid for the advertising. So I got a nice theatrical release for the film.

ME: *I imagine that is what you intended because Blockbuster merely specialized in rentals.*

DJ: Yes, even though it was good in the sense that if you get a movie on Netflix now it is great because so many people can watch it. But when you have it in the theaters we got reviews and Spirit Award nominations, which helped my career.

ME: *Talk us through the production of the film. Was it a difficult shoot, especially as the film was self-financed? Did that cause you issues?*

DJ: Yes, that caused me issues! [Laughs.] It is funny how that works. On the one hand, you make cheaper movies, you have more control as there is less at stake.

ME: *You did* Criminal *for around $12,000, didn't you?*

DJ: Yes, that was a student film and everyone worked for free and we got equipment from our film school. We were just paying for film stock and processing. In terms of the production of *Dahmer*, it was good in the sense that I had complete control over what I was doing, but then you don't have control in terms of money and budget limitations, which meant that we had a small crew. I had a really good DP and Jeremy Renner was great in being so "on" and we did a lot of the scenes in one take. One of the funny things we did to make it cheaper was to buy "short ends." When the big studios shoot films they may only use a bit of the film reel and then re-can it. Brokers would then sell those partial rolls. So we used a lot of "short ends" when shooting Dahmer. It is cheaper but then we would be shooting scenes and we would be getting to the perfect moment—with Jeremy doing some fantastic scene—and then the DP would shout "Roll out!" So we lost takes that way and had to go back and do it again. That was frustrating. There were certainly Art Direction things that drove me mad.

There was one day when the crew had a meltdown, I remember. A lot of people not getting paid much and long hours. There were scenes that caused us problems. For example, the scene in the chocolate factory was something we did later. I remember we were given the whole day to shoot there and then I was told that the people who operate the machines were only going to be there for half the day and then some of the crew turned up early and then we were left with an hour to get on those shots! We also had issues with cars that wouldn't start. By and large it was reasonable. But at the time it felt like everything was going wrong. One of the advantages that we had was that the Screen Actors Guild had a new contract coming up and then there was a strike. When that happens the studios are aware that it will happen, so they do all their productions during the first half of the year, so that when the strike happens they don't lose too much production. So this was in the summer of 2001, and no one was working. As an independent film, we were non-union so we got a free camera package from Panavision. We got many good deals because of the strike.

ME: *The casting for the role of Jeffrey Dahmer was one of the most crucial elements of the film. How did you come to cast Jeremy Renner? He is sublime in the film and it is no small wonder why he has become such a huge star in Hollywood.*

DJ: Back then, since I wasn't going to get a movie star, I cast in the old way, like I did for my student film. I put notices out. We did have a casting director, which helped bring in actors. However, it was mostly people who hadn't been in much. I don't think Jeremy had been in a great deal of movies prior, and at the time I auditioned around fifty guys for the part. Jeremy was one of them. As I narrowed it down he was one of the actors I was really keen on. We had another actor who looked a lot like Dahmer. He wasn't bad. He was pretty good and he looked like him. That was the only issue I had about offering Jeremy the part. Jeremy was so great in his auditions—and so powerful—every moment felt very real to me. I think I called him back around four times to read more! I think that drove him a little mad. It was also funny, too, because the casting director also managed actors and she had a conflict of interest because she kept pushing her own actors for the parts! When I came to my decision she wasn't happy with my choice! So I went against her judgment. It was great to audition people in that way because I learned so much about my role and saw different people play the character. Jeremy was just so powerful and it is funny because when you hear some actors playing the part you think, "God, my writing is so bad." Yet when an actor like Jeremy comes in and reads the scene you are like, "Wow, my writing is really good!" [Laughs.] It is amazing how a good actor can make the writing work. That's one of the geniuses of good actors—they understand the scene and what you are writing about.

Once we were making the film Jeremy was incredible. He was so well prepared.

10. *Dahmer*   125

He always did something great on the first or second take. The most takes we did was probably three. A lot of time it was just one take because Jeremy Renner was so good. I kind of made fun of myself by saying I was like Ed Wood because I shot a lot of the film in one take. [Laughs.]

ME: I liked the way you directed the film. How did you approach the visual stylization of the film?

DJ: I had all these pictures of underground French sex clubs that were all lit in red and those pictures really inspired me. I tried to get that look into the sex club that Dahmer is in [in the movie]. I tried to do lots of formal shots in the film and shots that were still, as I was inspired by the work of Hitchcock at the time. In terms of building tension I find that if the camera is moving quite slowly you build tension into the narrative. Nowadays every movie has frenetic cutting and camera movements and this doesn't help build tension.

ME: I agree. I think there is a stillness in your film. It has a very European feel.

DJ: I was always into still photography and I think in some ways that influences the way I shoot my films. I am very interested in precise composition. When we made the film we talked a lot about the lighting of the film and we did a lot of low-key lighting in the apartment. We did have a thing going on in the apartment because as so much of the film was set there we wanted to change the lighting throughout. It goes from a light and illuminated set at the beginning to a low-key lighting by the end. That was deliberate.

Dahmer (*left*) takes a drill to the head of one of his victims Dion Basco (courtesy David Jacobson).

ME: I was going to touch on that because in the film Dahmer's apartment seems to take on different characteristics depending on his emotional state. At the start his apartment is naturalistic and somewhat dour yet by the end of the film his apartment is drenched in neon reds.

DJ: Yes, that was a deliberate plan. Also, when filming the flashbacks we used different film stocks. In the present day and the apartment we used film stock with a faster speed so we could shoot in lower light. I wanted it to look more grainy and lurid. Then when filming flashbacks from his youth we used slower film stock that was daylight balanced because it was a way of making Jeremy look a little bit younger. I actually thought that worked well as you get a sense of aging with his character.

ME: One of the scenes that sticks in my mind is the scene in the club when he is raping his victims. The way you filmed and edited that sequence was excellent. I thought the strobe lighting was effective as well as your choice of music ("More, More, More" by Andrea True Connection). It reminded me of the paintings of Francis Bacon with Dahmer's twisted torso and the red hue in the background.

DJ: I can't say that was deliberate, even though Francis Bacon was one of my favorite painters growing up. I don't remember using that specifically; I didn't set out to do that intentionally.

ME: But that scene was brilliantly edited. How did you achieve that?

DJ: That was one of the scenes my editor put together and it was really exciting when he did it. The part with the strobe took a while to get some of the cutting before the strobe part right. Actually, that was a very funny production moment. We were shooting the scenes when Dahmer is humping those guys in the back room and I kept saying to my line producer for scenes in the bar that I needed lots of extras. I have to have twenty-five extras. So that bar scene we did originally had twenty to thirty extras but we only had them for an hour! We shot all night so I had to figure out quickly how to film it! So we shot wide angles first and then we kept losing extras so we had to get tighter and tighter and tighter. That was partly the way it was visualized, but still, it was hard! If you look at the extras you will see in one shot Jeremy is by the bar with an extra next to him and then he looks over his shoulder on the dance floor and the same extra is dancing next to him on the dance floor. Those kind of things drove me mad.

When it came to doing the scene in the back room that was a different day and I kept telling my line producer that I needed five extras and they were basically being butt-fucked by Jeremy! I said that they can't just be anyone. It is not a simple "extra" role. On the day of the filming, I was told by my line producer that she didn't have the extras but not to worry as she would get them! We were filming in downtown LA and she got people in off the street! But she didn't tell them the nature of the scene! She just said, "Do you want to be in a movie?" These guys were like, "Yeah, sure," and she took them upstairs to me and I had to tell them that they would need to lie face down on the bed and a guy would come in and get on top of them and have anal sex with them! [Laughs.] It was so bizarre and funny because some of them were like, "OK, cool," and some were saying, "Is anyone going to see this? I wouldn't want my wife to see this!" I said, "Don't worry, I won't show your face." Then Jeremy had to come in and mount these guys. He was pretty good natured about everything but he was a little bit like, "Oh, man!"

I remember working a lot on the editing of that strobe moment and then the editor did something with the strobe that was really cool. I can't explain it…. I was always excited by that scene. It worked out well.

ME: *The choice of music added to that scene as well.*

DJ: We ended up with a pretty good music track especially when working with a relatively small music budget. We had to get rights to everything. Some of the tracks I had to change, like Sigur Rós.

ME: *I wanted to ask you about the violence in the film. In* Dahmer *the violence is honed in and you hint toward the depravities Dahmer sunk to. I felt this was a far more effective device because using the power of suggestion for his ghoulish crimes was more powerful than being explicitly graphic and exploitive. Was that your intention?*

DJ: Yes, and I always thought that everyone, especially in the U.S., came to the movie already knowing what he did as it was reported on and they already have that in their head. My feeling has always been that when you actually see violence it throws you out of the story and it becomes more about the violence and not the story or the emotions. So that was definitely thought about.

One of the violence scenes I love is when he is chopping up the body of one of his victims. Jeremey played the scene so well. You don't even see much, but his reaction and body movements made it so real. I was amazed by that. That was funny, too, because I filmed the sequence in my mom's house on her kitchen floor. All Dahmer's childhood scenes in the film are where I actually grew up. Actually, it wasn't even location because my stepdad insisted we give him a contract and that if we made money that we would pay him, which we did. He got a $10,000 location fee!

ME: *I thought it was interesting that you shied away from the monstrosity of Dahmer's crimes, like cannibalism and necrophilia.*

DJ: From my research, and this is the funny thing about research into true crime, you realize you don't really know what happened or how much he ate [of his victims], because it is all his own account. His own account says he didn't really indulge in that much cannibalism. He tried it but it wasn't a major part of his practice. His biggest thing was trying to turn these guys into these docile sex zombies. He wanted to have complete control over them.

ME: *And that's the horror, in a sense. You don't have to have a film showing fifteen grisly murders. The horror is how he manipulated and preyed on these people. You know what is going to happen to them. A good example of that is the opening of the film in the department store and you know how it is going to end. That is more horrifying than seeing someone brutally murdered on the screen.*

DJ: Yes, definitely. Seeing violence in cinema is ultimately an aesthetic experience because it always fails what it sets out to do. The horror and violence becomes an aesthetic experience as opposed to an emotional or dramatic one.

ME: *We touched on the humanizing of Dahmer's character in the film earlier. How did audiences respond to this "humanizing" of his character? Some viewers went in with the expectation that this film was going to be an exploitation-type film. How did they respond?*

DJ: Very, very mixed on that level. It was very divided. Some people didn't like the fact I had humanized him. People were disappointed that it wasn't a film about him eating his victims and vivisecting them. And then there were people who really got the film and appreciated it for what it is. In some sense that was one of the difficult things I had when making the sale to Blockbuster. The original title of the movie, even through the shooting of the film, was *The Mind Is a Place of Its Own*. Then I got convinced, after I had made the sale to Blockbuster, to change the title to *Dahmer*. That was a hard choice to make at the time and I felt bad about it. I understood why and I rationalized it by saying that a lot more people will see the film with the new title who might not otherwise see it. And what is true about the Blockbuster release was that if it was intended as an indie-arthouse film it would have had a limited audience. So I thought with this new title all these people would get to see my film who might not otherwise would. Even Blockbuster's marketing campaign saw them take Jeremy to a studio and take pictures of him with a knife. It was very unlike the film I had made. Again, I felt a lot of audiences would be disappointed because the film isn't how Blockbuster tried to advertise it.

ME: That's interesting, because I have the Dutch DVD version of the film and they have advertised the film as Dahmer: The Cannibal. *So it just goes to show that even though there is nothing in your film that hints towards cannibalism it is funny how they still marketed the film in that way.*

DJ: That's really interesting how they marketed the film!

ME: I thought you portrayed the gay community well in the film. You handled that with great sensitivity. I understand that the gay community was demonized in the press in the U.S. when details of Dahmer's crimes emerged.

DJ: Yes, that is true. It was seen as, "Look, this is what gay people do." There was definitely an element of that and the heinous depravities you'd see in a gay club. It was as if what Dahmer was doing was standard gay club behavior! That is interesting, because I was also anxious as to whether this film would hurt the gay community by portraying this because he is a gay serial killer in gay clubs. What was quite surprising was that there was this gay film critic in New York who really loved the film and he was one of the first people to see it. He was excited to see this kind of gay character in a movie because he is sick of the *Will and Grace* treatment, that if you show gay characters that they have to be perfect people.

ME: Dealing with such a sensitive subject matter, did you encounter any opposition from the victims' families?

DJ: No, we never did. I was very worried about that, at the time. I even talked to Dahmer's father, just before the film came out. I asked him if he wanted to see it, but he declined. He didn't put up any block or anything. In one of the theaters it was supposed to play at, in Milwaukee, the theater owner didn't allow it to be shown because he didn't want to deal with any issues that might arise, like protests. There is still a bit of feeling there, even though he died in 1994, when it was coming out it was 2002. Time had passed but the owner was still worried about a backlash there. So it wasn't shown theatrically in Milwaukee.

I definitely had my own issues during the writing of the script. First I read the father's book, which is more about the emotions than the gore, then I read the more exploitative accounts on Dahmer, and when I was reading those at times I got really sick and questioned myself. "Why am I doing this?" I had a lot of dreams during the writing and shooting of the film where either I am the killer or I am helping Dahmer cover his murders and his tracks. Other people who worked on the film, like Jeremy, had dreams, too. We used to say, "Have you had your Dahmer dream yet?" [Laughs.] I had a lot of worries about that. Trying to humanize someone like that is difficult. He is horrible yet you are trying to understand that. I felt I was always trying to walk this very narrow line. I was trying to say that he had human qualities and he wasn't just a monster that we should put on an electric chair and kill. I think if you simply label him as a monster then you will never understand how and what made him.

11

Gacy

An Interview with Director Clive Saunders

John Wayne Gacy, Jr., holds the dubious distinction of being one of America's most cruel and vicious serial killers. Both a serial killer and serial rapist, it is estimated that Gacy killed at least 33 teenage boys from 1972 to 1978 in Cook County, Illinois. His victims were lured to his property either by force or by deception, where Gacy would sexually abuse, torture and murder them. His signature mark was to kill all his victims, bar none, through asphyxiation or strangulation with a makeshift tourniquet. The majority of the murders occurred after his divorce, when Gacy was free to indulge in his sick practices and his activities were easier to conceal. Twenty-six of Gacy's victims were buried in the crawl space under his ranch house in Norwood Park. Deemed a model citizen in the local community, Gacy became known as the "Killer Clown" because of his charitable work, fundraiser events and willingness to dress up as Pogo the Clown at children's parties. Gacy was finally caught and sentenced to death. He was killed by lethal injection on May 10, 1994, at Stateville Correctional Center.

In 2003, actor and director Clive Saunders brought Gacy's chilling story to the screen, as Blockbuster was keen to capitalize on the influx of true-life serial killer films that had hit the video shelves. Mark Holton plays Gacy Jr., a portly resident of Chicago's suburbs who is known in the area as model citizen and a man with powerful friends. On the surface, everything seems fine. A wife, kids and a steady business. Yet, beneath this thinly veiled air of respectability lurks a man of vicious monstrosity. Saunders quickly shows us that this is a mere façade, a man with twisted violent sexual impulses and a penchant for young teenage boys.

The film charts Gacy's downfall as his marriage falls apart, after which point he is allowed to spiral out of control into a depraved cycle of rape and murder before his ultimate apprehension by the police. Young men are duped, deceived and forced back to his home where they are sexually assaulted or murdered, their bodies dumped into the insect-infested crawl space under his home. Saunders does a good job of charting how the authorities failed to act and stop Gacy and how he managed to conceal his activities for so long. Atmospheric, and with an unnerving sense of horror that increases as the film goes along, the film is further accentuated by the fine acting of Holder and the supporting actors.

That the film has slipped into obscurity, and has received unfair criticism, is partly due to the nonsensical editing and studio tampering on the film. The film was intended

11. *Gacy*

to be a dark and blackly comic meditation on Gacy's life, a scathing indictment of seventies America and a look at how such a mass murderer could get away with his crimes for so long. With Mark Holton cast perfectly as Gacy Jr., and a cameo from Adam Baldwin as his father, the film remains a creditable stab at unraveling the story of one of America's most prolific killers. Yet it is a film spoilt by studio interference which ultimately unraveled the power of Saunders's vision. Critics were quick to slate the film without fully understanding how much Saunders's vision had been violated.

In August 2017, I had the pleasure of interviewing Clive Saunders about his film and the hardships and struggles he endured making it. The film was edited without his input and the version currently shown on DVD and television is not the cut that Saunders intended. Rightfully upset, Saunders spoke openly about the troubles he encountered and how the studio ripped out the heart of his movie by making editorial and narrative changes that were detrimental to the film.

Matthew Edwards: Can you tell us a bit about your background? You are known primarily as an actor.

Clive Saunders: That's correct. I have directed as well. I went to Hollywood in the nineties with a theater company to do some theater. While there, I tried to make a film about Charles Bukowski. I did a play first in London. I decided to adapt a load of short stories and put them on the London Fringe and this led me from one thing to another and led me to meet some people and this took me to America. So, this little Fringe play that I did back in 1993 took me in a direction, which I went with. I never considered doing a Hollywood career. The thought has never occurred to me. I wasn't really in Hollywood as I was in theater. It's an obscure act there because everyone is trying to get into the movie industry. The only time people do theater is to showcase or there is a fuck-you, avant-garde movement, which I was part of inadvertently because it is not a town noted for its theatrical traditions. Eventually, I met the widow of Bukowski and I said I wanted to make

Promotional artwork for Clive Saunders's *Gacy* (courtesy Clive Saunders).

a film of one of his short stories, called *Love for $17.50*. It was a way of showing the widow that I could make a film and be trusted in her husband's legacy because she was precious about it. While that was screening, a producer called Larry Rattner saw it in Los Angeles. He was dating the producer of that short, and she had recommended it to him. Larry Rattner had just produced *Dahmer*, which was directed by David Jacobson. In fact, I helped out a little on that film, and the *Dahmer* script was actually quite an interesting script and Jacobson's father was kicking him money. A lot of these low-budget films just want you to fill a video box. They don't really care about the quality, but that film got picked up at the Film Independent Spirit Awards and it started getting taken seriously. And that was the first real-life serial killer film that I was aware of. It wasn't really my thing as I am not really a horror guy. The horror films I like are more psychological like Polanski films. The slasher films I wasn't interested in. If you are in Hollywood, as a filmmaker you are only going to get horror thrown at you as a starter. I was trying to make off-beat Bukowski films, not very commercial, not appealing to many film companies. Then there was this slew of real-life serial killer films coming out. The producer of my little short was then brought on as Executive Producer with *Dahmer*. So she dragged the producers down to see my film because the original director of *Gacy* had pulled out. *Gacy* was really a follow-up. It was supposed to be a cash-in movie because *Dahmer* was doing so well. It got picked up by all the video companies and it was also financed partly by Blockbuster. At that time, they were financing films to help fill up their shelves. They were a right-wing, quite uptight, Midwest company. They had a big list of what you could and couldn't say.

I got the job because someone wanted to cash in quickly on *Dahmer* and there was a script already written on *Gacy*. Susan Rodgers, a friend of mine who came out of theater with me, she produced my first short and she gave me the script of *Gacy*, which was written by David Birke. I read it and I didn't like it at all. It wasn't my thing, so they gave me three weeks to rewrite it.

ME: *You came on quite late to the film, didn't you?*

CS: Yes, I think they were like, "Who the fuck are we going to get to do this thing?" I was this guy who had done a few short films. For me it was great. At that time, it was all film and I was using 16mm. The cameras were huge. So, you couldn't do what you do now with those small cameras. *The Blair Witch Project* was the first film to use those small cameras. We couldn't do that. I used 16mm because I liked the grain but on *Gacy* I was given 35mm and a full crew. So, I had to take that step. The weird thing was that all the Bukowski people thought I had sold out. So, I rewrote the film.

ME: *What did you change and what did you not like about the original script?*

CS: What I can remember about it was that there was a scene which had Gacy looking at his hair falling out and angsting about it. I thought that can't be the reason for him committing the crimes that he did! He killed 33 kids! The big problem when you write these serial killer scripts is that you have some kind of conscience—a lot of the victims' families are still alive—and you have a sensitivity issue. I come from a fringe, off-Broadway, to be confronted with a Hollywood sensibility that just wanted to make money and not worry about the body count. In fact, the more the merrier. I was a squeamish Brit. I was really concerned and I talked to Jacobson about *Dahmer*'s victims. Gacy's victims were killed in the '70s–'80s and their family members may still be around. So I didn't want to simply use the victims as cannon fodder. My choice was not to do it or do it. Because I was living couch to couch this was my opportunity of a big shoot to take a big career step.

However with the film I was accused of not having enough blood or thrills. My take was very different. It wasn't a kill after kill thrill movie. In the final cut I was replaced by a supervising editor. I turned up to work one day and I was told I couldn't come into the editing room. The guys from Blockbuster never even read my script, they just gave it the green light. I wouldn't say the script was subversive but it was a story about why Gacy got away with this for so long: thirty-three boys over seven or eight years in that Springfield, Illinois, area. Surely somebody would have noticed or cared. Really they didn't because they were low-rent boys or guys who worked out at the Greyhound stations. They were vulnerable and mentally ill. He picked off at the fringes. What angered me about it was no one seemed to investigate. From what I researched, the police investigations were very lax and they didn't give a toss about these boys. So my premise was this: If you are going to put thirty-odd kids in the crawl space of your house then there is going to be a hell of a smell. Someone has got to pick up on this … or why did no one pick up on this? In my working cut it was completely different, before I was replaced. When I sat down at the screening with actor Charlie Weber he turned to me and said, "Did we shoot this film?" In my cut we had this preamble—which was all removed—about his first kill. It showed him as a sleazy guy going for rent boys and there is a scuffle with a knife in a motel room and he stabs the kid and leaves him in the motel. For five years he was shitting himself and nobody came for him. In those five years he ended up running a Kentucky Fried Chicken franchise. So I put all this stuff in and it was taken out about the evolution of a serial killer. And everyone asks about the film, "Why didn't you get into his head?" But nobody can really get into the head of someone else so all you can do is put your take on what you think it is. For me, I didn't want to go down the road because it was an unpleasant place to dwell by trying to contemplate what sickness there is, and that's just another meditation on the nature of evil which we don't know and can only guess. So I thought let's just go with that angle and explore it, because I didn't have that much time to develop the script. Then when the story picks up in the final cut—when Gacy is having his Thanksgiving dinner—that is around fifteen minutes into it in my cut. That's the point when it starts to unravel for him because he is such a mean guy. It was his pathological stinginess that brought him down, which is still in the film. So much of it wasn't in the film, which is really about the banality of evil. He did it because he could get away with it. I was forced to put those police guys in because they turned up occasionally. So that's the story, at the start I was in the editing room and then I was out.

ME: That's interesting, because in the final cut of Gacy *his first kill in the motel is shown as a flashback during the ending of the film.*

  CS: Yes, they brought that kill into the film in flashes and it didn't make any sense. I also think there was a little bit of the Kentucky Fried Chicken scene.

ME: There is very little. There's a shot or two with him eating a piece of chicken next to his new franchise. Again, this appears quite late in the film. It is alluded to.

  CS: Can you imagine watching your film and seeing it all cut up? At that point, I had enough of Hollywood and I came back to England. I was going to stay and do more but I had a pretty unpleasant experience in Hollywood and I gave up on the Bukowski as well. You think Hollywood is the culture of abuse but it is even worse at the lower levels when people are trying to get into the industry, where people are even more desperate and frantic. They try to pull these films in on very little money, yet these companies were making huge profits. We shot this film in a couple of weeks. From inception 'til we stopped shooting, it only took around two months. It was very quick. I got a rough assembly cut going and then I was dropped. Looking back, I don't think Blockbuster liked where I was coming from, really, from day one.

ME: Did they want the film to be more exploitive?
CS: Completely. That's the nature of the beast, isn't it?

ME: I thought you approached the film rather well, in that respect, because you weren't particularly gratuitous or overtly violent. With these types of films it is so easy to go down that route. In fact, the film opens by showing Gacy being abused by his father.
CS: Yes, that's right. You have to have a stab at why you think Gacy was like the way he was. The production company went after this guy called Adam Baldwin, who was in *Full Metal Jacket*, and they wanted him in it. The film implies that the father beat the shit out of his son and kicked him in the tent and did horrible things to him—not sexually—and the implication was that that might have been the case. Then the next day I had another scene when they go home and they are packing up the trailer and the dad is remorseful and says, "Son, I am sorry about last night," and he hands him an effigy of a clown and he takes this clown, like some Rosebud device that set him off on this clown thing. I thought it was a bit clunky but I was trying to subvert this with an element of British humor. When I looked at the final edit I thought it was a car wreck and I recognized bits of my movie but they took everything out of sequence and repatched it. When they do that—and I knew it was a B-movie/exploitation movie—you still want it to resonate with something you set out to achieve. It was an interesting experience but it put me off living in LA and I came back home. I had been putting too much fight into it and I was sick for a year after that. I had a pretty rough time and I never went back.

ME: It sounds like the final cut of Gacy *was not the film you intended. That must have been very gulling for you.*
CS: It is not the first time it has happened nor will it be the last. It is not a place for anyone who has an auteur vision, unless you really stay on the independent tracks. This was an independent film pretending to be an independent film because it was a corporate film trying to get into the mainstream. These guys all wanted to get into doing studio work. There was a great push to sell and make money and move on.

I was concerned that we can't be too glib with the actual victims—we changed the names and everything—but not that much. Those kids were composites and were pretty much based on real people. That was my dilemma. I had a hard time with that, you know, recognizing the fact that these kids have mums and dads and brothers and sisters. I didn't want to linger on the fetishization of the killings, or the pornography of death, if you will. That doesn't interest me. I am much more into what Polanski does with the mind psychologically. I was interested in how Gacy would try and manipulate these boys.

ME: That does come across in the film that Gacy is this manipulating bully.
CS: Yes, he really is. For me the greatest achievement of *Gacy* was all the guys and girls who I acted with on the fringe, like Rick Dean, who played Ray the plumber, he was this force of nature. He was a very troubled individual and he was from our theater

company. He was your big, bad, nightmare guy. He always played a heavy and he used to do a lot of work with Roger Corman. So there is a lot of Corman actors in the film. I wanted to bring actors like this in, those who never really quite made it, because they are all great actors. When I look at that film now I see that some of these actors have passed away now. Working with them was a joyful thing, but the rest of it, when I look at the content, I just see how the financiers mutilated the film.

I also didn't really get on well with the lead actor, Mark Holton. Both he and I didn't click, so to speak. There was another guy I should have used. Oh well. I showed the movie to someone about a year ago and there are still some good sequences in the film. It got panned of course, during the early days on the net. It was the early days of everyone kicking you on the internet. The authenticity of it not being in Chicago annoyed people. Though I wanted to show that artifice. I wasn't trying to hide the fact that LA—we shot this in Pasadena—was trying to duplicate for the suburbs of Chicago. I had a really good director of photography called Kristian Bernier. He said should I cut the trees and I said, "No, fuck it. Leave all that stuff in." It's an exploitation movie, so we show the rough edges. I didn't want to get anal about that; I wanted to show the core of it. That's what I was aiming for. But I think some of the core of the film I was aiming for survives. There is no point lamenting what could have been. Those early sequences that we shot were my favorite, especially the motel scenes. Mark Holton was actually at his best in those scenes. That's the nature of this business. You have to roll with the punches.

ME: *I thought you did rather well, especially now that I know more about the circumstances behind the making of the film and the problems that you faced and the conditions you were working under. Stylistically, how did you approach shooting the film, because working on a low-budget period film is always tricky?*

CS: I remember I got a really good costume designer called Oneita Parker. In the beginning she was showing me Hawaiian stuff for them to wear and I said no, because I wanted a washed-out, downbeat seventies vibe. I am fifty-nine so I was around in the seventies. Those kids, and I didn't know them, I cast them because they reminded me of people I knew back then when I was at school. So I approached it from a very personal angle. I thought, "Let's get this guy because he reminds me of Cliff, Mike, etc.," and I wrote that because I couldn't write for abstract people. So I put my schoolmates into the script. I wasn't too concerned with the look because I knew the wardrobe girl got it. So I left her to get on with it because you have to delegate. I wasn't that controlling on that. The look, the cars—which were old, beat-up relic cars that they dug up from some place—I remember Gacy's car, every time we turned it on billows of smoke came out! We had a blue work van in the film for one sequence and you couldn't drive the fucking thing! We had to add sound effects and roll it down the hill.

The look of it just came together and my Art Director went mad halfway through the shoot! We were mates and we lived in Venice Beach in an old cluster of shacks. In those days it was low-rent stuff. It was Edward G. Robinson's old beach house and they had chopped it into the units and nine or ten of us lived there. All the set builders/set designers were renting these units so I moved in with that lot because I preferred them to the actors. They are salt-of-the-earth types, regular guys. One of them, Ben Edelberg, was my neighbor. We got on really well. We directed the Bukowski film in that enclave and he did the set design on that short film. He was great, however, he joined some cult!

The problem with LA is everyone somewhere is getting involved with a cult. I can't remember this one but he started sabotaging the crawl space. Actually, the original title of the movie was called *The Crawl Space*. It wasn't going to be called *Gacy*. I knew then the producers were toying with me. So we built the crawl space on a soundstage and he actually brought in real mud in a lorry. I remember seeing this pick-up truck dumping tons of mud and soil. "Wait a minute, he can't do this," I thought. There was dust everywhere and the producer went absolutely ape-shit. What the fuck was this guy doing? We didn't need real mud with polythene crap. Ben said he wanted authenticity. That set us back a few days as we had to get rid of it all because the health and safety people said you can't breathe this as everyone will get sick. So Ben was fired. That set us back a lot, though he was instrumental in the look of the whole movie. So he was fired and I couldn't defend him on that. He was my main collaborator. Him and I discussed on Venice Beach what we wanted to achieve with *Gacy* and we did want the same things. We wanted to have a kick at society. The reality is Gacy got away with it because Gacy is you. He is Donald Trump. He is Middle America. Gacy is the Americans who don't care about their children and who sacrifice their children. Our backers didn't want to hear that. They sort of picked up on that when they saw the edit and what we were really trying to say.

I recall that there was one scene with the two little girls that was cut—I loved it when I saw them because they reminded me of the girls in Kubrick's *The Shining*—where the bugs come through and they stand on the toilet. We shot that and the rushes went off—this was before everything went digital—and we waited for a few days and suddenly we got a memo from Blockbuster saying to take that scene out of the girls on the toilet and reshoot it. They didn't want underage girls standing on lavatories. How sick of a mind to object to a girl standing on a toilet! I couldn't even begin to work out where they were coming from. That to me was the horror. The people who were trying to clean it up and the psychology behind that I found very disturbing. Then I ignored them and I think ultimately that was the reason I got pulled off. I was getting shouted at by my producers and I had never directed a film before. Even on a low-budget film the pressure is enormous. There is no etiquette there. There is just people laying into you. The crew was good, though, and they were behind me. I also had a good assistant director who helped hold things together. He was solid and without him I wouldn't have got to the end of the shoot. But we did! Anyway, I wanted to show why the fucker got away with it and that's what you see in my version. After I had been replaced I was out. I was just looking in from the outside. I was allowed to come in once a week to look at the film and what they were doing.

ME: *So you were pushed to the fringes....*

CS: I was just kicked out. After two weeks of cutting the film I was a goner.

ME: *That's a shame because I feel there are some very good elements to the film. I know you said that you didn't see eye to eye with Mark Holton but he does deliver an excellent performance in the film.*

CS: Yes, he does. I put that down to the fact that I was green. I had only directed short films before or with my mates, so that was easy to direct. I also came from a different background to acting. I came from a method background so I hadn't learnt how to adjust to that. In the end I gave up and left him to get on with it, which he did very well because I realized that he was a strong actor and he had his vision of [the character] and I wasn't going to change that in any way. There was one scene we filmed that really pissed him off and that was the scene when he was in the toilet and Rick comes in and he wants his money. Rick was really going for him and I felt sorry for Mark. I could have helped him a little more, I felt. Rick was a dangerous actor. No director can handle him and that's why he never got into the mainstream and worked mainly for Roger Corman. He would attack people....

ME: He sounds like Klaus Kinski!
   CS: Yes! He was Hollywood's version. Unfortunately, he died in his early fifties, which was a real tragedy. He was a good friend of mine.

ME: I really liked the way you filmed the crawl space. That was particularly eerie with all the bugs.
   CS: The crawl space parts, I think, we shot some of them in the original mud but the dust kept fucking the camera up! So that's what held the shoot up. That's what put us over budget and my demise was set from that point for bringing Ben on. I never really got on with the producers after that and quite rightly. You don't bring in thirty tons of mud onto a sound space and dump it from a pick-up truck. Hey, we did! The crawl space itself was where I wanted a lot of the action. There was a lot more stuff that was cut out. I feel the crawl space stuff really worked and the cameraman did an amazing job. Mark was really good and he got in there and crawled about. Upon reflection, I feel I handled him wrong. In hindsight, he did do a very good performance.

ME: He suits the part.
   CS: Actually, the kid who plays young Gacy was a PA and he was just lurking around when we were casting for young Gacy's. No one looked like him and I looked at him and I asked him if he had ever acted before. He was a ringer! So we used him and he was great.

ME: Structurally, it sounds like Gacy *would have been entirely different.*
   CS: There would have been less jolts and it would have been more of a drama-doc. I didn't want that cop turning up asking questions. I fought that. I had two hippie cops in it and I guess I was being a bit like David Lynch at times. It was my first film so I was being a bit derivative. I was heading more in that direction but Blockbuster wasn't having any of it! They didn't even read the script! If they had they would have known what I was going to do. However, it was an interesting experience and I wouldn't want to go through with it again. I am glad you have reappraised it. I wasn't ashamed of it; I just felt it had been violated.

On Sunday, September 10, I was kindly invited to London by Clive Saunders to watch his cut of *Gacy* at his apartment in Hampstead Heath. The working cut of *Gacy* was a work-in-progress cut and roughly assembled 2 to 3 weeks into the editing of the film before Saunders was unfairly removed from the film. Having not seen his cut for more than fifteen years, Clive had to get the working cut transferred from VHS to DVD so he could show it to me. As we opened a bottle of red wine, Clive stated that I was one of only a handful of people who had seen his intended cut of the film and that he didn't know what to expect from the film as he had not wanted to rewatch it in the intervening years. He needn't have worried, for while the final cut showed *Gacy* to be a decent film, undone slightly by some strange editorial choices with regard to the film's structure—for which the studio bears full responsibility and not Saunders—Clive Saunders's version takes *Gacy* to a wholly different level. Cinematically it fuses image and sound perfectly, creating a foreboding horror that has been diluted in the studio cut. Further to this, Saunders demonstrates a brilliant understanding of cinematic language and narration, especially in the way the film was edited. Saunders also layered the film with a rich strain of humor that was seemingly lost on the studio. Saunders's version shows cohesion and a narrative timeline that hints as to why Gacy was allowed to get away with his crimes. In the studio version, the jumbled narrative and excessive use of flashbacks detract from the story and its place in Gacy's life and timeline. It is almost as if they didn't know how to structure the film and realize its full potential.

Saunders's assembled workprint opens with extended scenes with Gacy's father (Adam Baldwin) in the woods before we cut to Gacy's first kill in the Pink Motel during the credit sequence (which is crudely tacked on to the end of the studio DVD version in a clumsy flashback). Here Saunders shows us from the get-go that the start of Gacy's murderous reign begins when he stabs and kills a rent boy he has picked up. Saunders shows that the killing was not premeditated and shows a distraught Gacy in tears and slumped on the floor as the boy lies bloodied and dead in the bathroom. In an ingenious cut, the film flips from the dead boy (meat) to a number of years later when Gacy is carving up a turkey during a family Thanksgiving meal. In this, Saunders showcases a deftly comic touch that parades throughout his version of the film as we switch from one dead meat to another. "Gacy the sitcom. That's what I was going for while also being respectful to the dead."[1] This underlying strain of British humor was quickly cut out of the final film, which is one of the most notable differences between the films. This is particularly true of the opening of the film, which is layered with multiple tongue-in-cheek gags. This is an excellent tool employed by Saunders, for once the killings begin to take shape, the comical element is removed from the film, immediately unsettling the audience. Saunders said this was a deliberate choice. During the opening twenty minutes, the film is littered with comical moments that has the viewer question whether the movie is a comedy or not. When Gacy gets beaten up by Stevie (Jer Adrianne Lelliott) and a group of hoods, for the money that Gacy owes, Saunders comically plays "In the Still of the Night" by The Five Satins as Gacy is kicked and pounded to the floor. Later, at the BBQ he has thrown for his friends and distinguished members of the local community, Gacy is seen talking about his many achievements and contributions to the town, whereby an airplane flies overhead. Saunders cuts to everyone looking up and the sound of the plane taking over the soundtrack as Gacy's words become inaudible. Everyone tunes out, for despite his good standing in the community, the locals find Gacy tiresome and a tad creepy. It was this type of humor that Blockbuster found hard to swallow, much like the scene with the two girls standing up on the toilet seat—"which Blockbuster went ape-shit at"—that sowed the seeds of alarm that eventually forced Saunders to be removed from the editing suite.

Another noticeable difference between both versions is Saunders's use of music and his way of manipulating sound in order to elevate the film. In Saunders's cut, when Gacy's wife finds the dirty mattress, clothes and rope in the garage, he fills the soundtrack with the sound of a dysfunctional air conditioner. As she probes further into his domain, that ominous sound is replaced with an eerie quietness just before Gacy pops up from the hatch to his crawl space. It is a cleverly realized scene and shows a filmmaker with an understanding of how to produce cinematic scares. At first the ominous drone creates an uneasiness which is further accentuated by the seedy room she has stumbled upon. This lures you into the scene and then, as that sound fades into a foreboding stillness, Saunders unleashes his cinematic scare. Clearly this approach was not to the studio's liking, as Saunders noted: "Films like *Gacy* are not the place for an auteur vision." In contrast, this tension has been replaced in the studio cut with a standard piano and synthesizer score that fails to deliver the same effect or increase the tension. If anything, the score actually hinders the scare that is about to transpire, for when Gacy pops up from the hatch the synthesizer heightens its pitch so to help telegraph that that there is a shock coming the audience's way. In a sense, the music in the final cut is typical of music used in mainstream cinema in that it is used to dictate the mood or feelings of the audience, whereas Saunders's manipulation of sound and music shows a filmmaker more in tune with the avant-garde who is willing to use experimental sound as a means of heightening tension. Clearly Blockbuster didn't agree. They wanted a more conventional approach and a standard "by the numbers" horror flick. With musical choices such as "Albatross" by Fleetwood Mac, and music by the Faces, The Alarm and cult European outfits such as Nü, Saunders was clearly going in a direction that was alien to the producers and financers. "It was too European for them," Saunders recalled. "They didn't get it. It is unlikely I could have got all the music but I could have got something similar." The use of underwater sounds during panning shots of the crawl space couldn't have helped his cause, either. With regard to the use of sound, Saunders said:

> I was trying to bring in the sound of ordinary things like the a/c and the glopita-glopita slime extractor to enhance the idea of his insanity deepening. Also with the extractor as a source of black humor, the madder and deeper he sinks into his depravity the crazier he gets, the more blasé he gets and the use of sound greatly enhances this. I also wanted to give the house and the crawl space a personality of its own ... make that part of the claustrophobic vibe I was going for. At the Gacy household, fridges and fans are a good way of doing that.

One scene that was heavily edited in the final version is the scene when Gacy's wife discovers his collection of male porn magazines, handcuffs and dildos. In the final version we are only shown snippets of the items in his collection. Gacy's wife Karen confronts him on his gay paraphernalia all the while enraged because she knows he has been bringing back young boys to his garage. After a brief scuffle, we cut to her leaving with the children. In the studio cut, this section of the film seems a little off-kilter because the dialogue between Gacy and his wife seems forced and labored. In contrast, in Saunders's cut we see Karen going through the gay paraphernalia in more detail, especially when she picks up the black dildo, which is completely cut from the studio print. We then cut to the scene when a tearful Karen confronts her husband. In a masterstroke by Saunders, he opts to present this scene without sound. No words can express the betrayal. Saunders shows us that dialogue is not necessary and the viewer is left to imagine the extent of the conversation. No words can ever placate his wife. There are shots of Karen holding the dildo, again, cut from the final print. Saunders here shows the power of cinema as a visual medium and that what is being said is not important. The audience is left to imagine; left to imagine what they would say in that situation. Saunders confirms this was his intention:

> Those scenes were always intended to be cut without dialogue.... We shot with dialogue because the producers insisted I shot what was on the script but I never intended to use the dialogue for the Karen confrontation or the pick-up scene involving Roger. I didn't want all the obvious yak yak yak we see on TV. The studio cut is the televisual friendly version with all those bleeding obvious lines we've heard thousands of times before. I just wanted Karen to pull out that 10-inch black flexible dildo and wave it menacingly in his face.... Really, what more needs to be said after that!

Cut to Karen leaving with the children. Gacy is now left alone. "Now he can get on with his work. Now he is alone."

This part of the movie raises another interesting point about how Saunders's version has a greater narrative flow compared to the studio cut. In particular, the scene when Gacy attacks Dave, one of the young men who works for him, with a hammer precedes the scene when Karen finds his gay porn collection. In Saunders's version, the attack on Dave occurs after his wife and kids have left him. This makes much more narrative sense because Gacy is now alone and his behavior has become more erratic and he has become prone to act on his violent impulses. After the attack, a guilty and repentant Gacy buys Dave's silence yet it signals a man teetering on the edge. In the studio version, the attack happens prior to Karen finding his collection. The studio version then cuts to a strange scene that features a bloodied Dave walking out of the property while Gacy hollers "and don't be late for work!" This was added in by Blockbuster and Saunders was not impressed. He stated that that scene felt contrived and that "it changed the tone." The studio cut then shows Gacy driving in his car and returning home on Mother's Day with a bunch of flowers. As he walks into the house, Karen confronts Gacy about the gay paraphernalia in his possession. The handling of these two plot strands is clumsy and not wholly believable. Saunders agreed and was scathing about the way his film was edited. He stated, "The splicing was fucking awful! Those bastards just butchered my version. Hitting Dave with the hammer happens way after the wife and kids have left. It is part of the unravelling of the man and he's become a victim of his impulses now. He feels at this point of the story he can do anything as nobody came looking for the kids so fuck it.... They also added in dialogue for the hammer scene which totally negates the whole point."

Saunders's version shows numerous flashback sequences of his time opening his KFC franchise and implies that he was raping young boys during this period of his life, whereas in the studio cut only brief snippets are hinted at regarding his former life working at KFC. The act of cruising around and picking up boys is detailed in both versions, but here in Saunders's edit he again uses sound and image to make his point more forcibly than it is made in the studio cut. When picking up the male prostitute Roger (Joseph Skiora) the scene is played out without dialogue. There are neither formal introductions nor does Gacy state, "Wanna get high?" The viewer once again doesn't need to hear the banal interactions between the pair. We know what Gacy is up to and his intentions to kidnap and rape the boy ... or worse. Once he has his prey, we cut to the apartment where he is doused in vodka and strung up in a rack before being set free. Analyzing both versions, Saunders's editing of this sequence packs the greater punch. Dialogue is used sparingly and this is an effective tool in showing how predatory Gacy was. Interestingly, both versions do show how arbitrary Gacy was with his victims. Not all of Gacy's victims were murdered. Some were set free after Gacy had finished with them, much like the character Roger.

One scene that appears in Saunders's cut that is totally omitted from the studio version occurs 1.35 minutes into the film. The scene in question sees Gacy walking through a military cemetery looking for his dad's grave. We next cut to a scene of a young Gacy with his father on their hunting trip. As they pack away their equipment into their SUV, his father gives Gacy a clown ornament. "I am not sure that scene should have been in," Saunders said of the inclusion of this scene in his cut. "It was a tender bookend moment. I liked it." Saunders then cuts to Gacy crying next to his father's grave before we see him arrested and taken away to jail. In a sense, the scene tries to make some connection with Gacy's estranged relationship with his father and his fascination with Pogo the Clown. It is a nice moment and hints toward the internal demons that plagued Gacy, humanizing him momentarily as not merely a monster but as a man who just craved the love of his father. However the studio didn't agree with the link and removed these scenes entirely from the studio edit.

The ending of the film also caused consternation for Saunders. Watching his version left him a lot more satisfied as opposed to the final edit. In Saunders's version, as the cops swoop in and dig up the bodies in his crawl space as a pounding electro score plays. Then, in a poignant moment, members of the cast arrive outside Gacy's property as they slowly bring out black body bags and gently rest them on the grassy verge. It is a powerful moment as all the cast silently come together and bear witness to the crimes committed by Gacy, all the while Cat Stevens's song "Trouble" is played over the scene. Saunders's version ends with Gacy's dead-fish eye peering through a crack before we cut to the crawl space. There is no sound. Just an unnerving silence. Cue credits. Saunders was scathing about the ending of the studio version and the inclusion of Detective Kay (John Laughlin) during the final scenes. "That cop wasn't in it! Blockbuster insisted on hiring him because he was a famous T.V. actor. I didn't want him in it. His role made no sense!" Saunders said, "It just ends in a dreadful montage. Both I and Charlie Weber (who plays, Tom) couldn't believe it when we saw it. That's not what was intended." Saunders was rightfully critical in his assessment of the ending, especially when you compare it to the ending in his cut:

> Well the ending was just the worst.... What they did with that feeble montage, my God! Well I wanted there to be an exhumation of all the bodies and all the cast standing on the lawn watching as the body bags were taken out to the sound of a Cat Stevens song ... a sort of indictment of all of us. My ending was inspired by watching b/w footage of the death camps being liberated after WW2 and all the villagers were made to watch ... and then we have Gacy in jail taunting us.

Despite the studio cut of *Gacy* having its flaws and bouts of nonsensical editing, Saunders's work still manages to shine through and shows that there is a film of great potential lurking in what is left of Saunders's vision. However, Saunders's version shows us what the great film *Gacy* could have been and the brilliance of Saunders as a filmmaker and as an artist who was willing to experiment with both image and sound. The biggest tragedy of Saunders's removal from the film is that the whole experience led him to give up directing feature films until recently, when Saunders directed one short film and landed a hitman-screwball comedy set in Thailand, currently in the works. What is a shame is that for most people they will only encounter the "violated" version of *Gacy* and never see what the director truly intended.

After rewatching the film, and before cracking open the whisky, Saunders had this to say: "The final cut brings all the memories back. I wasn't trying to crawl into the head of a serial killer. I was trying to show that people knew but did nothing. I wanted to show that Gacy had all these connections and that he was able to get away with his crimes. The film shows that when he is in trouble he goes to his powerful friends." With respect to his cut, Saunders said, "In retrospect, I'd be lucky if they let me cut it my way, though I'd do the same again. After making the film I didn't want to do any more horror shit. I did want my name removed from the film."

12

Ann Rule Presents: The Stranger Beside Me
An Interview with Director Paul Shapiro

The term "serial killer," widely attributed to FBI Special Agent Robert Ressler after he used the term "serial homicide" in a 1974 lecture to British police at Bramshill Police Academy, sought to define mass murderers and their penchant for continuing their murderous desires over months and even decades. Though historians have argued that the usage of the term "serial murderer" was used before Ressler coined the phrase, with examples being that of German criminologist Ernst Gennat describing Peter Kürten (aka The Vampire of Düsseldorf) in his 1930 essay as a serienmörder ("serial-murderer"), the term would accurately and neatly describe killers of this ilk. That the term serial killer, and all the connotations that come with it, perfectly fitted the crimes of America's most infamous killer, Ted Bundy, was not what troubled and frightened people the most. It was Bundy's failure to conform to stereotypes associated with the types of people who supposedly commit such crimes that raised eyebrows and fear among the populace. Ted Bundy wasn't the odd goofball, loner or freak who lived alone down at the end of the street. Bundy, in contrast, was considered charming, intelligent, handsome and politically active. His persona was the antithesis to the attributes associated with such killers. People who knew him were duped, never suspecting his involvement in the reign of terror he inflicted on young women across the states of California, Colorado, Florida, Idaho, Oregon, Utah and Washington between 1974 and 1978.

Of those people who failed to pick up on Bundy's true nature was law enforcement officer, and later crime writer, Ann Rule, who penned the bestselling book *The Stranger Beside Me*, which was subsequently turned into an excellent TV movie by veteran director Paul Shapiro. The film charts Bundy's life and crimes, his work with Rule at the Seattle Crisis Hotline Center in 1971 and their subsequent friendship. Though made for TV, the film effectively highlights how manipulative and charming Bundy could be, allowing the viewer to get a greater sense of how he evaded being caught for so long. To begin with, Rule refuses to believe that Bundy could be the killer and her failure to adjust to the notion that she had been duped all along. Shapiro's portrayal of Bundy (Billy Campbell) is impressive and viewers are given a clear picture of how he used his charm and good looks as a means to reel in his victims. Though not overtly violent or graphic, the film does not shy away from Bundy's murders, though the film's real feather in its cap is how it effectively shows Bundy to be a sociopathic monster who was manipulative and cold-blooded but also a man deluded by his own arrogance, as shown in the court scenes that make up the final part of the film.

That the film has slipped into obscurity, overshadowed by Matthew Bright's widely outrageous cult film *Ted Bundy* and the excellent *The Deliberate Stranger* (1986)—both of which are still critically assessed by scholars and film writers—is a shame. As a new Bundy picture, *Extremely Wicked, Shockingly Evil and Vile* (2019), directed by Joe Berlinger, hits the cinemas, one hopes attention will turn to Shapiro's underrated flick and not exploitative trash like *Bundy: An American Icon* (2009).

In 2018, I had the pleasure of interviewing Paul Shapiro about his film and the crimes of Ted Bundy. I thank him for the generous amount of time he put into the interview and I hope the interview encourages a new wave of filmgoers and scholars to check out this impressive televisual work.

Matthew Edwards: *How did the opportunity arise to direct a film based on Ann Rule's bestselling book* The Stranger Beside Me?

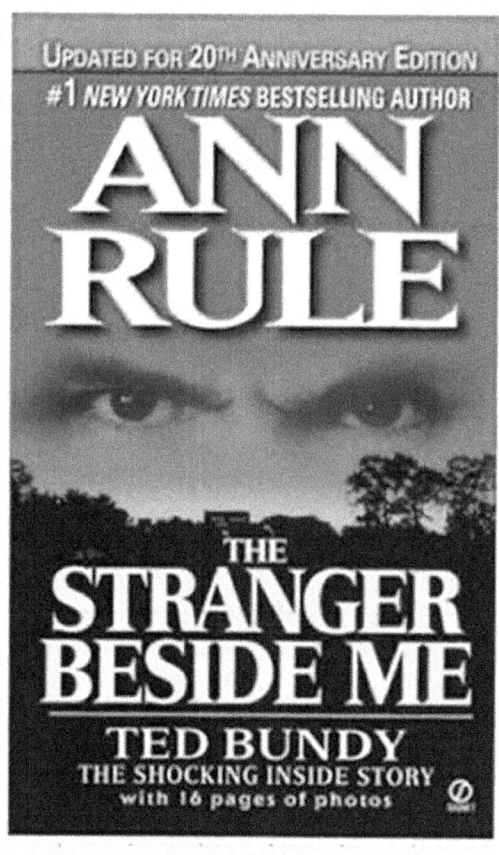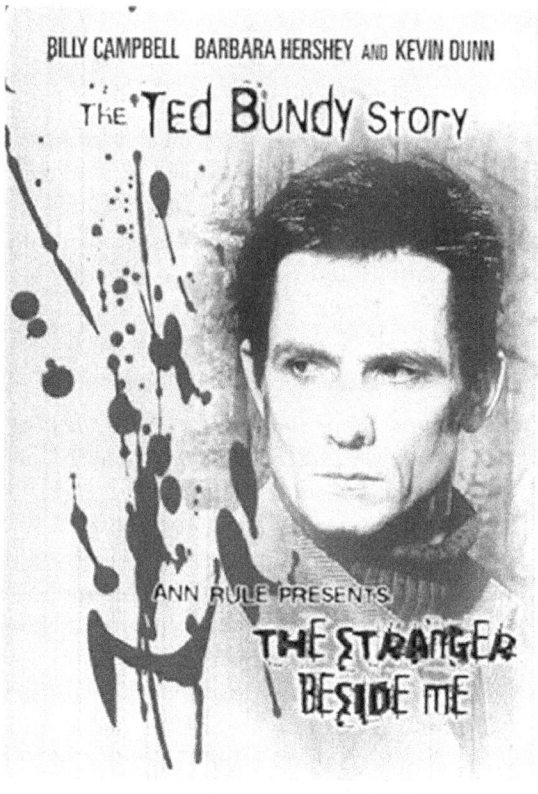

Billy Campbell in *Ann Rule Presents: The Stranger Beside Me*, directed by Paul Shapiro (courtesy Paul Shapiro).

Paul Shapiro: Well it's not a highly entertaining answer: usually projects come to you and you decide whether it is something you can make something out of or not. It was a project that dropped out of the sky, as they always do, and I was intrigued by it. So I took the film on. Once I get involved, I get involved in the script and all that stuff, but in terms of how it happened I just happened to be the right person at the right time with the right project.

ME: Had you read Ann Rule's book beforehand?
PS: No, I had not. But I did meet Ann Rule. She showed up on the set when we were shooting.

ME: What was it like meeting her?
PS: She is a really lovely person and very down to earth. In a way what you would expect given her background. My recollection is that she was a big fan of the film. She loved being on the set and seeing what was being done with her material.

ME: Ted Bundy is one of America's most notorious serial killers. When the project landed at your table did you have any reservations about making the film, considering the subject matter and notoriety of the case and Bundy's crimes?
PS: It is a good question. No not really and that is largely because in a sense it is not really Ted Bundy's story. It is, but it is told from the point of a friend, which is Ann Rule, obviously. It is not straight on a Ted Bundy movie. It comes at it obliquely which is interesting all on itself.

ME: Yes, because the film/book is equally about Ann Rule and how she was manipulated by Bundy.
PS: Yes, you're right, but not only manipulated but also betrayed. It is the only thing that separates or makes it different from any of the other films that have been made about Ted Bundy. Even though the film does track his story carefully, there is always that point of view you come back to, that of Ann Rule's, which makes it a very personal story. At the end of the day it's a film about betrayal and it goes beyond all the heinous things that he did outside of their relationship.

ME: How important was it to keep the film both accurate to Rule's source material and to the crimes that Bundy committed? Did you undertake extensive research into both his crimes and subsequent trial?
PS: Yes, it was. If you look at the film, Bundy's crimes— which are not all dramatized, but a lot of them are—are directed from a dispassionate, third-party observer's eye. It doesn't seek to get into his mental state. It doesn't seek to elaborate on what could have caused him to have that severely split personality. It doesn't really go there. It just documents it. The commentary is really Ann Rule's commentary. So yes, it was important to do both of those things in the film. Also, to be honest, Billy Campbell is a really interesting actor and he brought all sorts of other levels to the Ted Bundy character. As a person and an actor, he is a very charming guy. You then add another layer of madness to him and it is compelling. It was a great cast. Barbara Hershey was wonderful. We had some really good people on that movie. That always helps.

ME: As you said, Billy Campbell was excellent, and wholly convincing, as Bundy in the movie. He is both frightening and tragic at the same time. How did you set about directing him for the role and transforming him into an infamous psychopathic killer? Did you let Billy interpret the character in his own way?

PS: It was a collaboration, as it always tends to be. I think both of us were pretty clear on what we wanted to do with the character and what the character does in effect is pretty clearly written in the screenplay. He does have this enormous seductive charm and that was part of his ammo and we had to be faithful to that, that's for sure. Of course, Billy has that … not that I'm saying he's Ted Bundy! [Laughs.] Billy is a very charming guy and we fed off of that and we made the killings in a sense that they are almost banal. They are not highlighted for their gruesomeness. They are not exploitive. They are just simply a record of what he did. If you see the film you will see that. We are not trying to judge him. That was Ann Rule's job. As much as we could the effort with Billy was to make it credible and to try and understand, if we could, the charm that masked the demon underneath it. I think Billy did that. He had all those qualities, along with a vague resemblance to the real Ted Bundy.

ME: I thought that was a masterstroke. Billy Campbell conveys that charm effectively in the film. I think you pulled that off brilliantly; not only does he look like him but we see the charm and the way he manipulates his victims or the people around him.

PS: Exactly right. Then on top of that, when the walls start closing in on him, you start to see the anger and brutality in him. I think that is accurate, not even so much for the story itself, but for human nature. That was something Billy was great at. He really understood that he had to unravel his character a little bit in order for an audience to start to see what was going on with Bundy underneath it all.

ME: I agree. One of the major strengths of the film, and a successful strand pulled from both the book and what we know about Ted Bundy generally, is that you convey Bundy's duplicity and his gift of charming and manipulating women. That is one of the frightening elements of both the film and crimes of Bundy. That behind this charming façade lurked this sociopathic monster. Were you pleased with the way you conveyed Bundy on-screen?

PS: Generally, I would say yes. When you are making a film and working under enormous pressure and time constraints there are always things you might have done differently in hindsight, but I think in general the film is where I thought it should be. It has quite a grittiness to it, which I like and which seemed right for the film and the period, which is mostly the 1970s. I am generally happy with what we did and I would just say with more time we might have done more but we didn't have that. During this era, these films were done really quickly. I can't remember exactly but we had a fourteen-, fifteen-, sixteen-day shoot. That is very fast to shoot a movie. There are always things you don't get to do that you wanted to do but that's life. Given all those parameters I am happy with it. I will say, honestly, from my perspective, the film has gone largely unnoticed in the U.S. I don't know why. I don't know if it was promoted properly. It is definitely underappreciated for what it is. It wasn't promoted well and if your film does not have a buzz about it for whatever reason then people just don't know about it.

ME: Film is all about the marketing now. It doesn't really matter about the content of the film; it is what you can market in a trailer or a soundbite. All companies seem to care about is can they get two minutes of decent footage? If yes, it is rammed down the audience's throat. Studios aren't overly interested in the quality of a film but whether or not it will sell.

PS: That is totally true. What that means is that the films that are outstanding won't get a chance to find an audience.

ME: *I think your movie is excellent and I hope this book encourages others to seek it out.*

PS: Thank you, that would be wonderful. It certainly deserves more recognition than it got at the time. Keep in mind that it is now fifteen years old. It would require a new audience to assess it and also I would like to point out that one of the things that made the Bundy case so sensational in its day, with the trial and everything, was that he seemed too intelligent and charming that it contrasted with the crimes he was convicted of. I think that is at the center of what made this such a sensational case. He wasn't on outward appearance somebody you would consider to be a monster and in a sense that's what makes it the most frightening for audiences. He could be anybody. He could be your neighbor, your bus driver, your flight attendant—he could be anybody. That is a very sobering revelation, I think. Up until then most serial killers were more overtly monsters; you could see their day-to-day demeanor and disposition and say, "Yeah, I get it. I see it there." Not with Bundy. That's what was so new to the world at the time.

ME: *Also his arrogance. He represented himself in court.*

PS: Yes, he did. In the movie, the judge talks about that. He said he wished he could sit across him as an equal, as a legal mind. I think the judge was being honest. That's what he felt.

ME: *Talk us through the production of the film. Was it an easy shoot, given the short time frame you mentioned earlier, and especially as you were essentially making a period film? Was it difficult to capture the look of the '70s while working on a modest budget?*

PS: Generally it was very good. That's partly because we were able to get an extremely strong cast. Once you have that on your side you are well ahead of the game in making something special. I had a wonderful production designer and the support team was good. As I said earlier, it was a highly-pressurized environment. There is no time for second thoughts or restaging scenes. You just don't have it. There are occasions in any situation like that where your first instincts might be great but they don't produce exactly what you think they should be. It's not possible to change things as you go. The time pressures are just too much.

ME: *I think you captured the look of the '70s really well, considering the budget. The production design was good, as you said. Aesthetically, were you pleased with the way the film turned out?*

PS: Yes, I was. We put a lot of consideration into how we were going to portray the seventies and that goes for every single set or location that we worked with and with every period car that we chose. All of those things were spot on with what we were attempting to do. What I liked about it was that the seventies seem grounded in the film but it is not in your face. It is just there. That's the most successful part of it, we weren't trying to hammer the point. We were just trying to get the audience to live in that world.

ME: *You touched on this briefly earlier, but Bundy's crimes have been depicted in many films over the years, many of which have slipped into the exploitation terrain. Were* *you cautious in not proceeding down this route when making the film? Did you have to show some restraint when showing the murders, as the film was primarily made for a TV audience?*

PS: I think it was deliberate, though you have a screenplay in front of you and your network has approved it so you can't stray too far away from it. We can in some instances but generally not. Like I said, what makes it not exploitive is that it is not Ted Bundy's point of view. It is not even an audience's view of Ted Bundy. It is a particular person's point of view of him and because that is the abiding notion of the movie it removes the sense that you are watching something for the sake of the gore and the titillation of the violence. Like I said, we did not set out to glorify any of that. If you remember in one of the opening scenes, Bundy is carrying one of the girls that he has killed and he is holding her in his arms like a baby. It has that counterpoint all the way through it. He has just killed this girl and he is treating her so tenderly. For me, that's the creepiest part of this whole movie, in terms of his character.

ME: I agree, the film is very creepy and unnerving at times yet it doesn't resort to gore. I believe you can sometimes say more by being suggestive without being overtly violent or explicit.

PS: I agree with you. There was nothing to be gained by revisiting every gory detail of what he did. It is more about how he seduced these women into his possession. That's what the movie focuses on, less so what he did with them.

ME: Another interesting element of the film was that you touch upon the guilt experienced by Rule for not heeding the signs that Bundy was implicated. Do you think she should be criticized for not seeing that and for being manipulated by him? Or do you think, like the quote at the end of the movie, "We think we know evil when we see it, but we don't. It just exists." Do you think that rings true? Do you ever really know someone?

PS: Yes it rings true and it also harkens back to what we were talking about a minute ago. That is one of the elemental parts of the real story and of the film, that here is a guy who walks among us. He is not a monster. That's what defines his role in history, in all of these events and everything that happened around it is precisely that idea: he was just a guy who any of us could be with, hang out with, which is what makes it the most frightening to an audience. He was just a guy and you could put him in front of a camera and he could be articulate, witty and confident. You would never have guessed he could have done those crimes.

ME: I think you are right, a lot of audiences find it hard to accept that these killers are human. Sometimes it is easier to say they are monsters, are inhuman, when the reality is a lot more complicated than that.

PS: I think you are right, and that's the most frightening part, in my mind.

ME: What is particularly frightening and unsettling, which you show in the film, is that Bundy worked in a crisis center in Seattle fielding calls from vulnerable people or those in need of help. This brings into play a fascinating contradiction as well as questions about his mental psychosis. Was he warped, unhinged or did he feed off the pain of others?

PS: That's an excellent question, and in addition to that he was very engaged in politics for a long time. All of those things make you feel that he was always like that and that, in a way, he had this incredibly mad, psychotic personal life contrasted with somebody who on the surface was empathetic and got politically involved, which most people don't do in the United States. It is again a very stark contrast in his reality. The movie suggests, though we don't know for sure, that his first murder was a girl he lured from a porch swing when he was fourteen years old. That's a pretty long history of the same behavior. It is almost like a psychotic fetish for him that he couldn't control. I don't know if anyone has suggested that but that's what I have felt about him as a character.

ME: The film implies that Bundy's first victim, when he was 14, was 8-year-old Ann Marie Burr, who vanished from her home in Tacoma in 1961. There is some contention with regard to his involvement in this murder.

PS: I don't think anyone has actually proved he killed Ann Marie Burr. All the speculation indicates he did. He was the paperboy and she disappeared from the front porch, never to be found. Again, all of that stuff goes back to hiding this monster behind this very pleasant, charming façade. If you think of it as two trajectories, his personal life verses his private life, this is something that is common in our culture and we can't ever really know what happens behind closed doors, even for the most successful people. That's what the film says very starkly, in my opinion. Again, that is what's most chilling about it.

ME: I felt that the editing of the film was particularly interesting, especially the scene when you cut between two time frames: one of his murders and one of Bundy returning home to his girlfriend. Both demonstrate his ability to manipulate people and situations. I felt this was expertly done.

PS: Thank you. Again it was a way of juxtaposing the banality of his killings and his private life. Intercutting those two ideas exactly dramatizes the point you are making, which is that there is this carnage and evil going on in one corner of the frame and in the other corner is Bundy inviting Rule out to dinner or he had bought groceries and was going to cook her dinner. The contrast was just so absurd. Yet, that is kind of what the movie is about at the end of the day.

ME: I thought your film was a realistic portrayal of Ted Bundy and how he got away with his crimes instead of glorifying his crimes for entertainment. Some filmmakers make that mistake.

PS: I wouldn't put it all at the hands of the filmmakers. This is a long, complex process usually with many, many voices. There is what the network wants to do or the studio wants to do, there is what the producers want to do and what the audience seems to want. There are all those factors in how a movie gets made and you can't necessary put it all in the hands of the filmmaker because they generally are people who were hired to do a job. It is risky for directors to walk in and demand—in this format at least, television movies—wholesale changes to suit their own tastes. It happens, but not very often because it is a very risky road to walk down, especially if it fails. There are a lot of cooks in the kitchen when you do a film like this and your main job as a director is to distill the material through your own sensibilities and make choices that fit your sensibilities and tastes. That's where a director really makes a difference. In a funny way, when you hire a director to make a movie you're banking on that person's sensibilities as an artist and a human being to be an arbiter of what is shown on-screen and how it is shown, because every choice is going to go through that director's sensibility and in a sense that's what you are hiring: their take on the material and how to execute the material. It is all about personal vision. If you can be true to the material and you have a vision then you are going to make something unique to you even though you may not have conceived it. It will still be your work.

ME: Did you face any opposition from the families of the victims, some of whom would have still been alive at the time the film was made?

PS: Not that I remember. These true stories go through exhaustive vetting in terms of what can and can't be said about people, especially people who are still alive. It would be rare for something to slip through the cracks and you need to get an insurance writer in for these movies. They go through an exhaustive process saying what can and can't be shown or suggested in a movie. This is why at the end of the movie, with the death of Ann Marie Burr, it is specifically implied or suggested but not stated as a fact because there is no way of stating that as a fact. It has never been revealed to be a fact. Also, because it was based on Ann Rule's book, it would have had to have some sort of clearance for everybody who was described in the movie. I think they were on pretty safe territory most of the time and if there was anything I was unaware of it.

ME: Though you imply that Bundy killed Ann Marie Burr, Bundy has claimed he has killed more than 100 women. Yet he was such a liar—are we inclined to believe him?

PS: A lot of the lies are about self-aggrandizement. I think it is somewhere in the middle. There is no question that he killed on many occasions. What the number is, I am not sure we will ever know. It would be like him, once he saw the noose tightening, to exaggerate his prodigious behavior. That makes sense for that kind of personality.

ME: You show in the film that he was becoming more and more drawn to the limelight his case was attracting. I believe the film brilliantly conveys how Bundy began to enjoy the celebrity persona that arose after his escape and recapture. He seems to revel in being in the limelight, which is further shown in the film during the court scenes, where his arrogance rises to new levels as he gets "to play lawyer"! Was that your intention?

PS: There's no question and that's part of what made his original case so fascinating. He was a showman. He reveled in it. If you think about it, it was a once-in-a-lifetime opportunity for a guy like him.

ME: He took it.

PS: Yes, he took it and it is fascinating. If you see any of the archival footage taken of the real guy he was like a carnival barker. He was amazing.

ME: The real footage is frightening. His arrogance is unbelievable.

PS: Yes, it is unbelievable.

ME: Though Bundy's crimes were committed in various states in the U.S., I understand that the majority of the filming took place in Vancouver, British Columbia? Is that correct?

PS: Yes, it was all shot in Vancouver. We were shooting in the wintertime and what happens in Vancouver, like in England, you have very limited amount of daylight hours to shoot. It is cold and wet but on the other hand it was interesting for the movie. I don't know if you remember the scene in the film where Bundy is in his VW Bug and he is stalking a girl in a parking lot?

ME: Yes, I do.

PS: That was written as him on a beach with all these girls in bikinis. It was impossible to shoot that in Vancouver in the winter without endangering the safety and health of the people in front of the camera. I will tell you, the network was very upset that I didn't shoot it!

ME: Were they?

PS: Yes, because primarily they wanted to see girls in bikinis. Honestly, between you and me I think that is true. [Laughs.] In order to satisfy their lust we had to have a scene in a health spa, just before the girl goes into the parking lot. That was never in the original script but that was because we failed to put people in bikinis on a beach. For my money, the parking lot is much more interesting and more chilling because it is sort of the everyday rather than the exotic. This is what I mean about having a lot of cooks in the kitchen when making a movie like this.

ME: That's the type of area Bundy played on. Correct me if I'm wrong, but I don't recall Bundy scouting victims at the beach.

PS: One of the most interesting moments is when Bundy is out at that University campus looking at all these girls coming out of a music class. For me, that is a completely chilling scene. It is visually very electric and that scene encapsulates everything about Ted Bundy.

ME: That's the scene that I had in my head, just then. Bundy is like a predator looking for his next victim.

PS: Yes, but in this case there are multiple targets and he just happens to light on one of them. In the other scenes, there aren't really multiple targets. There is just one girl that he lights on. That's what makes this scene so chilling because he is fishing in a trunk pond.

ME: What was the critical reaction to the film?

PS: I don't really know because it was severely underpromoted. There were reviews but I can't remember them. Keep in mind that the network who produced the film, USA Network, here in the states, was a very young network at the time, and I don't think they knew what they had or how to promote it and I think that is the prime reason it fell between the cracks.

ME: Did the film get aired again? What happens to movies made for TV in the U.S.?

PS: This isn't across the board, but generally they only play once. The reason for that is that royalties involved in multiple airings are very, very high. So unless they have a compelling reason to air it more than once they don't tend to. With cable, they buy a number of rights over a period of time. So on cable you can see a movie multiple times but generally almost never on the networks.

ME: Are you proud of what you achieved with the film?

PS: Yes, I am proud of what we did. Like I said, there are things I would have done differently and there are always things you would have revisited if you had the time and resources. But I don't think of that after a movie is made because what you were able to create in the time you had is what you get. There is no other way of judging it. I am proud of it and I think it is a good, solid and essentially nuanced film.

In my mind and I will say to you, if it's of any value, I wasn't really interested in the gore and the details of what Bundy did to these girls. It would have been harder to tackle it solely from Bundy's perspective without getting into the gore. What interested me about this movie was the duality of it. The split personality. The banal set beside the incomprehensible. That to me was the only reason to make the movie.

13

Starkweather
An Interview with Director Byron Werner

Considered one of America's most notorious murder sprees, the case of Charles Raymond Starkweather transfixed and shocked a nation in the late fifties. The crimes were committed by two teenagers, Starkweather and his 14-year-old girlfriend Caril Ann Fugate, who served as his accomplice. That Fugate's mother, stepfather and two-year-old half-sister were among the victims only added to the appalling nature of the crimes.[1] The pair's murderous spree began in December 1957 and ended in January 1959. Their bloody road trip took them through the states of Nebraska and Wyoming, where they ruthlessly killed 11 people. Upon their eventual capture and trial, Starkweather wound up on the electric chair and was executed on June 25, 1959. Fugate was imprisoned and released on parole seventeen years later, where she tried to slink into obscurity by working as a janitorial assistant and later a medical technician.

Unfortunately for Fugate, the notoriety of the case has been hard to suppress. Just as the Columbine shooting had a profound effect on the U.S. in the late nineties, so did the Starkweather–Fugate killing spree leave an indelible psychological scar on the nation during the fifties. That the violent crimes were committed by two teenagers played a decisive role in the infamy of the case, along with the sheer motiveless nature of the killings. Unsurprisingly the crimes of Starkweather and Fugate have inspired multiple media depictions ranging from music, to literature, to visual arts, to film, to television. With regard to the latter, Starkweather's and Fugate's murderous spree has served as the inspiration for a number of high-profile films such as *The Sadist* (1963), Terence Malik's seminal *Badlands* (1973), *Kalifornia* (1993) and Oliver Stone's controversial *Natural Born Killers* (1994). Though fictional, all the aforementioned films were clearly inspired by the Starkweather case, even if director Terence Malik didn't acknowledge it at the time of *Badlands* release, despite the glaring similarities with the case. Operating outside the mainstream, the late eighties saw the production of the low-budget film *Stark Raving Mad* (1981), starring Richard Stark as Starkweather and Marcie Severson as Fugate. This cheap exploitation flick, directed by George F. Hood, served to present a fictionalized account of Starkweather's crimes with reasonable success. In the nineties, Tim Roth starred in the decent TV movie *Murder in the Heartland* (1993).

For more than a decade Starkweather adaptations went quiet. Then the late nineties and early noughties saw a flurry of low-budget films churned out to capitalize on the demand for flicks based on infamous American killers, many of which were penned by

Director Byron Werner (*right*) with actors Brent Taylor (*middle*) and Shannon Lucio on the set of *Starkweather*. Taylor and Lucio portray infamous spree killers Charles Starkweather and Caril Ann Fugate (courtesy Byron Werner).

scriptwriter Stephen Johnston (*Ed Gein*, *Ted Bundy*, and *The Hillside Strangler*). With many key killers already ticked off the list (Dahmer, Gacy, Ed Gein, and Henry Lee Lucas), attention naturally turned to the bad boy of crime who was instrumental in introducing American citizens to the notion of spree killing: the case of Charles Starkweather.

Billed as a truthful adaption of Starkweather's life and crimes, the film follows Starkweather and Fugate as their crime spree unfolds across America before they are finally apprehended by law enforcement officers after a high-speed chase across the country by Sheriff Merle Karnopp. With a good '50s vibe, solid direction by Werner and excellent central performances by Brent Taylor (Starkweather) and Shannon Lucio (Caril Ann Fugate), the film makes a decent stab at accurately recreating Starkweather's crimes, despite its obvious low budget, time constraints and inclusion of a few fictitious elements (more on that later). While not overtly graphic, the film doesn't shy away from depicting all of their killings, with the murders of industrialist C. Lauer Ward, his wife Clara and their maid Lillian Fenci particularly unnerving. Though billed heavily on posters and DVDs, Lance Henriksen's only contribution to the film is the use of his voice for Starkweather's alter ego, "The Mentor."

Helmed by cinematographer and director Byron Werner, *Starkweather* can be considered a good low-budget piece of filmmaking that tries to delve into the fractured psychosis of Starkweather and highlights his lack of compassion for human life. One of the interesting elements of the film—though some viewers will find this a weak point—is

Director Byron Werner (with crew) directing a scene featuring the mysterious Mentor in *Starkweather*, 2004 (courtesy Byron Werner).

that Starkweather is presented as a man suffering from schizophrenic tendencies that manifest themselves in the form of a shadowy figure called "The Mentor," who encourages Starkweather to act out his violent impulses and killings. Though there is no evidence to suggest that he suffered from schizophrenia or a split personality, the film presents Starkweather as a person always on the brink of sanity, or insanity. From a pure cinematic viewpoint, "The Mentor" adds a creepy undercurrent to proceedings, though purists may not buy into this element of the film. That said, the film undeniably succeeds in presenting the volatile rage that ate away and consumed Starkweather, though it does shy away from the causes that this brought on other than hinting towards a damaged psychosis present early on in childhood and a man at odds with society and his social standing within it (the excessive bullying he experienced at school and how this saw him bully others who he disliked is not explored in the film).

The film ultimately succeeds in its portrayal of a remorseless, cruel, sadistic killer, and his horrifying rampage through the heartlands of America. In contrast, Fugate is first presented as a naive and infatuated girl who was easily manipulated by Starkweather and who gets sucked into his bloody vortex as his rampage spirals out of control. Yet, the film shows, as the killings mount up, that she knew exactly the crimes he was committing, and the film makes no apologies for contending that she was fully complicit in knowing and assisting in the spree. In that sense, *Starkweather* is a difficult film for audiences to watch, as both leads are thoroughly unlikable and seemingly remorseless of their actions. Director Werner should be praised for this because ultimately the film doesn't pander to the killers, or try to inject an element of glamour into their murderous spree. Werner clearly presents them as the unhinged, cruel killers that they are and their doomed relationship. It is for that reason that the crimes of Starkweather and Fugate still continue to capture the public imagination and why they have left such a cultural blemish on the nation's psyche.

In March 2018 I had the pleasure of interviewing director Byron Werner about his underrated and brilliantly acted film. I thank him for the generous amount of time he gave up to be interviewed for this collection.

Matthew Edwards: *How did you get involved in film? You have worked primarily as a cinematographer, I understand?*

Byron Werner: Yes, and that is still what I primarily do. As a matter of fact, I have directed three movies and they were all super low-budget and they all came about because there was a producer who came to me and said, "Do you want to direct a movie?" The movie industry has got so difficult in terms of getting financing and getting good things done. Basically, I don't really pursue directing anymore because the only way to get a movie done is to work really hard at it! That's what you have to do as a director. That's why I work as a DP, as I don't have the time or energy to get my ideas off the ground. So, the short answer long is that I generally work as a DP and I direct and shoot commercials, though no longer movies. It may happen again—and I may do it again—but I believe the true problem is that I don't know how to separate [being a director and a cinematographer]. I think for me to truly become a director, and to do a good job on a movie, I need to separate the visuals from the acting/story. When I read a script I just read it as visuals and I have so much trouble separating it. I think I'll have to quit being a DP if I want to pursue directing! But it is great to be able to talk about *Starkweather* with you as the film didn't get much exhibition and it no longer has a life. The film was never mastered in HD.

ME: *The killing spree of Charles Starkweather is one of the most infamous cases not only in Nebraska, but in the U.S. What attracted you to the project and how did the opportunity to direct the picture arise?*

BW: I had been working for a producer named Mark Boot and he did a lot of low-budget movies around that time. I was trying to make a name for myself as a DP and I worked for him on a number of movies. This was before the digital age and it was hard to sell films digitally, so everything was shot on 35mm film. I felt the only way I was going to be able to make films was to just go ahead and learn how to do it. I was making very little money. That time it was less than what tradesmen, or crew, make on bigger movies, but I did these films so that I could learn how to make movies. So, I did a bunch of movies for Mark Boot and he must have thought I had a good eye for directing and he said, "Would you be interested in directing a film?" To be honest, the films I was doing with him at that time were like Skinemax movies. They were rated R but they had soft sex scenes in them, and things like that! [Laughs.] I finally said yes and I directed, and shot, a movie called *Starstruck* (2000). It was basically taking the idea of *Body Heat* (1981). It wasn't a remake, but the writer tried to move it into the film world where this guy was a soft-core porn director. It kind of made fun of *Body Heat*, anyway. I got to direct the movie and that was great. So, when *Starkweather* came about, the same writer of *Starstruck*—Stephen Johnston—brought the script to Mark Boot and said, "Do you want to do this?," and Mark approached me to direct it. I said I wanted to be DP but I love the idea of this movie. I love the genre and the style. So, I said that I wanted to do both. He agreed, which I think for this film was a good thing. That's what really attracted me to the film, the opportunity to both direct the film and be DP.

I also liked overall idea of Charles Starkweather and making a film about his killing spree. That was very interesting to me. Looking back now, I also liked the idea of having this guy in his head telling him to do it. I feel that with our culture today, especially here in America, with all these recent shootings, this is not a nurture thing but a nature thing. I think it is just in people's heads. Obviously, that wasn't real and made up by the writer. I do think it made the film interesting and it helped drive home the point that this guy did this—or it was our take on it—because he was deranged and fucked in the head. He would have done this regardless of what happened.

ME: I did like that element in the film. "The Mentor" was an interesting addition to the film and fits in with comments made by his former friends saying he could be really kind then flip to being really cruel. In a sense, "The Mentor" is like his schizophrenic alter ego. Is that what you were trying to get across to the audience? A man with a fractured psychosis and how he could change from one person to another?

BW: Yes, absolutely. Stephen Johnston did a really good job of researching this movie. Even though we didn't shoot it in Nebraska—we couldn't—and everything isn't perfectly accurate, the people, the murders, the order it happened, those details are all fairly accurate. The locations may not be, but a large part is. The thing is, Starkweather wasn't a serial killer. At that time there was no name for it, but later he was labeled a spree killer. His story was made famous by *Badlands* (1973), but really, in terms of the spree portions of it, by *Natural Born Killers* (1994). The fact that he could just flip in a second helped drive that part of his character home. I think that's what makes it an interesting part of the story, because he was a nut who didn't think or premeditate anything—he just went on this killing spree. Something had to flip in his head. Synapses must have been firing in his brain to have made him do this. From what I could tell, there was nothing in his life that led him to this. He didn't have a bad life, nor was he abused. What we were saying with the film was that this was always in him and he was going to do it no matter what. No matter what upbringing he had he would have gone down this path. At the beginning of the film we see him with the frog and "The Mentor" tells him to kill the frog. When his father confronts him on why he killed the frog he simply says, "The man told me to do it." So, you basically have that set up there that this kid had problems from an early age. It obviously didn't come from his father but from himself.

ME: The only issues I found he had growing up were that he was bullied at school. That is something you allude to in the film during conversations between "The Mentor" and Charles.

BW: Yes, that is true. We do say at the beginning that the kids bully him. That's a good point, I feel that is an element that pushed him, but I don't believe that other kids bullying him or feeling less about himself drove him down that path. I don't think that is going to make somebody kill people. It probably didn't help. I think if it is in their head they are going to do it no matter what. I think with Charles Starkweather, no matter what happened in his life, he was always going to do this, and you would never have been able to cure him of it. It was bound to happen at some point. Perhaps the bullying led him down that path, but it seemed like it was always going to be inevitable, in my opinion.

ME: Starkweather's crimes have been depicted in and have inspired many films—like Badlands and Natural Born Killers—*to television shows and other media, such as music and visual arts. Was there a specific side of the Starkweather story you were looking to explore in the film?*

BW: I think the idea was to just make the movie specifically about Starkweather. The same producer had success with making a movie about Ed Gein (*Ed Gein*, 2000) but these movies were popular at that point, especially with low-budget filmmakers. I would love to say I was an auteur and that it was all about the "art" but the only way to get some of these movies made was to ensure that there was a name to sell it. *Starkweather* had a real low budget but they were able to get the money going because they knew they could recoup their investment. The film was more of a financial one, as opposed to artistic. There again, this was a great story that hadn't been told fully about Charles Starkweather. Or a film calling him Charles Starkweather.

ME: Scriptwriter Stephen Johnston had previously written scripts for Ed Gein, Ted Bundy, *and* The Hillside Strangler *before writing* Starkweather. *So, he was well-versed in writing films about real-life killers. Did you think it was an accurate account of Starkweather's crimes and the relationship between Starkweather and Caril Ann Fugate?*

BW: Everything we know about them, other than the guy in his head [The Mentor], and that we shot in Nebraska, is a fairly accurate representation of what happened. It is interesting that Charles's relationship with Caril Ann really makes the movie work. It is the two of them and they are portrayed by two really good actors in that whole relationship. We can't explain her in the same way that we can with him. Starkweather had some synapses misfire, or something. How do we explain Caril Ann? Obviously, she is deranged; she is crazy. However, she did say later on, and we show this in the movie, that he made her do it, or forced her into it. We don't know the real truth about that. I think she is still alive today....

ME: Yes, she is.

BW: She got off scot-free! We are saying that she was complicit in the killings. I don't think anyone knows the real story about that. Who knows, but their relationship is the most fascinating part and her complicity works for the movie.

ME: Well it does, because at the beginning you show her as being a naive teenager, but as the film goes on she is drawn more and more into the crimes and complicit in the killings.

BW: Absolutely! We start off with that innocence; the innocence of both of them. I liked the fact that Charles falls in love with Caril Ann at first sight, which you don't see much anymore. That was very much a thing of those days. She is innocent because she's innocent, and she is young. That relationship and innocence I started in that scene at the drive-in. We had no money to shoot in a drive-in so we shot in a parking lot and faked it! I thought to myself, "How am I going to show the movie? I can't film them at the drive-in and have no movie." So, I thought that if it starts raining then it doesn't matter about the movie. What the rain did was it got me out of a low-budget problem, but it also helped pushed them into that car together. It helped that connection and made it all about them. You have the other couple making out at the back, but it still drove home the connection between the two of them. I love how that low-budget problem made everything better. From then on you have that connection and that kiss. Then they are off and running together as this couple.

ME: *I felt that worked really well and then slowly her character changes.*

BW: Yes, she is so impressionable. I guess you buy it. She knows right from wrong. I think that if this wasn't a true story I don't know you could sell the fact that she killed her sister. We don't know if she did it, or Charlie did it. Or the pair of them. And her parents! To kill your parents is one thing, but the kid is like … even when I rewatch the movie I wince when I see her hit the kid with the butt of the gun. It is crazy and then you see her going outside and you see her sister's little feet laying there. It is heartbreaking. If you made that up I don't know if it would work. I think the fact that that actually happened shows that she did go from this innocent girl who was infatuated with Charles and to something else. She was so impressionable that he got to her. Either that, or she had that little person in her head, too. We didn't explore that in the film but perhaps she always had that, too! Then again, I haven't heard that she has killed anyone since then, so who knows!

ME: *She is still alive, though on August 5, 2013, she was seriously injured in a car accident, which killed her husband.*

BW: I didn't know that.

ME: *When making the film, did you strive to make the film as historically accurate as possible? How difficult is that when making a fictionalized version of a true-life case or when working on a low-budget period film? How difficult is it to marry those two elements?*

BW: I think it is really hard. I think with any movie you never have enough money and in this case there was none. I think the movie was made for around $125,000, which is insane! It was shot on 35mm film and I think they gave me about 25,000ft to shoot with, which is next to nothing. I had one camera and I shot the film in twelve days. That was unheard of back then. You can do that with low-budget horror films but with the amount of locations that we had and with the amount of actors—and with what we were trying to achieve—it was crazy! Trying to be historically accurate, and get the period cars, and all period details that you need, on top of the film stock you need to shoot the movie—it was pretty nuts!

I tried to make it as accurate as possible and people say, "Well you didn't do this," and "You didn't do that" and "You didn't shoot it in Nebraska," but we couldn't! I say that you have two choices. You either make the movie or you don't. It is like now with *Star Wars* with people bitching about it saying they are ruining it. I say to those people that you have two choices. Either you have nothing, or you can have *this*. You can't bitch because they weren't doing it and now they are not doing it perfectly. So, I had an opportunity to make the movie and I had very limited resources and very limited time. I had to make it in California. I did the best I could to make it as historically accurate as possible but knowing some things you just had to concede. So, there wasn't much I could do. I wanted to open the movie with an overhead shot and they got me a helicopter.

ME: *That was a lovely shot.*

BW: Well I strapped in the camera and hung out the side of the helicopter and shot that car! Okay, it looks like the Californian desert and maybe not Nebraska but at that point you can't stop doing the things you want to do because you may be criticized. Well, I think if the story is good enough, and people aren't just jerks or trolls from the internet, then they are going to get over that sort of thing. You just got to make the movie as best you can with what you have.

ME: Perhaps that is why the film has been better received in Europe, because they have been able to concentrate more on the story as opposed to the accuracy of the terrain/ landscape. I imagine a lot of European viewers wouldn't pick up on the fundamental differences between Nebraska and California, unless they had specific knowledge of the areas. I am pretty sure that an American viewer of a British film wouldn't pick up on geographical differences in the UK.

BW: I wouldn't know the difference between Liverpool and Manchester. You are exactly right.

ME: The thing is, with low-budget filming you have to shoot where you can. It is like guerrilla filmmaking. If you have to shoot in LA to make the film then that's how it is.

BW: Yes. You are right. It is like guerrilla filmmaking. You got to shoot fast and you just got to get the shot and move on. You sometimes only have a couple of takes. I have a philosophy on that. If the actors are great, I can get a shot and I can move on and maybe I can do two more takes. I am not going to do a third take because I'd rather have a couple more set-ups to help tell the story than shoot the same thing.

ME: You managed to secure Lance Henriksen's voice as "The Mentor" in the film. I liked the way you kept his character in the shadows and never revealed his face.

BW: We got him later. That wasn't the intention at the beginning. We had a guy who did the voice, but we always knew we were going to replace him. We didn't know who with, at that point. We never wanted to show "The Mentor's" face in the film. Lance wasn't the actual actor in the film, it is just his voice. We got Lance later, which is really funny because I noticed in Europe—in places like Germany—that Lance Henriksen is on the box as one of the main actors! We only used his voice and in Germany his voice had been over-dubbed, so he wasn't even in it! [Laughs.]

ME: I liked that element. You can clearly tell it is not Lance in the film, but I liked the way you shot "The Mentor" as this shadowy figure either at the end of his bed or at a window. I thought that was well done and I liked the way you didn't reveal this alter ego.

BW: Yes, the alter ego in a sense is Charlie Starkweather in some form—maybe it is him when he is older, maybe him in another life. I don't know. It is him. You can't show the face because that would bring to life a whole other person. The Mentor has to be a reflection of him, in a sense.

ME: So, how did Lance become involved in the film?

BW: I was speaking to the producers and we talked about getting another name attached to the film. Someone with a really good voice. At that time Lance had just finished *Millennium* (1996–1999), the TV show. He was pretty popular at the time and the producers managed to get him. I set up an ADR session with him and we voiced that stuff! It was pretty awesome. Lance is like any big actor. You can give him some guidance, I guess, but he just went in there and killed it! I just shot a movie with Samuel L. Jackson. It is the same. He goes in there and does Samuel L. Jackson! That's great and you are not going to tell him to do it any differently. I felt Lance was the same. Lance did Lance and he did a friggin' great job at it!

ME: Did he add the profanity to the character?

BW: Yes, that may have been him. I actually can't remember. I think the dialogue was similar, and we changed a few things in the ADR session, but yeah, he added a few extra F-bombs!

ME: The casting of Charles Starkweather was a central component of the film. How did you come to cast Brent Taylor and Shannon Lucio in the lead roles?

BW: Basically, through the casting agent and casting auditions. We cast Brent after a casting session with a bunch of people and we saw him, and we thought this guy was great, and he just fitted the part. He was the right guy for it. I thought he would have gone on to be a big star, but he didn't. Funnily enough, Shannon was the same. She was genius in the movie and so good. I think we got them to read together after we had cast Brent. Shannon did a TV movie after and I thought she would go big, but she didn't. The funny part is that the guy who was the biggest out of everybody, who went on to be successful, was Keir O'Donnell, who played the friend. I think it was one of his first acting parts and he went on to be in *Lost*. He was the brother in *Wedding Crashers* (2005). He was the one guy who made it big! He was great, too. Overall, and I am going to be completely honest, and I won't hype the fact, but I was the director and the DP and the camera operator. It was a twelve-week shoot and I was busy as hell. I didn't give Brent and Shannon too much direction. I probably told them where to go, and gave them some ideas, but from take to take I let them do their thing. I didn't do a lot. They were so good I just felt that I just had to capture it. I bet if you asked them they'd say I didn't direct them at all! I really didn't! I am not embarrassed by that. I'd probably approach it differently now and be a little more interactive with them, but they were so good, the shoot was so fast and I had so much to do, I just don't think I had any brain power or time to try to change something that was working. One of the biggest successes of the picture was the casting of Brent and Shannon and without them the film wouldn't have worked.

Starkweather and Fugate broke into the house of wealthy industrialist C. Lauer Ward and his wife Clara. Here, Starkweather (*left*) attacks Clara played by Tacey Adams (courtesy Byron Werner).

ME: Did you give them any guidance as to how the characters change through the course of the film? How they become more ruthless, while on the flip side more devoted to one another? Did you try to get that across to them, during pre-production?

BW: I can't honestly remember. I guess we did speak about it but as it was such a small movie we didn't have time for rehearsals. As soon as we got on set we just had to go and shoot. I'm sure we did have discussions about the characters and how they should be and talked about an arc and a change. But those two [Brent Taylor and Shannon Lucio] were so good. I am not sure whether I should say this, but I will, as I don't care! But the biggest problem I had with the film was the part of the sheriff (Jerry Kroll). I spent so much time on that part and I never got it right. He financed the movie and he had to be in it! Al Sapienza, who plays the deputy and is a fine actor who had been in tons of stuff, he was great. I don't know if I love him being the dumb guy in playing that role, but he wanted to do that. So, I thought, "Go ahead and do your thing." Al Sapienza was fine but Jerry Kroll…. Well, I am very thankful that he financed the movie, and we wouldn't have got it done without him, but I wish he didn't have to be in it as the movie could have gone to another level—or been a festival movie—had he not been in it. Maybe I'm kidding myself, but I feel the film would have been better received if it wasn't for him. He brings the film down. Every scene with him in it is awkward. Everything he says he never gets right and I didn't have the time for him to get it right because I didn't have the time.

ME: Was Jerry Kroll's character in the original script?
   BW: That's a good question.

ME: Did Jerry write a part in the film for himself? Were there always going to be two sheriffs?

Al Sapienza as Deputy Dale Fahrnbruch in *Starkweather* (courtesy Byron Werner).

BW: That's a good point. I don't remember. I do recall that a part was made up for him and that originally there was only one sheriff. I think we had to split the part up, to make two, and then beefed up his character. I think there was always a cop in the original story.

ME: I think his part does draw the viewer away from Starkweather's spree during the film.

BW: I don't mind the story point of the sheriff, or having someone after him, but the crazy part of this movie is that the protagonist is in a sense your antagonist. He is killing people, yet he is so likeable. They almost play both sides, so you do need a true good guy, or a hero, at the end. It should have been just Al, or a better actor than Jerry. God, I hate to throw the guy under the bus after all these years! [Laughs.] I feel his part is the weakest part of the film.

ME: Were there any other problems during the production of the film? What about trying to capture the look of a period film using such a low budget?

BW: Yes, everything was a problem! Every day there was a problem. Not enough time, not enough money, not enough film and not enough rehearsal time. So, all that stuff! We found some locations out in a location called Acton, California. It was out towards the desert. It was the closest we could find that resembled Nebraska. We found some older places that we could use and based ourselves in one general location, which meant we didn't have to move too much, as that kills time. When we had to go back into city, especially when we filmed at the house where they kill the husband, wife and maid, yes, at that house I had to stay tight. I was only able to shoot one house on the corner, in order to make it look period! I could only put one car in there! But that was OK, because you can shoot foreground instead, and shoot through the car and do that kind of stuff. You can hide the fact that you have limited resources and make it look like a period film.

Once again it goes back to the fact that you can either make the movie or not. If you complain that you don't have enough money, don't do the movie. If you embrace the fact that you are going to do it then accept it will be difficult and that you can't do everything you want. I don't think that is possible, anyway. Even in films like *Rogue One: A Star Wars Story*, the special effects guys complained they didn't have enough money to do certain shots! Another friend told me that they were going to do a big car chase sequence in *Spiderman*, but they couldn't afford to do it as big as they wanted to! Well, if those guys can't afford certain things then low-budget movies have to suck it up and try and make it work! Besides, it is the story that counts. You can't say it isn't good because you didn't have this or that. In the end, nobody knows or cares. Nobody knows the battles or problems you had when making the film. It is irrelevant, in the end. What matters is what ends up on-screen.

ME: Stylistically, how did you set about shooting the film? I understand that it was shot quickly and that you photographed and directed the film. Was that difficult or was it easy for you to get the shots you wanted? There are some beautiful shots in the film.

BW: Yes, I wanted it to be warm. I wanted a warm color palette, earthly tones, stuff like that. I felt that look lent itself to Nebraska and that era. At that time, I was hung up on sunset grad filters. You can call them cheesy, but I felt they looked cool. If you don't have a ton of money, then you need to utilize the light and make it a little prettier. My philosophy is to just go for it. For the interiors, I tried to use warm lights. Often, we would pick locations that had wooden cabinets and had a rustic Nebraska feel, as opposed to '40s–'50s LA. We didn't use many gel lights. It didn't think it was necessary, aside from the scene at the drive-in, where we used some red gels. We just tried to keep it simple, and we didn't have the budget for fancy shots and lighting. We just tried to build everything around our resources.

ME: I thought there were some interesting camera movements in the film.
BW: I like to keep the camera moving. I shot with a zoom lens, so I could work fast. I wasn't into handheld and *Starkweather* didn't feel like a handheld movie to me. I wanted it to be more elegant, even though it was gritty. My AD would go crazy at me as one minute I would be filming a wide shot then I would zoom in real tight, and he would have to change focus! He was a young guy, but he did an amazing job!

ME: Was it difficult shooting that final chase sequence?
BW: Yes, that was the one day when we brought the helicopter to shoot the opening and we brought out a second camera, and I brought a buddy of mine out, and we shot with a process trailer, so we could put the camera on. So, they did give us a few things! At that time, you didn't tend to have multiple cameras when working on 35mm. The process trailer allowed us to mount the camera during the driving footage and having the helicopter allowed us to do some overhead shots, which was great. I think I only had two days to film all the stuff on that road. It was tough but planning it out, and doing it right, and not going too crazy, it worked out pretty well. Having the second camera to bring out was great, because at that time it wasn't digital. You couldn't use the same camera and do slow motion. I was able to bring out an ARRI 3, which was able to do slow motion. I felt I was able to combine all these resources, which helped the picture.

Behind-the-scenes shot of the finale in *Starkweather* (courtesy Byron Werner).

ME: *I thought the soundtrack was another interesting piece to the film. It seemed very apt.*

BW: I was inspired by Neil Young's score on *Dead Man* (1995). My cousin is a musician and I asked him for a very guitar-driven score. I feel it works. Very unorthodox but I am happy with the end result.

ME: *You don't shy away from depicting Starkweather as a ruthless killer. Was it important that the killings were pretty graphic or was there some pressure from the producers to tailor the film to horror and true-crime audiences?*

BW: It is a movie about a killer, so we needed to see the blood. You needed to see the horror of their crimes. I will say we were making a low-budget film, so we couldn't afford to see the bullets hitting people. We didn't have easy digital effects at the time to enhance the film. I couldn't afford squibs. For instance, when Starkweather kills Fugate's parents, I used slo-mo, and you see him go out of frame and then you cut to a shot of Caril Ann. I think it was more effective that you were on her reaction of her parents getting killed instead of seeing them getting shot. That was a function of low budget, but I think cutting it that way worked better. Sometimes the reactions, and what you don't see, but what's imagined by the viewer, are more graphic than what you actually see. Also, *Starkweather* is not a horror movie. We weren't trying to gross them out. We wanted them to have the emotional impact of the killings and understand it. This is a deranged person killing people, but you don't need to see gore and guts flying out. That's not going to help the story.

ME: *Being more suggestive packs a bigger punch.*

BW: Yes, it does. As I said, that was partly a function of the way the story should be told and not having the money, even if we wanted to, to show everything.

ME: *The killings of the maid and the husband and wife really stick in my head, not because of what is shown on-screen, but the brutality of it.*

BW: Yes, especially in that scene because everyone was innocent. They did go into other people's houses and kill them but this one was especially brutal. This might sound weird, but the crime was committed in the city, not the country. For some reason, that packs a bigger punch because you feel safer in an urban area. This world is so crazy, but you at least feel safe in your own house. The fact that these guys came to the city and picked out that house randomly and then killed these people is crazy.

ME: *When making a film like this, do you have to be sensitive to how you portrayed the characters and victims as some of them and their families are still alive?*

BW: Yes, we tried to. I would often bring this up with the producer, "Do we need to worry about this going into the public domain?" I always felt that because we were using their real names that we needed permission, but we never did. I think because it had become part of history for so long that it was fine. I did have concerns that we might offend someone but that was only in the back of my head and it never became a reality. No one complained about the film. Caril Ann is the only one who is alive who we made look bad. If you want to argue that she didn't do it, or that she wasn't complicit, or that Starkweather lied and she didn't do it, then she is the only one who we would have done a disservice to.

ME: Did you ever receive any feedback from her?

BW: No, we never heard anything from her.

ME: How was the film received critically? Was it shown theatrically?

BW: No, it wasn't shown in theaters. It was bought by ThinkFilm before they went bankrupt [in 2006, while a division of David Bergstein's Capitol Films]. They put out some good films at the time, but it went direct to video. DVD was big, and obviously you couldn't watch things online. At that time, these films sold big overseas and would have big lives in places like Germany and in England! More so than the US! Some people wrote about the movie, IMDb was out, however there wasn't much feedback on the film. There were some reviews from *Fangoria* when it came out, nothing amazingly positive, but the bottom line is *Badlands*, *True Romance*, and *Natural Born Killers* are all better movies than this! But that's fine.

ME: I think that's a tad unfair, considering the resources you had to work with. Those aforementioned films, especially Badlands, *aren't specifically about the case, though clearly inspired by it. I think the film holds up!*

BW: Thank you, that makes me feel better! I'm just reading a review on Scary-Minds where some guy gives it 8 out of 10! Obviously people enjoyed it, which is great, and if people can take it for what it is then I will be happy. I don't think people should give it a break because it is low-budget but if they enjoy it, great. None of these films are ever perfect, there is always something that goes wrong. If they can get over whatever hiccup affects them—mine was that actor—then great. Then you are always going to get those who complain about the film that it was not shot in Nebraska or who don't like Lance's character, "The Mentor."

ME: There have been versions where it has not been shown in its correct ratio, which has seen the mic boom visible on some prints.

BW: Yes, that's not true at all. I know what happened there. What happens is when you shoot on 35mm with the full aperture you crop it down. So, at some point somebody made a mistake and released a version in full frame (where everything can be seen) and without the mask on it. That's total BS. That was a technical mistake a distributor made. Hopefully those copies aren't in existence anymore. I'm proud of the film and I did my best to honor the story.

14

Killer Scripts

An Interview with Screenwriter Stephen Johnston

While there are numerous cinephiles with a passion and interest in serial killer flicks or true-crime movies, there are those folks who have made a living penning such fare for the screen. During the early noughties, one man in particular was responsible for writing a number of infamous films of the era. These included Matthew Bright's *Ted Bundy*, Chuck Parello's *Ed Gein* and *The Hillside Strangler* and Byron Werner's *Starkweather*. The fellow responsible for these scripts is none other than American scriptwriter Stephen Johnston. With a reputation of delving into the minds of some of America's most vicious mass murderers, Johnston has the dubious distinction of being a bona fide expert in this grisly field. In January 2019, I was afforded the opportunity to interview Stephen Johnston about his craft, his fascination with serial killers and on how he set about bringing some of America's most grisly crimes to the silver screen. A true gentlemen, I thank Stephen not only for taking time out to be interviewed for this collection, but for also providing the forward to this book.

Matthew Edwards: *You have written four screenplays for films relating to real-life killers....*

Stephen Johnston: Yes, I have a bit of reputation! [Laughs.]

ME: A good reputation!

SJ: You should also know that I have another film in the pipeline on the Moors Murders,[1] which is supposed to be done in the not too distant future in your neck of the woods.

ME: Have you completed the script on that?

SJ: Yes, I guess you would say the film is in pre-pre-production with my old friend Hamish McAlpine who did *Ed Gein*, *Ted Bundy* and *The Hillside Strangler* with me.

ME: I hear Hamish is a character!

SJ: Yes, he is, but in a good way! I have been friends with him for some twenty years or so.

ME: He did Tartan films.

SJ: That's right. To some degree, he was instrumental in the whole explosion of Asian cinema on video. That was very much their stock and trade, especially Asian horror.

14. Killer Scripts

ME: *Tartan Video originated here in the United Kingdom and they specialized in world cinema before going down the extreme route of Asian horror and then he began producing films in the early noughties based on real-life killers.*

SJ: My original screenplay for *Ed Gein* was actually called *In the Light of the Moon*. It is cribbed from the band Slayer. They had a song and in it they had a lyric that said, "In the light of the moon…." When I was in college in Chicago I wrote the script for *Ed Gein*, though originally it had the previously mentioned title. I don't recall how, but at some point the subject of Ed Gein came across my radar. Ed Gein was like a character; there were all these movies that touched upon the story like *Texas Chain Saw Massacre*, *The Silence of the Lambs* and *Deranged*. I thought to myself, "Why doesn't somebody just tell the actual story, instead of something loosely based?" His story is certainly interesting enough, so I started researching it. I wanted to very much write it like it was a horror film and not just tell his story but approach the material as if it was supposed to be a scary horror film. So that's what I did.

Ultimately, I ended up meeting Hamish and selling the script, then for commercial purposes it was retitled *Ed Gein*. You know, nobody would know what *In the Light of the Moon* necessarily means! By the time I had sold the script I had moved to Los Angeles and I had some success as a writer. I had been asked to rewrite a few scripts and then I was hired to write a few erotic thrillers and I think you can find them out there on occasion … not that you would want to! [Laughs.] That's how I made some money back then. The fateful day occurred when I was with my friend and producer Mark Boot, who I was working with. He introduced me to Hamish, and that's when Hamish had his Tartan offices here in Los Angeles. It was my friend Mark who met up with Hamish with regard to distributing movies and Hamish actually had a bust of Ed Gein on his desk. When Mark saw the bust he said, "My buddy wrote a movie about that guy," and Hamish was immediately intrigued and said that he wanted to read the script. So Mark called me and said you need to send your script over to Hamish, which I did, and about two weeks later I had lunch with Hamish and I agreed to sell the script to him. About six months later we were in pre-production.

ME: *What really interests me about your script, and you touched upon this earlier, is that it is one of the first films that is a truthful, historical account of the Ed Gein story. You don't up the murder count or have the victims as young, good-looking women. How did you go about researching and writing the script? What goes into writing a script based on a real-life killer?*

SJ: With Ed Gein there were a couple of books about him. There was a book called *Deviant* by Harold Schechter and many others. The particulars of the case were very well established. The things we know happened, we know happened. Then I took the basic facts but I tried to approach the material elliptically and tell it like a ghost story. Not all of that makes it into the final product, by the way. The original script is by and large the movie as it exists. I took a—dare I say it—very gothic approach. Within the context of the script, the ghost of Ed's mother is very much like a character. She doesn't necessarily speak, but she is very much a ghostly presence in the movie. My approach was to tell the story as it actually happened but to also delve into the idea that Ed was this haunted guy and I think what made the script work was that it was scary. One rule for screenplays is that if it doesn't jump off the page, then it will never make it to the screen. What made the script work was that if you read it then it had a visceral response and I think that is why Hamish read it and wanted to make the movie.

ME: *The quality of your script must have shone through because* Ed Gein *was the first film that Tartan produced. There must have been something in your script that made Hamish want to make the leap from distribution to film production.*

SJ: Yes, very much so. I think part of the reason was that Hamish was also a provocateur. So he liked the fact that the material was provocative. It was incredibly gratifying for me, because *Ed Gein* was so successful, financially and critically. We won best picture at the Sitges Film Festival, and I won best screenplay at a few festivals, including Fantafestival. For the amount of money it was made for it did incredibly well on video. In fact, if I remember correctly, *Ed Gein* was the biggest rental DVD that was a non-studio release. It was on the top twenty-five highest grossers and it was the only film that was a genuinely independent film.

ME: *Chuck did a great job directing the film, too.*
SJ: Chuck had a very good understanding of what we were trying to do.

ME: *With the success of* Ed Gein, *Tartan wanted to build on that success with* Bundy. *Is that correct?*
SJ: Precisely. Yes, because *Ed Gein* was so successful, and not to put this into horrible mercenary terms, when something is that successful what do you then do? Well, you make another one! I think it was Hamish's idea to do Ted Bundy. After *Ed Gein*, Hamish approached me about doing *Ted Bundy*. He already had the idea.

ME: *How did you approach that from a scriptwriting perspective, as you didn't originate the idea? I'm assuming you were naturally interested in true crime, anyway.*
SJ: My first love has always been horror films. My heart has always belonged to the genre. With *Ed Gein* I always felt I was writing a horror movie that also happened to be a character study. After *Ed Gein* was so successful, and Hamish approached me about doing another, of course I said yes. Remember, and let's be realistic, when you are a starting screenwriter and people are offering you money you say "yes" no matter what it is! [Laughs.] It just so happened it was a subject I was interested in anyway. Unlike *Ed Gein*, Ted Bundy had actually been written about. There were around seven or eight books about him, one of which was written by his girlfriend. So there was much more material for me to familiarize myself with that story. The thing I took away from the girlfriend's book was just the idea that you could have this guy who was in so many ways this friendly, affable, likeable guy who of course did extraordinarily unlikeable things. Ed Gein was apparently likeable but an odd fellow. We also have to remember, and not to diminish the things that he did, but he only killed two people that we know of for certain. He was an oddball character and a grave robber. Whereas Ted Bundy was this charming and politically active man who did awful, awful things. So I approached the material that way. To show the darkness that human beings are capable of.

ME: *In many ways, he redefined what a serial killer could be. He wasn't like Ed Gein, the goofy, oddball person. Bundy was someone on the surface who was charming and intelligent and yet capable of doing these terrible crimes.*
SJ: It was Robert Ressler, who was one of the FBI agents with the FBI's Behavioral

Science Bureau, who coined the term serial killer with reference to Ted Bundy. Ted Bundy has the distinction of having the term serial killer named to describe him.

ME: When you were presented with the opportunity to write this script about Ted Bundy, did Hamish have any stipulations as to where he wanted to script to go? Were you given free license?

SJ: If my memory serves me correctly, he basically said, "Go do what you did before." That was partly due to the success we had had with *Ed Gein*. I think he felt perfectly comfortable turning me loose on it. I don't remember any real strictures. I do recall him saying to me to make it "rock and roll." Imagine approaching the movies with a music analogy in mind: if *Ed Gein* was some kind of '50s Doo-Wop song, then Bundy was supposed to be rock and roll. I remember us saying that the Ted Bundy film was going to be like a Rolling Stones song.

ME: There is definitely a different vibe to the Ted Bundy film in comparison to the Ed Gein movie.

SJ: Very much so. I have no great interest in writing the same movie over and over. Again, although Ed Gein often gets lumped under the heading of serial killer, he really was not. Ted Bundy was the actual, literal definition of a serial killer. In terms of approaching the material and the storytelling we tried to make it totally different. I think Matthew Bright did a great job with the material as director [on *Ted Bundy*] because he understood it had a strain of black humor to that movie. If overdone it could come across as disrespectful and off-putting, but I actually think it works perfectly. It could have very well fallen on its face. Often when you take that approach, where you have to be very careful with the material, you end up going too far in one direction. Assuming you do your job well, the payoff can be that much greater.

ME: Interestingly, with Bundy *did you use different names for the victims?*

SJ: Some names are correct and some names are totally made up. Then there is that sequence with Tom Savini, as the detective, which goes into the overtly comedic because he is just throwing out names [of victims]. That was a rip on the idea that even today we have no real idea how many people Bundy killed. We definitely know some of his victims but there is every reason to surmise that for every one we do know there could be two or three that we don't know. He may have killed upwards of one hundred women. It's remarkable. There were so many possible victims in that elongated scene with Tom Savini, where he is just rattling off this list, it's horrific to think of how many women Bundy may have murdered.

ME: Were you pleased with the final outcome of Bundy?

SJ: Yes, very much so. I would actually go as far as to say that it is my personal favorite, just in terms of how everything came together. Michael Reilly Burke did a great job at playing Ted Bundy and Matthew Bright did a great job, especially with his approach, understanding and handling of the material.

There is one scene in that movie after Ted has been arrested and he is sitting in the common room and his girlfriend is there. His girlfriend visits him and there is a moment when she is talking to him, and through Bundy's body language, and the way he tries to insist he didn't do anything … but because she knows him so well she just looks at him and there is this dawning horror on her face when she realizes, "My God, he did do it." The way I wrote that in the script, it was one of those things that I thought people were either going to get or they aren't going to get it. The moment I knew the whole movie was going to work was when I saw that scene. Matthew, as the director, was able to interpret how I saw that scene unfolding.

ME: *I think it is a great little film.*

SJ: Yes, everyone has their favorites but people seem to really respond to *Ted Bundy*. I think the film fires on all cylinders.

ME: *There are also nice little touches in the film, like the nod to Ann Rule, who wrote a book about her experiences with Bundy in* The Stranger Beside Me. *It demonstrates how much research you have done into the Bundy case.*

SJ: I always think, and I don't know if it is a product of laziness, but when people retell real-life stories they can't always be bothered to research all of the stuff. There could also be an innate human need to "improve" on things. When telling the story of Ed Gein or Ted Bundy there was enough stuff there that you don't really need to invent things. Just tell the story as it exists. In my mind, part of telling the story as it exists is all of that material. It is all the little minutiae and weird little connections. It is building that world. All the facts and minutiae are the bricks that help you build that world.

ME: *When you start writing your scripts do you begin by researching the topic/killer then trying to piece together a narrative? How do you go about it?*

SJ: Yes, you do the research and absorb the material. I tend to go into it with no real idea or conclusion and I let the story wash over me. I want the material to dictate to me how it wants to be told. Usually, in terms of the mechanics moving forward, I write big scenes. I take the things that I know have to be there and then I try and find the connective tissue that might be able to connect it all together.

ME: *Did the film do good business for Tartan?*

SJ: Yes, it did quite well, though the only thing with that film was that it got some backlash because people accused us of glorifying the Bundy case. I think the problem is that some people want their stuff to be sanitized, in that if you are going to tell a movie about a serial killer then you are supposed to make him a *bad* person. Which, of course in context, he was a bad person, but some people want things neat and tidy. The analogy I always make when people try to accuse us of glorifying serial killers is that when The History Channel airs their documentaries about World War II, are they glorifying Hitler? So that was the only backlash that *Ted Bundy* got. I guess that strange, knee-jerk response is to be expected.

ME: *You raise an interesting point, and one I have raised with other film directors in this book. People find it hard when you humanize these killers. They want filmmakers to merely present these people as monsters.*

SJ: Precisely. Of course the great irony is that was my entire intention all along. What makes those stories as horrific as they are is the fact that they are human beings. That's why they are scary! They're not these salivating monsters with fangs that we can all look at and say, "Stay away from that person." What makes them terrifying, especially with films like *Ted Bundy*, is that he was so charming. He was this ladies man kind of guy. My wife and I watch a lot of crime shows and we often remark how frequently people will say, "Well, he didn't look like a serial killer." I mean, what is a serial killer supposed to look like? [Laughs.] It is actually dangerous that you have to explain to people that they don't have serial killer tattooed on their forehead! [Laughs.]

ME: People have it in their minds what a serial killer should look like and how they behave. They have to be the odd-bod down the road with the gammy eye or toothless grin. Unfortunately, serial killers don't fit that profile—look at Ted Bundy. He does not fit that profile.

SJ: Precisely, and again it goes back to the idea that people want things to be neat and tidy. It is an inherently scary notion, the idea that your next-door neighbor, that nice guy you have coffee with, could also be a homicidal maniac. That is a scary notion so I think people like to imagine that they have this internal radar that will go off when they are in the company of evil. That's just not how it works.

ME: Some people go into these films with an expectation of what path the film should follow, especially when presenting these killers. Yet the best films on true-life killers don't adhere to this.

SJ: Look at *The Silence of the Lambs* and the character of Hannibal Lecter, which is one of cinema's greatest characters, but let's be realistic, there is nothing about that character that reads real. He is a great cinematic character but nothing more than that.

ME: I agree. One of the interesting facets of your scripts is that you delve into each individual that you focus on and each time you present something different and new. Of the four scripts that you have penned, each one is different, as shown by The Hillside Strangler, *which doesn't hold back, does it?*

SJ: No it doesn't and this goes back to how each film evolved and my conversations with Hamish. After *Ed Gein* and *Ted Bundy*, Hamish approached me about doing another one. It was a conscious decision to not hold back because we thought this would be the coda on it; this would be the exclamation point. With Ed Gein, though he gets lumped under the heading of a serial killer, he really wasn't. Then we had Ted Bundy who was the literal definition of a serial killer. Then we thought if we were going to make a third film the idea would be on one of the rare serial killing partnerships. Again, this gave me a different story to tell and I thought if this was going to be the last one then we are going to pull out all of the stops. Also, though it doesn't fit chronologically, *The Hillside Strangler* was meant to be our postmodern final statement on the serial killer subject. If Ted Bundy was our rock and roll film then *The Hillside Strangler* was our heavy metal film. It was Black Sabbath!

ME: There was definitely a different vibe to that film. You get a real sense of the nastiness of the killers in that film.

SJ: After the initial screening of the film my friend said, "Boy, that's not a date movie!" [Laughs.]

ME: You present both killers as two abhorrent and vile individuals. During the film, when you see their crimes, which are graphically explicit, you are left sick in the stomach.

SJ: Going back to Ted Bundy, what made him so frightening was that he was a charming, likable guy. But when I did the research into the Hillside Stranglers case, neither of those two guys [Kenneth A. Bianchi and Angelo Buono] could be described as charming or likeable in any way! So, initially I thought this was going to be a challenge.

How am I going to spend ninety minutes with these two characters who were utterly detestable? They weren't even interesting.

ME: They were scummy.

SJ: Yes, they were scummy and wholly uninteresting. So I kind of embraced that. I was like, well, if there is nothing about these characters that is remotely interesting then I will embrace the fact that they are uninteresting. The only interesting thing they had was their perversion. So I kind of went with that. Credit to Nicholas Turturro and C. Thomas Howell for pulling those characters off!

ME: Looking at the two films you did that were directed by Chuck Parello, Ed Gein seems very restrained in terms of content....

SJ: Yes, very much so. Again, with *The Hillside Strangler* we decided to take the gloves off. Part of the thing with *Ed Gein* was that we had cast Steve Railsback. He very much had his own ideas about how the film should play and he was interested in it being a character study. Some of the restraint came at the request of Mr. Railsback. So by the time we got to *The Hillside Strangler* it was balls to the walls! That's not to say that was wrong. The way Chuck approached that material was exactly what that material needed. It wouldn't have worked if Chuck had exercised the lack of restraint as we did with *The Hillside Strangler*. Steve Railsback was not interested, or would want to be in, a film like *The Hillside Strangler*.

ME: As I said earlier, you adapt each script well and each one has its own identity and each film is specific to each killer and era. You don't churn out the same movie.

SJ: Thank you for noticing. Again I was very adamant that each movie had to have its own thing. Hamish understood that there had to be some king of progression. In the first one we had Ed Gein, in the second we had Ted Bundy, then the Hillside Stranglers. They were different stories and not the latest iteration of some homicidal maniac. They were different stories. Each film had its own structure. I approached each film trying to give each movie, based upon what they were like, their own personality. That's why with the *Ted Bundy* film you have weird black humor to it, because that was what Ted Bundy was like. He was a charming, erudite guy who did these horrible, horrible things. *The Hillside Strangler* winded up having the personality it did because it was about two total cretins who were devoid of personality!

ME: I think you laid the foundations for all your films, which is why I feel they turned out so well.

SJ: Thank you. You are right. As one of my instructors said at college, "You can make a bad movie from a great script, but you can't make a great movie from a bad script." If the script doesn't work, and I don't care how pretty your film is, it is not going to work.

ME: After the trilogy of films with Hamish, you stopped collaborating, and if I recall, Tartan soon went bankrupt.

SJ: Yes, unfortunately they did. Again, not to be horribly mercenary, but if money kept pouring in then we may have considered doing another serial killer film but it never really happened. I was fairly ready to be done with it. However, the two movies I have coming down the pipe are on the Moors Murders and the Golden State Killer, who was identified and arrested recently. So I am currently writing a script for Lionsgate about the Golden State Killer. Oddly enough, I still can't quite get away from serial killer films. [Laughs.] The difference with the Moors Murders is of course that it is male–female killers. You will be very familiar with the case....

ME: Yes, they were carried out by Ian Brady and Myra Hindley.

SJ: Exactly. That is a case that Hamish always had a fascination with, and some time ago he approached me about doing a film on the Moors Murders case. He actually intends for it to be his directorial debut. Our approach to that material was because it is a heterosexual couple who engages in murder and perversion we felt the script should be told as what I would call "a corrupted love story." So our movie ends just before they kidnap their first victim. We had to approach the material very differently. Also, because their victims were children it is difficult to try and pull that off. You can get away with adults being victimized on camera. I don't think you really want to attempt to do that with children.

ME: Actually, there has been a lot of protests about the Jamie Bulger[2] short film being nominated for an Academy Award. Are you familiar with that case?

SJ: No, I am not.

ME: They have nominated the Irish film, Detainment *(2018), by director Vincent Lambe. It is a dramatization of the killing of James Bulger in 1993 by two ten year olds, Robert Thompson and Jon Venables, in Bootle, Merseyside, England.*

SJ: Yes, I remember that!

ME: The film director has come under fire from the media, an outraged British public, and the mother of James. She wrote a personal letter to the filmmaker asking him to withdraw it from the Oscars. Lambe has stood firm, and despite apologizing to the family, insists he will not withdraw the film.

SJ: There you go. As an aside to the whole story, Hamish always had this fascination with the Moors Murders and wanted to make a movie but his mother made him promise that he would not make it while she was still alive. She didn't want him to make that film. She passed away a few years ago and Hamish said he is now ready to make it. I find it amusing that even as a middle-age man that you still listen to Mom. The film is still in pre-production at this stage.

I inhabit an interesting space with the authorship of these movies. Wikipedia referred to myself and Hamish as the inventors of the serial killer biopic! I am not sure who wrote that, which is somewhat true. Even though I didn't direct any of those movies, they do bear a certain stamp of authorship. I am not being egotistical, but it is a statement of fact. [Laughs.] I am the only guy, as far as I know, who has written all these damn things, with the exception of my friend David Birke who wrote *Gacy* and *Freeway Killer*. I have a weird reputation. When people ask you how you get into these things you say because they make money! That is the reality. We made one and it made money so we made a second. Commerce is a fact of life.

ME: Did you come to England to research the film on the Moors Murders?

SJ: I have been to England but not in the context of that project. So in terms of research, I got numerous books on the murders and familiarized myself with the material. What is interesting, as an American writing about these British serial killers, is that I have come to learn that if you say the Moors Murders to people in the States then nine out of ten people have no idea what you are talking about. Whereas it has become very evident to me that in the UK, even though it happened decades ago, it still has this resonance. I found it a unique challenge writing a script set in that time [1960s] and imagining what the dialogue should be. As a weird complement, Hamish has given that script to numerous people, a DP and a composer have signed on and at no point has anyone realized it was written by a yank. [Laughs.] I take that as a compliment! I must have pulled it off!

ME: *It's an interesting case, here in Britain. There is a real hatred for Myra Hindley, who lured the children to their deaths at the hands of Ian Brady.*

SJ: Yes and that's what I've said to people. That's what is fascinating about that story. In the script we don't really deal with the killings. The movie fades to black when they are about to kidnap their first victim so it is all about their devolving and corrupting love affair. There is every reason to imagine that if Myra Hindley had not hooked up with Ian Brady then she may well now be an old grandma someplace. There is something inheritably fascinating about the idea that somebody could be that malleable and they'll do the vilest acts at the behest of someone else like that.

ME: *I think the way you are tackling the Hindley–Brady case is an interesting one. We don't need to see their crimes. They speak for themselves....*

SJ: It is not just the fact that it is something distasteful in showing children being victimized, but what I find fascinating about their story is that it actually ended when they started committing their crimes. It was all about the two of them and their weird, corrupted love affair and the energy that they fed off one another. To me, that was far more interesting. By the time they started committing their crimes that aspect of the story is almost mundane. For the lack of a better comparison, think of a movie like *Sid and Nancy* (1986). It is a bleak love story.

ME: *You say that you have recently hooked up with Hamish again, but between the Moors Murders film and* The Hillside Strangler, *you wrote* Starkweather, *which I felt was a good little flick.*

SJ: *Starkweather* was a different beast. My friend Mark Boot, who had introduced me to Hamish, asked me if I had anything else. I said, "No, but that I could certainly do something." That film was done as a favor to Mark, though I did get paid for it. Mark had facilitated my meeting with Hamish and when Mark approached me about doing another film I was happy to oblige.

ME: *I feel it is a good little film.*

SJ: Very much so. It sounds like a backhanded compliment, but I was surprised with how well it turned out.

ME: *I know Byron had a few budget problems* [see interview with Byron Werner], *but he did really well despite the lack of funds.*

SJ: Very much so. When working with such a minuscule budget it helps having the guy behind the camera who knows what he is doing. That was Byron. Byron was the guy who was able to figure things out and improvise. When you have the director and director of photography behind the camera pontificating as the sun goes down you can't really make a low-budget movie that way. Byron very much understood how to make things happen.

ME: *Again you did well with the script in telling the Starkweather story from a historical* *perspective. Similar to the Ed Gein story, it is one that has inspired other films but has never been told accurately.*

SJ: Yes, that's true. Many people have touched upon the Charles Starkweather and Caril Ann Fugate story with *Badlands* but nobody has told the story as it actually happened. That script dictated its own approach. It was meant to be a fast and compulsive story because that is basically what it was. Once they went on the run, they were on the run. So I wanted the narrative to have that same compulsiveness. Credit should also be given to the two leads. Their performances were very good. There is one scene where Charlie kills the woman in the root cellar and Caril Ann (Shannon) is looking down at him and she says to him, "Why are you hard, down there?" Charlie claims he only killed the woman in self-defense but Shannon challenges him by saying, "Why are you hard?" I forgot that was a great moment and tells you everything you need to know, right there.

ME: What can you tell us about your script about the Golden State Killer?

SJ: In a nutshell, when I first started having discussions with Lionsgate, I tried to find what defines the Golden State Killer as a story. What I realized, as far as I know, serial killers do not typically retire. They are either active and get caught or they are sent to prison for something else. Whereas, Joseph James DeAngelo was actually retired. The last crime that we know he committed was in 1986. So to me there is something fascinating in the idea that this elderly man was this retired serial killer. His neighbors would say that he was the crotchety old guy on the block and they would hear him in his house at night yelling at nobody. There was a little girl who lived next door to him who referred to him yelling at the aliens in his attic. In my mind, perhaps the aliens in his attic were his victims. So my pitch was that he was this retired serial killer who was haunted by his victims. Then I started thinking about it: He had three definitive phases of his criminal career, if you will. He started as the Visalia Ransacker, where he would break into houses and ransack them. Then he evolved into the East Area Rapist, where he didn't just get off on ransacking houses, he started raping women. Then he evolved into what is known as the Golden State Killer, where he took to murdering. So he had these three distinct phases to his criminal career. So I had the idea of *A Christmas Carol* where Scrooge is visited by the ghosts of past, present and future, so my idea is instead of Scrooge you have the Golden State Killer, and he is being visited by ghosts from the three phases of his criminal career. Lionsgate jumped at that. That's what I have been working on. I just wanted to bring something new to the material, creatively speaking. If his last crime was committed in 1986, as an old man and you are sitting in your chair in your home watching the sunset and thinking about the things you have done in your life, what goes through your head if you are that guy? You know?! When you look at your past, and we are all haunted by one degree or another by the ghosts of our past, that guy literally has ghosts from his past!

ME: Any plans to go behind the camera, in the director's chair?

SJ: I do, and in fact before I sold *Ed Gein* it was my intention to direct the film and make it myself. It was going to be a low-budget down-and-dirty kind of thing. So I do have the intention but I am interested in directing something I have written. In other words, I am not one of those people who is like, "What I really want to do is direct," I am actually more than happy to work at my craft and get better at my craft. I always consider myself to be a screenwriter first and foremost but I would step behind the camera as an evolution of my screenwriting.

15

Gacy and *Freeway Killer*

An Interview with Screenwriter David Birke

Screenwriter David Birke is a man who is no stranger to the world of serial killers and their portrayal on screen. Known in the horror community as the man who helped shape the serial killer film genre, Birke penned a number of key titles that would hit the rental shelves or DVD market during the early to late 00s. Uncredited for his work on David Jacobson's *Dahmer* (2002), Birke would go on to write the scripts for *Gacy* (2003) and *Freeway Killer* (2010), a trilogy of films that focused on serial killers that preyed on young, vulnerable men. In February 2019, I was afforded the opportunity to interview David Birke about his contribution to this increasingly popular off-shoot of the horror/crime genre and the process behind bringing these crimes into a filmable script. I thank David for being interviewed for the collection and sharing his anecdotes about the trials and tribulations of bringing his work from the page to the screen.

Matthew Edwards: *Studying your résumé, your work has been drawn to both the horror and thriller genres and true-life crime, as shown by the TV movie* A Kidnapping in the Family *(1996). What is it about these subjects, particularly true-life crimes that draws you to them?*

David Birke: Well, first, I should admit *A Kidnapping in the Family* was not my idea. All those ABC TV movies I did were works for hire that I just grabbed at because I wanted to get paid to write scripts. In general, though, like just about everyone, it seems, I am very interested in true-crime stories. For me, the beauty of them is the chance to explore those crimes. Also, *A Kidnapping in the Family* was an interesting project because of the research trips. That was particularly interesting because the kidnapper happened to be a waitress in the coffee shop of the motel where I was staying. She was actually a very ordinary woman and it reminds you that the most lurid true-crime stories are just very quotidian domestic situations where one element has been dialed up to eleven.

ME: *You were billed as an uncredited scriptwriter on David Jacobson's excellent film,* Dahmer. *What was your involvement with the script and how did your involvement in the film come about? Was it through Larry Rattner, one of the film's producers, who you had worked with previously on the script* Horseplayer *(1990)?*

15. *Gacy* and *Freeway Killer* 177

DB: Yes, exactly, Larry Rattner introduced me to David Jacobson, who I should say is a really great guy in addition to being a brilliant and a terrific director. One of my big regrets is not accepting David's very generous offer to share screen credit because I was afraid of getting into trouble with the guild at the time because it was a very low-budget affair. (I was in, let's say, a stressed economic situation at the time.) It was generous of him to offer shared credit, I think, because most of my big changes to the script weren't really used. There's a gimmick I was quite proud of that has been done in the years since. Ultimately, and probably rightly, they decided to go with a more linear structure.

ME: With the success of Dahmer, was it your association with Larry that landed you the scriptwriting job for Gacy? You have intimated to me in our initial email correspondences that what we see on-screen "script wise" differs from what you had originally penned. Talk us through how the script changed and how you set about researching the crimes of John Wayne Gacy for the film?

DB: Yeah, *Gacy* rolled straight out of *Dahmer*. It's ironic that I declined to put my name on *Dahmer* which is actually a good movie and I'm the credited screenwriter of *Gacy* and there's I think exactly one bit in there that I wrote. A moment when Gacy shows his clown's license. As I think I told you, Clive Saunders was a good guy and I ended up liking him but he sent me an email at the time saying he couldn't believe what a piece of shit my script was and that he was going to completely rewrite it—which he proceeded to do. My favorite scene I've ever written was in that *Gacy* script actually. It was based on a true incident where Gacy went to buy a bike for his kids but ended up reducing the children to tears after he turned trying to wheedle a bargain out of the bicycle shop owner into this torturous, protracted negotiation/confrontation. It was just so perfect because these serial killer guys are always incredibly self-righteous and balance their aggressive pursuit of having everything their way with this paranoia that

Promotional poster for *Freeway Killer*, starring Scott Anthony Leet and Michael Rooker (courtesy David Birke).

somebody's trying to get something over on them. (They're also always highly litigious and sticklers for following rules, ironically—like the BTK killer was the incredibly petty and vindictive leader of his local homeowners' association.) Anyway, I thought that scene really captured that in a funny and horrifying way, but Clive in his email listed the scene as one of the reasons the script was such shit: "Why was there five pages dedicated to buying a bike?" [Sigh.] But Clive, a very smart director, had his own vision and for sure if he'd been able to realize it without the producers meddling so heavy-handedly (as they always do) it probably could have been a really good little movie. Oh well.

ME: In 2010, you penned a new script dealing with one of California's most notorious serial killers, William Bonin aka Freeway Killer. *How did this opportunity come about? Also, the film, and your script, suggests that part of Bonin's disturbed psychosis was born out of the troubled childhood he experienced as a young boy. While this does not excuse the awful crimes that he committed, from your research into Bonin's life, do you feel the neglect he suffered as a child, and the sexual abuse he encountered at the hands of his grandfather, were contributory factors to his sexual violence toward boys and young men?*

DB: That was again, I have to admit, more of an economic opportunity than anything else. I was on the verge of having my house foreclosed on and I think *Freeway Killer* was a way to hold off eviction for one more month. (I can laugh now of course.) Larry Rattner, the producer, always wanted to do a serial killers thing because they always made money and this was literally decided upon only because it seemed like the case hadn't been done yet. I remember I was trying at the time to convince him to do the Sunset Murders case but that one was deemed—probably correctly—too sick. Interestingly, Bonin and Butts were not ideal for the business model because they were gay and at the time this was potentially a negative element that had to be handled in a very, very constricted way. So, again, a lot of interesting stuff went by the boards because of the homosexual relationships—a pretty central thing in the story!—that might have kept the movie from being released in certain markets. I always thought it was funny that the cover of the video box shows Bonin picking up a female hitchhiker!

This film was kind of the inverse of my experience on *Dahmer*, where I wanted to explore more specifically his very unique personal sexual mythology and instead in the movie—great as David Jacobson made it—I think Dahmer comes off, for the most part, as a rather ordinary gay young man coming of age in the closet. That's not really a criticism because that's clearly what David was trying to do in that movie. I just always would have done everything differently (the cliché screenwriter's cri de coeur).

As far as Bonin's troubled past making him a killer, that he was abused as a child, that he was unable to reconcile his sexuality with the macho ethos he was raised with—all that molded him.

ME: Though not covered in the film, do you think Bonin's service in Vietnam had an impact on him? Your script touches upon an unstable home life and Bonin's sense of loneliness and issues with homosexuality, but do you think his tour of service as a gunner in the U.S. Army may have given him an even greater warped view of mankind and violence? Admittedly, he was treading down an unhealthy path prior to his involvement in Nam—with acts of molestation on young boys and committing theft and robberies in this teens—but what do you think made him cross that line from sexual assault to sexual violence and murder?

DB: I think there is no doubt his service in Vietnam exacerbated his pathologies or at least gave him his first opportunities to explore them. All those clichés are solidly based in truth, I think. I have witnessed personally how the proverbial cycle of abuse works. I don't know what it says about Northridge, California, but two people I knew as a kid wound up being murderers. One of them was actually a multiple murderer—he had moved to Northern California, rose to some modest position in city government, then one day killed his girlfriend and her daughter before committing suicide. (Funnily enough, when I told a mutual acquaintance about what happened, he was blasé about the murders but was stupefied by the news that he'd managed to get elected to something.) In both these cases, these were homes marked by serious abuse. I shouldn't say more to avoid venturing into tricky legal territory but in this particular case I know there were accusations that both he and his sister had suffered sexual abuse at the hands of their father in childhood. It's not surprising that that kind of damage marks you out as always a kind of outsider, and nothing drives rage like being an outsider. Just because these things have been said before doesn't make them untrue—the tricky thing, though, is that it does perhaps render them uninteresting in movie terms. I always try to do everything I can to avoid reductive Freudian explanations when depicting a serial killer or any aberrant personality (like the woman in *Elle*, for instance). Even though those sorts of explanations or the most banal sociological observations might have a lot of validity. To me, it's most important to preserve mystery.

ME: How did you set about adapting Bonin's story for the screen? What I found particularly interesting about the film, and your script, was how Bonin coerced others to participate in his murder spree: Butts, Kyle (I am assuming this is based on Gregory Miley?) and William Pugh. I think you did an excellent job with your script in conveying the hold Bonin had over these young men, in particular Vernon Butts.

DB: I agree that the most interesting thing about Bonin was the little community he created around himself. A lot of people kill, that's pretty easy. Getting somebody else to kill takes some doing. And Bonin was able to pull that off at least three times that we know of. Whether this speaks to Bonin's unique charisma or just the fact that he had the audacity to try and take advantage of the fact that the average person is "closer to the line" than we'd ever want to admit, I don't know. I suspect the latter. Absolutely if you look anywhere on the internet it makes you think the latter. I do hold to the belief that the average person is a serial killer held in check by laziness and a lack of imagination. Maybe that's a bit pessimistic. And yes, Kyle is Miley. I think we couldn't use his name because he was still alive.

ME: I felt the director John Murlowski did a good job at adapting your script. How involved were you in the filmmaking process? I understand that they filmed the exterior of your home which doubled for Vernon Butts's home? Is that correct?

DB: I was not involved in the actual shooting. John did a terrific job. He's pretty much a one-man band. He was his own cameraman and DP. I did let them use my house as Butts's house. This backfired a bit when the actor playing Butts tore out of the driveway in the picture van and crashed into a neighbor's car parked across the street. That car accident was probably equal to the film's budget. [Laughs.]

ME: All three of your films based on real-life serial killers have centered on mass murderers who have targeted young men. Is this merely a coincidence? Interestingly, when we think of serial killers our natural assumption tends to be that the victims are either women or children. Your scripts show that some of the most infamous killers have preyed on young, vulnerable men. Do you see any similarities between Bonin, Dahmer or Gacy and why they committed the crimes that they did?

DB: As I've said it's a coincidence I did three killers who targeted young men but I am glad of that coincidence because I think there is something uniquely interesting about those cases. Misogny is kind of clear-cut in a way. With a killer like Bonin there's an interesting angle where he's sort of serially killing himself, subjecting these young men to the abuse he suffered, ritualistically recreating and dominating his own self-image as a victim, reclaiming himself in a way, while at the same time worshipping these boys as objects. It's more interesting I think than the relatively straightforward incel thing that drives a lot of serial murderers.

ME: *There is an excellent scene in the film when William Bonin (Scott Anthony Leet) is being interrogated by Det. St. John (Michael Rooker). For a moment there is a flicker of joy in Bonin's eyes when he is told that he is being lined up as the "poster boy" for the first person to be executed by lethal injection in the history of California. Was that your intention? Were you pleased with the way that scene translated from the page to the screen?*

DB: Yes! I liked that scene a lot. That's one where what I intended on the page ended up on the screen in a way that I felt worked. The other is the framing sequence with an actress named Debbon Ayer. I thought she was excellent and she really captured the fucked-up dilemma of needing to butter up the murderer of her child in order get "closure" (which should always be put in quotes). Trying to manipulate him and letting herself get played at the same time. I always like scenes like that where there's a couple of things going on at the same time.

ME: *How sensitive to the victims do you have to be when writing a film based on real-life mass murderers such as Bonin, Gacy and Dahmer? Have you ever encountered any opposition from the families?*

DB: Well, I've got to admit I've never had any kind of conscience at all. I think when you're writing something you have to give yourself permission to go anywhere it takes you without any regard to consequences or implications. This is probably an indefensible position. I do think, though, that writing is always a bit like lucid dreaming, even when it's based on a real-life tragedy. In fact, as I said, it's mostly just been the breaks that people have often brought me true stories. Left to my own devices, I'd never do them largely because I think the facts have a tendency to get in the way.

ME: *It was great to see Michael Rooker in the film. How did he become attached? I also thought Scott Anthony Leet played his role well. Were you pleased with the way both actors brought your work alive on the screen?*

DB: Yes, Scott Leet was great and it was one of the big thrills of my life that Michael Rooker was in something that I wrote. I'm a huge fan of his. I never got to him! I wasn't around for some reason when his scenes were shot. I forget now why. I obviously regret missing that chance, though hopefully I'll get him for some future project and correct the mistake.

ME: *Looking back, are you pleased with how* Freeway Killer *turned out? How has the film been received critically?*

DB: Yes, overall, I am pleased with how *Freeway Killer* turned out. Though also for me it's very problematic in that they were really very faithful to the script and a lot of things didn't turn out so great, making it difficult for me to pin the blame elsewhere. [Laughs.] Like with *Slender Man* (2018) I can honestly say that has nothing to do with me even though I'm the credited writer. *Freeway Killer* is more troubling for me personally. To me the big problem was the pacing, it seemed monotone and very slow. I think I always imagined the big speeches being gotten through much quicker. Still, all my fault for having put in too many words! I've hopefully learned since then.

ME: Finally, do you think you will return to the true-life crime genre again? That said, your script Benedetta, *directed by Paul Verhoeven, sounds brilliant!*

DB: Yes. I always think I'm out of doing true-life cases but I keep getting pulled back in. [Laughs.] The movie I just wrote for Paul Verhoeven, *Benedetta*, is basically a true-crime story—just a very, very old case. It's about the trial of a nun in the 17th century. And a case that proves the lie to everything I was saying before—sometimes the best stuff you can't make up. For instance, her big crime was not lesbianism—which there was really no formal prohibition against—it was using a dildo! The crime was taking the phallus in vain!

16

Jack the Ripper (2016)
An Interview with Director Sebastian Niemann

The murders of Jack the Ripper are unquestionability one of the most talked about events in criminal history. That his identity has never been revealed has strengthened the mythology and intrigue around the killings in Whitechapel, making it a ripe subject for artists, writers, comics and filmmakers in all forms of the creative arts to explore and exploit. A quick search reveals a magnitude of films inspired by, or using the Jack the Ripper moniker. These include *Jack the Ripper* (1988; see in David Wickes interview), *The Lodger* (1927), *From Hell* (2002), and exploitation films such as Jess Franco's *Jack the Ripper* (1976) and Hammer's *Hands of the Ripper* (1971). Jack the Ripper even appears in a Jack Elam western called *Jack the Ripper Goes West* (1974). While some of the films were based on fact, or hypothesized the identity of the Jack, many used his crimes as a vehicle to explore other elements of Victorian Britain or to contemporize or reimagine the slayings in a variety of different locations and settings. Jack the Ripper has seen his life interweave with both real and fictitious characters, such as Batman (*Batman: Gotham by Gaslight*, 2018), Joseph Merrick aka the Elephant Man (*From Hell*) and Sherlock Holmes (*A Study in Terror*, 1965), to name but a few.

In 2016, a new version of the Ripper tale hit the small screens with the arrival of the made-for-(German) television movie *Jack the Ripper*, directed by respected filmmaker Sebastian Niemann. Weaving fact and fiction, Niemann's take on the Ripper story begins with the death of Jack the Ripper's final victim, Mary Jane Kelly, as its starting point before creating a fast-paced whodunit thriller that uses the squalor of Victorian Britain as a vehicle to conjure up a landscape of corruption, vice and sin before the explosive finale unmasks the killer in the midst.

The premise revolves around a young German photographer named Anna Kosminski (Sonja Gerhardt), who arrives in England looking for her mother and her brother Jakob. Upon her arrival she learns her mother has died of syphilis and that her brother is one of the prime suspects in the Whitechapel murders and confined to Colney Hatch Lunatic Asylum. With the police—notably Chief Inspector Briggs (Peter Gilbert Cotton)—satisfied that they have the right man, Anna refuses to accept the outcome of their investigation and sets about trying to prove his innocence and unmasking the identity of the Ripper. While visiting Jakob, he informs her that he was not present in London at the time of the murders but in Leeds, working with Le Prince on a revolutionary new motion picture camera. Buoyed by this, Anna enlists the help of local photographer David Cohen, a colleague of Jakob, and Inspector Frederick Abberline to clear her brother's name and her seemingly sinister landlord Samuel Harris (Nicholas Farrell). However, after receiving a number of threatening letters, Kosminski realizes that she has become a target for the Ripper, who wants Jakob to take the wrap for the Whitechapel murders. As suspicion and paranoia take over, and Anna burrows closer to the truth and the bodies begin to stack up—including that of her brother, Jakob—she begins to realize that the identity of the killer may be someone closer to her than she originally thought. Will the 8mm film footage she finds hold the key to the identity of Jack the Ripper?

Niemann's take on the Ripper case is an intriguing one, most notably for its subplot of weaving (much like Alan Moore did in his seminal graphic novel *From Hell*) of other key historical figures into the narrative. In this case, fusing the pioneering work of Louis Aimé Augustin Le Prince and the advent of cinema makes for a compelling side story. That Le Prince is acknowledged as the first person to shoot a moving picture sequence—on Leeds Bridge in 1888—before his own disappearance in 1890, makes for an intriguing take on the Ripper legend. What if the Ripper's crimes were caught on celluloid? While purely fictional, the film shows the power the medium of cinema, and photography to an extent, has on the viewer and its ability to capture moments of beauty and brilliance as well as those of the horrific and perverse. The grainy 8mm footage at the end, of the Ripper slicing up Mary Jane Kelly, recalls some of the black-and-white Holocaust images from World War II and images similar to this ilk. Reflecting on the film, one comes away with the notion that since the advent of cinema there has always been the fundamental desire to entertain and be wowed by the images on the screen, yet, overtime, the medium has been used to capture humanity at its worst (which the film shows by contrasting the seminal [but now considered mundane] film footage of Leeds Bridge by Le Prince, with the grisly mondo-esque death footage of Jack's handiwork). Niemann seems to suggest that with the advent of film we have always sought to push the boundaries of what is deemed acceptable to show on-screen (the titillating nude photographs

Sebastian Niemann's new take on the Jack the Ripper legend, for German TV (courtesy Sebastian Niemann).

served under the counter would soon give way to the rise of explicit pornographic films, or stag films), to the point that the capture of death was always seen as the final taboo. Sadly this seems no longer the case as we have become desensitized to the violent images presented to us daily from the mainstream (TV/film/internet news corps) to the underground web pages of the internet. Now we are bombarded with excessive images in our living rooms and on web pages across the net. We, the audience, are drawn to cinema's dark power, where images of death, suffering and sex have become the norm.

Purists may be less interested in this element of the film and ultimately find the film a shallow cash-in on the Jack the Ripper legend. That would be unfair, as the German hook is certainly a cinematic perspective worth exploring, seeing as a handful of the key suspects in the Ripper crimes have been of German origin. Secondly, Niemann does well at presenting a London of extreme wealth and poverty. Those with power are seen to manipulate those at the bottom rungs of society and we are presented with a London rife with corruption, squalor, sin, vice and violence, and those operating on the fringes, like homosexuals, relegated to the underground in fear of being caught and imprisoned. In contrast, London is a place of wealth, opportunity and entitlement for those able to tap into it. In a way, Niemann is commenting that little has changed in the last one hundred and thirty years.

In March 2018, I had the pleasure of interviewing director Sebastian Niemann about his work and the themes omnipresent in his version of *Jack the Ripper*. I thank him for the generous amount of time he put into the interview.

Matthew Edwards: *The Whitechapel murders have been the inspiration for countless cinematic adaptations on the killing spree of Jack the Ripper, each having their own theories on the identity of the killer. How did you become attached to the production and what were you looking to explore with this film, in relation to the Jack the Ripper killings?*

Sebastian Niemann: Jack the Ripper is probably one of the most notorious figures in criminal history. I have been fascinated by this subject for many years and had often contemplated developing a movie project about the mysterious serial killer. So naturally, when Marian Redmann and Thomas Gaschler, the initiators of the project, came to me with Holger Karsten Schmidt's great script, I was elated.

Gaschler and Redmann had been developing a first draft for a major German television channel (Sat.1) for some time, and since Holger was tied up in other projects, I jumped in as "ghostwriter" and took over writing the project up to the shooting script.

By that stage, the production company Pantaleon Films was already on board and with it two old friends and colleagues: Dan Maag and Simon Happ. Dan and I worked together on my first feature film *Bükenbrennen* and he also produced my first film for the big screen, *7 Days to Live*.

Executive producer Simon Happ has been by my side on almost all my projects and as well as being friends, we are a well-oiled machine. We have been making movies together for more than 20 years now and been through more than our fair share of adventures. Still, we knew early on that Jack the Ripper would be an especially challenging endeavor.

I knew from the very beginning that I wanted to approach the story from a different angle than earlier Ripper adaptations had done and during pre-production we were delving deeper and deeper into the subject. I was looking for a way to emotionally involve the main character in the case, as well as to invoke a feeling for that specific time and its circumstances. My aim was to tell the story from a less distanced perspective than a more traditional crime story would and introduce exciting facts at the same time.

ME: Holger Karsten Schmidt is a well-known crime writer in Germany. What attracted you to his script?

SN: Since Jack the Ripper's story isn't based on fiction but on historical facts—a series of brutal killings that terrorized the people of Whitechapel in 1888—there wasn't one clear, predetermined plot to follow, and Holger found a fantastic angle to tell this story from a completely new perspective.

What makes this angle so special is that we're not telling a classic murder mystery, where the plot follows a detective working a case. Instead, we experience the story through the eyes of a heroine, a young German woman, who is directly affected by the case and threatened by the killer.

ME: The film is set post–Ripper murders and brings a German perspective to the film with the character of Anna Kosminski. Was this element brought in partly because it was a German TV production and because some Ripper historians have pinpointed Aaron Kosminski (a Jewish-Polish immigrant whose family had lived in Germany), as a top suspect? Were you trying to approach the film from a German angle?

SN: Yes, exactly. The theory that Jack the Ripper may have been German opened up an additional hook for German audiences and I also thought that it presented a new and exciting perspective to tell the story from. Naming our heroine Anna Kosminski served several purposes: as a reference to the historic facts of the case and as a clear indication that we're not suggesting our story is 100 percent factual, which I personally would have viewed as misleading the audience. Plus, I think it always adds to a film to provide the audience with hidden hints, clues and the occasional Easter egg.

ME: With the character Jakob Kosminski (aka Aaron Kosminski) you have remained historically accurate to his life, in that he was omitted into Colney Hatch Lunatic Asylum. Yet, without spoiling the film too much for readers, you seem to dismiss him as a suspect in the film. Is that the way you see it?

SN: In 2014, Aaron Kosminski was considered one of the main suspects—there was even a DNA test performed on a victim's scarf. Since then, however, this particular theory has been called into question again and there are significant clues that point against Aaron as the murderer.

In any case, rather than focusing on complete historical accuracy, we set our sights on making a movie that was entertaining and exciting without ignoring the subject's historic background. I just felt that it's very emotional and thrilling that our heroine knows her brother has to be innocent and now sets out to find proof and save his life.

ME: In the film, I thought you presented Whitechapel, and London, effectively as a place of extremes. The city is seen as a place of wealth and one of profound squalor and poverty. I particularly liked the way you captured the latter, with its muddy footpaths and decaying wooden homes, shabby peeled walls and dank and underlit confined corridors. For me, you captured the right feel of Whitechapel as a fearful, impoverished place of sin and vices. Aesthetically, how did you set about recreating Victorian London?

SN: Thank you. As a filmmaker, I always put tremendous importance on the atmosphere and the mood of a film. I do a lot of research while I'm writing and preparing to shoot, and I try to let the visual concept convey a certain feel for the time and location that goes beyond the bare facts. In this case, I felt it was imperative to show how hard life was for the people of Whitechapel at that time, how they lived under crushing uncertainty and constant threat.

A successful, believable atmosphere doesn't just captivate the audience, it's already palpable on set and helps the actors with their performance. When the atmospheric foundation is just right, it allows everyone to empathize and put themselves into the London of 1888. That is why set design, costume and make-up are a crucial part of pre-production to me and I make sure to prepare every aspect with the heads of department. We work on very detailed concepts for every department—colors, textures and patina—to create a believable world for every story. During the shoot, the cinematographer can then adjust the lighting and complete the illusion.

ME: Talk us through the production of the film. What challenges did you face? I understand that the film was shot in Lithuania?

SN: One of the biggest challenges is always to create an entire world on a limited budget. When the project started, it was one of the first questions to come up: where can we build our late Victorian London? The original Whitechapel was out of the question—it looks nothing like it used to back when Jack the Ripper roamed its streets.

In Vilnius, we found our perfect location. Sure, we had to build and create a lot of the sets, but we also found houses, streets and backyards whose well-worn brickwork formed a perfect framework to build our sets in. Naturally we also had a pretty elaborate studio portion, but I'm certain that it's precisely this combination of genuine old buildings and quality set design that culminates in a very dense and truly believable atmosphere. And of course we used visual effects to boost up the image in quite a few places.

ME: Like Alan Moore's seminal graphic novel, From Hell, *you bring fictional elements into the script that touch on key characters of the era. One of the interesting elements of*

Sebastian Niemann on set during the filming of *Jack the Ripper* **(courtesy Sebastian Niemann).**

the film is that you bring into the film the pioneering work of filmmaker Louis Le Prince, who is accredited as shooting the world's first film, Traffic Crossing Leeds Bridge, and the dawn of cinema. I thought this was an interesting facet of the film, the idea that Jack the Ripper's final murder was caught on camera—in a sense, the first mondo movie. I felt that was a great tie-in, as both were operating at the same time. As a filmmaker, that must have piqued your interest in this adaptation?

SN: Yes, I was extremely drawn to that particular aspect. Holger had already touched on it in his script and I elaborated on it.

The conception of film as a medium is naturally fascinating to me as a filmmaker, but in this project, I was especially interested in how strongly the killer's motives are tied to the murders being captured on film and to the public's perception of the killing spree. This aspect also ties us over to today's times, where we record and film every little thing happening in our lives and how the lines between fiction and reality start to blur.

It also reflects what happened historically with the Jack the Ripper case: the Whitechapel murders were the first to receive this kind of massive media attention. For the very first time, the general public was suddenly exposed to details of brutal and gruesome murders, and many people had never heard of anything like it before. This kind of reporting obviously contributed to turning Jack the Ripper into the legend he is today. For us, nowadays, this media attention is everything but a phenomenon, its business as usual, but back then, it changed everything.

ME: The central theme of the movie suggests police complicity in the Ripper killings as a way of instilling fear into the local populace. I felt this was an interesting take on the killings, though one that may prove to be contentious. Is there any evidence to support this theory or is it purely a plot device/fictional take on the Jack the Ripper legend?

SN: Actually, there was a theory at some point that the Ripper may in fact have been a policeman. It's always one of the most pressing questions: how does a killer get his hands on certain pieces of information? How does he manage to always be a step ahead of the police? And while probing the case for possible angles, I personally felt it was a very interesting concept.

ME: The film posits the idea that those in authority, and power, are as corrupted as those pick-pockets and crooks at the fringes of London society. Take for example, the chief inspector and the gentleman that purchases "nature studies" photography from Anna's landlord. Both are abhorrent, yet both hide behind a guise of respectability. Would you agree?

SN: I can't help but feel uncomfortable with broad generalizations. Everywhere on earth, in every society, there are good people and bad people and most are somewhere in between. Obviously, it's especially disturbing when a respectable front hides an evil core or when power is abused.

But every front has the potential to fool us: the perception of power and authority can be just as misleading as the seemingly honest roughneck on the street. In my opinion, people should be judged by their deeds, not their covers.

ME: The film also touches on sexuality, including homosexuality, which was deemed a capital offense until 1861 in Britain. Yet, you show that it still held a vexed position in society and was relegated to the underground, as shown through Anna's landlord. Was that something you wanted to get across to audiences?

SN: Yes, absolutely. I always try to portray complex characters and put them and the times they lived in in a realistic context. It personally fills me with great hope and satisfaction to see our world become more liberal; to see barriers fall that seemed insurmountable only a short while ago. And making movies presents me with a great opportunity to shine a light on such topics and discuss them in their historic context. The character of Harris and the transformation he undergoes in *Jack the Ripper* presented just such an opportunity, to show a homosexual lead and do it in a self-evident, casual way.

ME: As the film was made for German TV, did you have to rein in the violent content and bloodletting of the film?

SN: Only a little—we were given a lot of leeway. We discussed it, of course, but everyone knew from the start that we were making a movie about a gruesome series of murders and that we had to tell that story accordingly. The focus of our movie, however, is not on the murders themselves but on our lead character Anna Kosminski. On the frightening experiences she makes while hunting the Ripper and how she finally ends up in his sights.

ME: I ask because a lot of Jack the Ripper's handiwork is shown via grainy black-and-white stills of his mutilated victims. Was this a decision forced on you? Or, going back to the point earlier about the advent of cinema and thinking about this in a wider context, as the film deals with themes of photography as the precursor to the cinematic image, was this a creative decision taken by yourself? Were you making the link between photography and the moving image? The work of Eadweard Muybridge, for example.

SN: The seed for this particular element was already planted in the first draft and it grew with the evolution of the project. Thomas Gaschler, who has a background in movie journalism and started his research many years ago, brought this particular idea and his extensive knowledge to the project very early on. We spoke about this aspect at length and I then proceeded to elaborate on it with my cinematographer Gerhard Schirlo.

As filmmakers, we are naturally drawn to such cinematic aspects, but we also have a responsibility not to get carried away with them. For me as a director, the historic facts usually present a veritable treasure trove of elements to choose from to tell an exciting story, and it is often a balancing act to give each element the ideal weight. In practice that typically means that we focus on select characters and elements to not lose sight of our main story, namely the criminal case, and to avoid confusing the audience. But at the same time, I want to leave enough room to at least touch on contributing aspects that add another dimension to the story, in this case the mysterious disappearance of Louis Le Prince.

I always try to captivate my audience and think about the emotions I can elicit by introducing such aspects in a certain way. And here, it turned out to be very effective to show the murders in grainy black-and-white photographs and film footage, since it provided the audience with the feeling that they had seen everything and yet left enough room for imagination.

ME: How has the film been received both in Germany and abroad? How have Ripperologists reacted to the film, especially with the film's theory on the killer and that only Mary Jane Kelly's death is depicted in the film?

SN: We were very fortunate in that our movie was extremely well received, especially by the Ripperologists, who noticed how much research we had done. I was particularly happy about that because it really has been quite a balancing act: putting a lot of work into studying the historic facts and simultaneously taking enough freedom to tell our story in an exciting and thrilling way.

So, we built a lot of bits and bobs into our script that hinted at and identified certain historical facts but also took great care to reveal where the facts end and fiction begins. Especially when it came to the question of the true identity of the Ripper, which is still among the greatest riddles in human history, we very consciously mixed actual suspects and mere speculation.

The interest in Jack the Ripper is still extremely strong, abroad as well as in Germany—which is evident in the great success of our movie: it enjoyed tremendous ratings and is the television channel's most successful production to this day.

ME: Finally (although presented in a fictional/cinematic way), do you stand by the film's findings or do you have your own thoughts on the identity of Jack the Ripper? Was he German? Merchant sailor Carl Feigenbaum has been labeled as a top suspect, too.

SN: I think the Ripper's true identity will remain a mystery for some time. The solution we present in our movie is deliberately designed to represent a new idea, but it in no way claims to be historically accurate or stand in judgment of anyone.

Whether Jack the Ripper was German is indeed an interesting question: Aaron Kosminski is still among the top suspects. As far as I know, only very little is known of Karl/Charles Ludwig, but he is still under some suspicion and Carl Feigenbaum's role, too, is very controversial.

There are new opinions and theories surfacing practically every year that sound very convincing and claim authenticity, only to be met with "foolproof" refutation by some other expert soon after.

17

Joel
An Interview with Director John R. Hand

While not widely known outside of the U.S., Joel Rifkin does hold the dubious distinction of being considered one of New York's most infamous serial killers. New York City folks growing up or living and working in the city will recall Rifkin's handiwork in the late eighties and early nineties. Active between the years of 1989 and 1993, Rifkin preyed on prostitutes working the streets of New York City and Long Island, where his dark and perverse interest in prostitutes, violence to women and strangulation crossed over from fantasy into reality. Described as a loner and an oddball, Rifkin was adopted during childhood and performed poorly at school, where he was diagnosed with a learning disability. Upon leaving school he worked as a landscaper and frequently paid for sex workers to get his sexual kicks. His murderous spree began in 1989 and all his victims were known to be sex workers. It is estimated that Rifkin killed up to seventeen prostitutes, strangling them before disposing of their bodies in a variety of ways. Some were dismembered and their parts scattered around the state, another placed in an oil drum, another thrown into the East River. Ironically, Rifkin was only apprehended on Monday, June 28, 1993, when state police attempted to pull him over as his truck did not have a license plate. Rifkin was in the process of disposing of the body of his final victim, Tiffany Bresciani, age 22, whose body he had stored in his garage for a week after strangling her. With the body rotting, and Rifkin's nose and handlebar mustache coated in Noxzema to block out the foul odor emanating from the corpse, Rifkin tried to flee from the police, but was ultimately apprehended. Once arrested, Rifkin willingly confessed to his crimes.

It is these final stages of Rifkin's murderous campaign that are used as the starting point for John R. Hand's effective micro-budget feature, *Joel* (2018), starring Arnold Odo as Joel. After his capture by state police, we see Rifkin brought in for interrogation. Interestingly, Hand eschews the normal approach to cinematic renditions about real-life killers and focuses solely on the killer, telling his story from Rifkin's own point of view. As he confesses his crimes to the detective interviewing him, the film chronologically charts his life, starting with his unhappy childhood and his unhealthy obsession with watching dirty films until the killings begin. By applying such an approach there is a coldness and haunting undertone to the film as we hear Rifkin's chilling words as he recounts how he progressed from watching simple erotica and films that showed sexual violence toward women to being a serial killer. That Rifkin charts his exploits in a matter-of-fact manner adds a haunting layer to the film, especially when we hear Joel coldly talking about his deeds and the problems encountered while disposing of the bodies. Seemingly without remorse, Rifkin tries to justify his actions and at times he presents himself as the victim. In one part he laments that people like him need help so they can return to society as functional human beings.

In this atmospheric and chilling work, Hand firmly directs his camera at our killer and it is his thoughts and actions that occupy the screen time. Little attention is paid to the victims and little is known about them and their backgrounds, other than they are sex workers and addicted to drugs. As the body count rises, so does the death count for our unfortunate sex workers. Invariably, the viewer witnesses the final throes of these poor women's lives, laying on their backs in the back of Rifkin's truck as he strangles them. Though there is scant blood shown on-screen, Hand's filming of the murders is unsettling. With Rifkin's hands wrapped around his victim's neck we not only see his handiwork in action but also his chilling commentary on the justification of his crimes.

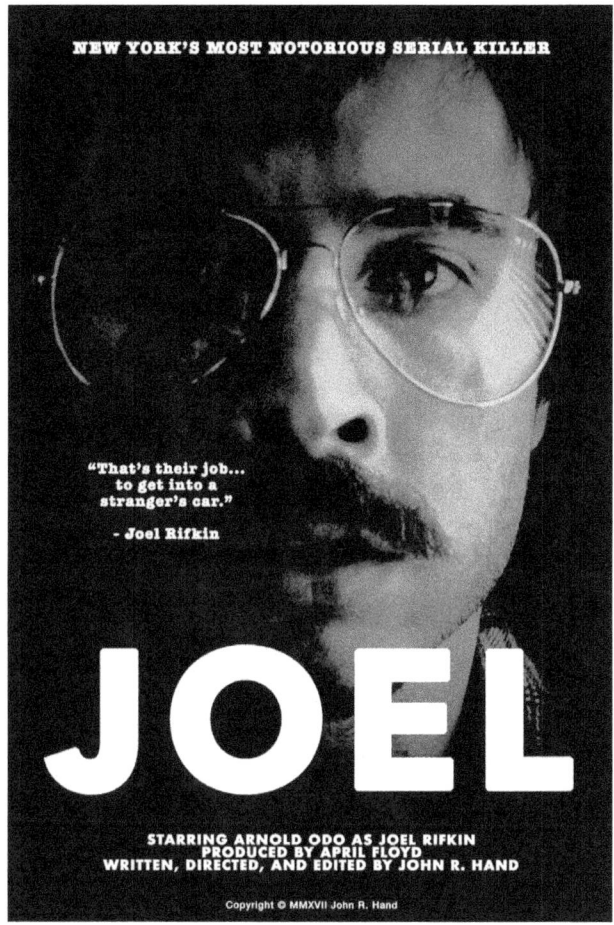

Promotional poster for John R. Hand's chilling serial killer flick *Joel*, 2018 (courtesy John R. Hand).

Joel is an interesting addition to the canon of films made on real-life and serial killers and one that deserves praise for presenting the material from the POV of the killer. Though no explanation is given as to why Rifkin targeted sex workers, aside from his perverse fascination with strangulation and violent sex films, what the film does show is Rifkin slowly loosing grip on reality. Shot similarly to that of a crime documentary, you'd be forgiven if you thought that the commentary was actually supplied by Rifkin himself and that the film was made up of staged reenactments.

In February 2019, I had the pleasure of interviewing director John R. Hand about his work. I thank him for agreeing to be interviewed for this collection and all the time and effort he put into the interview.

Matthew Edwards: *Your film* Joel *is based on one of New York's most notorious serial killers, Joel Rifkin, who is believed to have murdered 17 sex workers between 1989 and 1993. What was it about his crimes that made you want to make a film about his exploits?*

John R. Hand: I wanted to tell the story of Joel Rifkin because I found something in his life which was relatable and could allow me to create a full portrait of a killer as a real human being and not some one-dimensional slasher boogeyman. I've told this to people and they get a little nervous when I talk about relating to a serial killer. It scares me as well because in many ways Rifkin had a very average and ordinary upbringing and lived a very boring life up to the point where he went off the deep end. It reminds me of that Fassbinder movie *Why Does Herr R. Run Amuck?* (1970), where he's just this ordinary schlub with something bubbling up deep inside him and then some unexplainable trigger hits and boom, an explosion of violence. But before that explosion he was very average and relatable.

When you read about most serial killers they come off as complete assholes. Dennis Radar was this community enforcement officer who would take your dogs to the pound; John Wayne Gacy was some building contractor acting like a big shot showboating around town; Ted Bundy was the guy who shows up to your party on Saturday night and then is sneaking into your bedroom window Sunday morning to steal your stereo. Setting aside their gruesome crimes they're just not easy people to relate to. Rifkin was the kind of guy you might have a beer with at the local bar and never guess he was a serial killer. The relatability and humanity of Rifkin makes his crimes much more terrifying to me because you can't shove them away or distance yourself from them in the way that you can with some of the more outlandish or weirdo true-crime stories of dissolving people in acid or burying bodies in crawl spaces. To me that's the whole point of the film—getting past the tabloid façade and gaining empathy and understanding for both the victims and the killer.

There were other reasons to tell this story as well. No one had made a Rifkin movie yet so the story wasn't overexposed. Also, from a budgetary standpoint, Rifkin's story was easy to tell—it's just a string of murders in cars, hotels and his family house. Very simple to achieve as a micro-budget film. The most important reasons to make the film were the emotional components to his story. The fact it was new and budget-conscious was just a bonus.

ME: How did you approach researching the film and writing the script? I understand the process of research took more than three years.

JRH: I read everything about Rifkin, the interviews, the major newspaper profiles about him and then I watched that great A&E *Biography* television special on him over and over. I think the reason that it took so long to write was I had problems figuring out the structure of the film and which details about his life to include. In early drafts of the script I got bogged down in the details of his family life and his relationship with his parents, being bullied at school, and then all of these scenes of what happened to Rifkin after high school but before the murders. Every draft or page-one rewrite kept whittling those early-life scenes down until I was just focusing on the prostitution and murders exclusively. I'm convinced those nighttime sexual encounters, which turned into murders, were the only times he truly felt alive. He threw everything away to be out on those streets night after night. He spent every cent he had on these prostitutes and eventually started murdering them. It's what defined him as a real person as well as a fictional character in my film. Inventing some fake *Ordinary People*–style mainstream family drama scenes would've compromised the story in my eyes.

Also, when I had those scenes of young Joel Rifkin being bullied at school I think it generated a stronger sympathy for Rifkin as opposed to the final film where we don't see the abuse firsthand. We only hear Joel in voiceover moaning about being abused and the audience can make up their own mind whether he's being genuine about all the abuse or if he's stretching the truth.

ME: When watching Joel, *I feel you are particularly struck by the level of historical accuracy that has gone into the film and that you as a filmmaker sought to portray on-screen a truthful account of the crimes of Rifkin. Was that your intention? Because with this type of material it is easy to fall into the trap of exploitation, or add dramatic license, which this film does not do.*

JRH: I started out with the goal of one-hundred percent fidelity to the actual story but I quickly realized that I couldn't get there because of my budget and also we simply will never know the full story of how these crimes went down. We have the forensic evidence which can only tell us so much and then the interviews with a psychopath who won't let the truth get in the way of a good story. We'll never know the full truth completely.

Still, I was dedicated to telling the story as truthfully as possible because I think the truth is much more interesting than anything I could concoct and I think people recognize and respond to the truthful approach. Even though I had to cut corners and take some dramatic license, I think the one thing people really responded to in my movie was my approach of sticking as close to actual details and chronology of these crimes as I could.

I think people can sense when something is fake or invented. It reminds me of something that FX artist Tom Savini used to say about gore effects, about how he would reference anatomy books and try to create anatomically correct gore because an audience could somehow sense that yes, that's what viscera really looks like and they would respond to it. I think with true-crime films it's a very similar approach, that when one starts with the real facts and real characters it gives your work a kind of substance that people respond to.

ME: An interesting facet of the film is that you tell the narrative in first person, from the view point of the killer Joel Rifkin. Why did you take this approach?

JRH: I don't think there are many really great serial killer films that have been made but many of the truly best ones that inspired me, films such as Mark Blair's *Confessions of a Serial Killer* or David Bowen's *The Secret Life of Jeffrey Dahmer,* had this same approach of first-person narrative where you see the crimes laid out and then you hear the inner monologue of the killer. To me it's the best approach for this film, especially if you have lots of details about the crimes and interviews to pull the monologues from.

It's not the only approach and it's not possible with every story—for instance, you'd have to invent a lot of fake dialogue for a killer such as the Zodiac, where we don't know all the details—but with Rifkin there were so many interviews with him I wanted to use as many of his own words as possible. I wanted you to get a feel for this guy's weird rationalizations for why he's doing this stuff. He's obviously an unreliable narrator but even within all his psychopathic lies and justifications I think there's a kind of truth that emerges after a while.

ME: I do feel you effectively capture Rifkin's cold, unhinged mental state and it is particularly chilling when we hear him confess to the law his progression from watching "dirty films," and films involving women being tied up and beaten, to him acting out his perverse fantasies. As a viewer, you are stuck for 80 minutes with this essentially remorseless killer opening up about his crimes. I found this very disturbing and an effective way of portraying Joel Rifkin. Did you want the audience to come away from the film as if they had been watching a crime documentary?*

JRH: My motivation was definitely to make a very realistic, by-the-numbers, almost procedural film about this guy and his murders. I was highly influenced by a Kieslowski film which was part of his *Dekalog* series but released separately as a feature called *A Short Film About Killing*, where it's this very dry, dynamic story of a disaffected youth who strangles a taxi driver and gets caught up in the Polish capital punishment machine. I was looking to make something with a structure like, just portraying Joel's crimes, beat by beat, no mythologizing, just one vignette after another just telling the story. I think there's a power to just telling the truth of his story, the evil and mundane and tragic, everything interwoven.

ME: How did you come to cast Arnold Odo as Joel? I think he did a terrific job as Rifkin and he looked remarkably similar to him.

JRH: That was just serendipity, the movie gods, call it what you will but I couldn't have made the movie without Arnold. That was a big fear when I started this movie, "What if I can't get a guy to play Rifkin?" It kept me up at night. Luckily enough I live in Austin, Texas, which is a mecha for many young people wanting to become actors. Arnold had only been in town for a few weeks when he responded to some of my casting calls wanting to be a PA or crew, anything, but he had this full beard and I could see that if we just shaved that we could make him into Rifkin. The next question was "Can he act?" and from the time we shot the first scene he proved he was good, he had a specific and unique vision of the character and how he wanted to play him and it blew me away. Once I found Arnold I knew we couldn't wait—money or not, time or not, I just started running around shooting the movie.

Arnold Odo as serial killer Joel Rifkin in John R. Hand's *Joel* (courtesy John R. Hand/ JRH Films).

ME: *I understand you shot the picture for $3,000. How did you achieve that and how difficult is it making a picture for that kind of money, especially a film that is essentially a period piece?*

JRH: Many of my bigger ideas and scenes with lots of extras or production elements had to be cut, but as I said, once I found Arnold I knew we had to start shooting while he was available and nothing was going to stop me. I felt the story lent itself a very dingy, dark, claustrophobic feel which didn't require big sets or big money to capture. Most of the scenes were set at night and shot with very limited lighting, basically just street lights and then some battery-powered LED lights which we carried around in order to accent little details within the darkness.

Many of the actors were friends of my wife. Most of them were involved in burlesque and were up for this very indie no-budget project. The biggest expense was Joel's truck, which was this vintage little truck that we bought from this strange University of Texas professor. The truck came with that camper shell which was very important, because there are tons of those little trucks still around but good-condition vintage camper shells are scarce. My wife had to teach Arnold to drive stick—another crisis, "Can Arnold drive the truck?" He learned to drive it with no problem.

Purchasing that old truck that barely ran and babying it through the production was expensive but it was like a rolling set. Drive to a location, set up the lights and then "execute" a scene. There was no crew—I was a one-man crew—there was just Arnold playing Joel and then the actress playing the victim. Maybe a few other people but that was it. Very few distractions. The fact we were shooting these scenes in the dead of night really set a grim tone that Arnold and the victim really picked up on and played off. Again, if this had been a multimillion-dollar film I don't think we could've gotten this same kind of atmosphere.

ME: *Though you never see Joel's mother in the film, the film hints at no tension between the pair, only with the father. In real life, he was adopted at three weeks old, yet there is nothing to suggest in his life, nor the film, that he had problems with his mother or women. Why do you think Rifkin began targeting women, in particular prostitutes? Did his fantasies of inflicting violence of women, as the film suggests, simply spiral out of control?*

JRH: We'll never know for sure what was really rolling around in Joel Rifkin's head when he did these crimes but I don't think the reason was mommy issues. That's a theory that the forensic psychiatrist Park Dietz has always tried to advance about Rifkin, that he was tormented by being adopted or not knowing his real mother and that he was somehow trying to punish or kill his mother by killing these women. I think it's a fine theory which ranks up there with Vincent Bugliosi and his Helter Skelter theory as far as credibility, which is to say I don't think it's very credible at all. Why did he murder these people? I think it starts with a deep lack of self-esteem, the need for power and control in his life, which collided with his obsessions and then combined with other behavioral and biological factors into a perfect storm of madness and murder. I think if any one factor was out of place it probably wouldn't have happened; he just would've been an ordinary guy with the ordinary problems we all have.

Again, that's what interested me about Joel. Most serial killers have something in their early life, some kind of sexual or physical trauma (both Gacy and Richard Ramirez actually had head trauma) and they start acting out very, very early. There's nothing in

Rifkin's early life that was overly traumatic but then he gets into his early thirties and bam, he explodes.

ME: *Though your film shows a number of Rifkin's murders, all of which are chilling, the film is largely gore-free and restrained.* Joel *is certainly not an exploitation flick, and though some of the murders are harrowing, almost real, especially when we see Joel violently strangling his victims in the back of his truck, the film never becomes gratuitous. In fact, we learn very little about his victims, especially as the murders begin to rack up in the final third of the film. Did you deliberately film the murders in this way? Because apart from the first and second murders most of the victims are afforded very little screen time or information about their lives.*

JRH: There were a few gore scenes in the original script but when it came to shooting those scenes there was no time or money for the effects. Even then the effects I wrote into the script were very basic, like some severed hands or some basics wounds. Nothing that would've really changed the film. The lack of gore was intentional because that really wasn't a big part of Rifkin's story. He wasn't doing all this crazy stuff like Dahmer or doing any necrophilic things like Bundy. He just strangled these people and it was like, "Oh, well I gotta get rid of this body," and he goes about the disposal. If you read or watch any interviews with Rifkin he describes getting rid of these bodies like a butcher describes throwing out scraps of meat, very nonchalant, cold and terrifying.

From the serial killer's perspective his victims are one-dimensional objects. We don't get much background information about them other than Joel's sniveling commentary about this one being a junkie or seeing this other one in a sex show, very demeaning stuff, but I don't think it makes you feel less empathy for them. I was just trying create a realistic portrait of how Rifkin and many of these other serial killers view their victims.

Killers have to do this because if they stopped to think about this human being

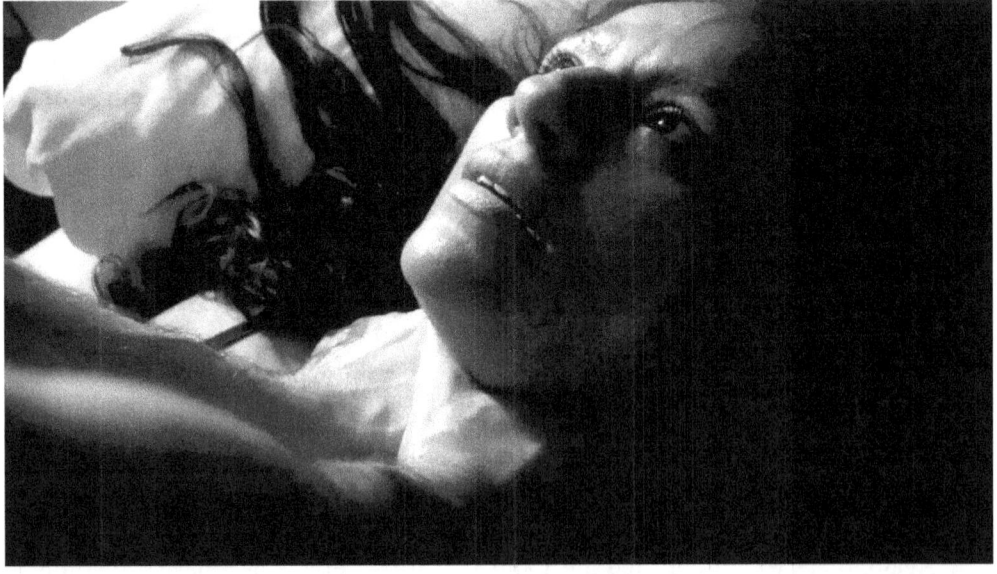

Jeannie Ramirez, as the unfortunate Macy, dying at the hands of Rifkin (courtesy John R. Hand/ JRH Films).

who is a daughter, mother, sister, a person with problems but still a human with a right to live, if they stopped to think about it they couldn't fulfill their selfish desires and do these murders. I think many serial killers actually do have the capacity for deep reflection and empathy but I think they can also compartmentalize that and do these horrible, irrational acts. I think contradiction in their behavior speaks to the mystery of human behavior in general.

ME: The film is shot on digital film though you intercut this with images of Super 8mm film and snippets of vintage erotica. Where did you obtain this material, especially the soft-porn/nudity footage? I even noticed footage from Carnival of Souls *(1962). Did you have to get permission to use the various footage in the film or was it public domain?*

JRH: Yes, all the archival footage was in the public domain. There were a few stock shots in the film I paid for, such as some scenes in a prison, and then there was a hospital room scene with Joel's father where I bought some stock footage of an old man in a bed and then digitally put Joel into the scene.

ME: The opening of the film is very stylized and, combine with the use of POV, grainy 8mm footage/erotica it works well, in my opinion. Stylistically, what were you trying to achieve with the film?

JRH: I love Super 8. I shot my first film *Frankenstein's Bloody Nightmare* (2006) on Super 8 and I'm always trying to get that look into any movie I make.

I think 8mm works because it has a gritty texture that we associate with something illegitimate and sleazy. It also evokes vintage home movies. It's like the texture of memory in a way. Initially I wanted to start the movie like the beginning of *Mean Streets* (1973), where you see all the home movie footage. I wanted to start with home movies of Joel's parents bringing adopted Joel home. I abandoned that idea a couple years into writing but I always knew I was going to include some 8mm somewhere in there. All the public domain footage was from a digital source so I dirtied them up in a few different

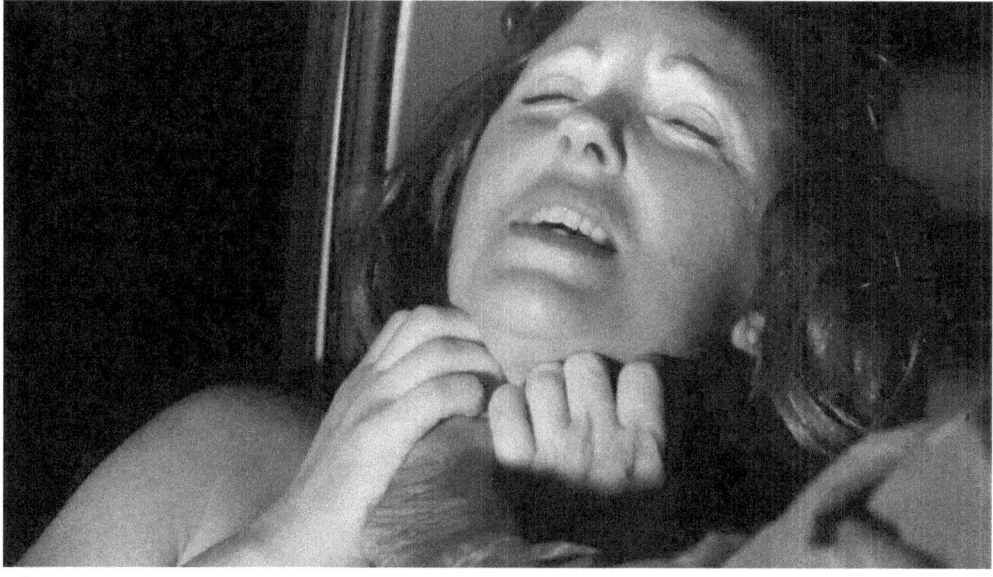

Julia Golden as Lola pays the heavy price of stepping inside Rifkin's vehicle as the killings pile up in *Joel* (courtesy John R. Hand/ JRH Films).

ways. Sometimes I took a video projector and photographed the projection off the wall. Other times I just put the footage up on my computer screen and shot it off the screen using a Super 8 camera app on my iPhone.

ME: *Though you have changed the names of some of the victims in the script, have you encountered any opposition to the film or criticism from the families of the known victims?*

JRH: I did change all of the names of the victims, even the fake prostitute names. I haven't encountered any criticisms from the families.

ME: *There is a scene in the film when Rifkin admits that he started fixating on strangulation after watching Alfred Hitchcock's* Frenzy *(1972). Is that based on fact? Where do you sit on the debate that violent films can have an impact on audiences?*

JRH: I think the fact that Rifkin saw *Frenzy* has been confirmed in numerous interviews. I believe he was also into other violent pornography on home video but that might be incorrect. In the beginning of my film we show some dirty loops and things but I think as a child Joel was more influenced by lurid detective novels and fantasy stories in a way similar to Ted Bundy. Unlike Ted Bundy I don't think Rifkin was sophisticated enough to blame his murders on porn or any other outside media. That's another reason I like Rifkin, you ask him deep searching questions and he just gives you a schlubby "I dunno" response as if he's totally oblivious, which I think he really is.

I'm strictly a layman in psychiatric matters but I think the debate about violent movies and pornography is overly simplistic and naive. It's more about winning votes and gaining notoriety than it is about solving problems or saving lives. Yes, movies and media affect people. Everything affects people. A Victoria's Secret lingerie catalog can affect people. Do you ban that? Or do you just ban the "rough stuff" so you can mitigate some of the harm? Who decides what is too rough? There's a lot of guessing and finger pointing going on.

One thing that has emerged for me through my research on killers is that much of psychopathic behavior is deeply biological. People don't like to admit this because they feel it will absolve these people of their crimes and they'll have a ticket to get out of jail. Again, naive and simplistic.

To me it feels like we live in this technologically advanced modern world but our attitudes on human behavior and mental health are stone-age. A few hundred years ago if someone had a seizure they might be diagnosed as being possessed by pernicious demons. We now obviously can pinpoint the specific deficiencies in our bodies which can cause epilepsy or seizures. Someday I hope we can have this same biological exploration of psychopathic behavior without all this crime and punishment, brimstone, "they must pay" nonsense which does no one any good. We're better than this, smarter than this and maybe someday we can realize that people like Rifkin are deeply ill and need to be studied from many different behavioral and biological standpoints.

ME: *Tell us about the use of music in the film by The Greys. I felt it added another dimension to the film that helped accentuate the horror on-screen.*

JRH: I composed and performed the film's score under the name The Greys, which is a name I've used on a few movies. I guess it's my professional movie soundtrack pseudonym. I scored the film with analog synthesizer sounds using CS-80 and Moog plugins, along with a bunch of the built-in sounds in Apple GarageBand. It's something

I've dabbled in on many past films and I love electronic scores, everything form Wendy Carlos to Tangerine Dream. The soundtrack for another great serial killer film, *Angst*, by Klaus Schulze, was another big inspiration.

I guess it's fitting that a movie about a cold serial killer should have a cold analog synth soundtrack but I think there's something deeper. I think it's beyond being just retro and hip. I think these sounds really get inside you. I have this crackpot theory about simple analog electronic music and how it can affect your body. It's like if you put a heartbeat on a soundtrack, the audience's ears will take that in and eventually their body will mimic that heartbeat and then *their* heart will start syncing up to the beat. I think electronic music is similar. It affects your central nervous system or brain in some way. I think electronic music can somehow model the electrical impulses going on inside your body and your body can recognize these audio pulses and then synchronize with them like they would a heartbeat. I think electronic music can be deeper than emotion, beyond emotion, deeper and more primal than traditional music with recognizable acoustic instruments. I think when you're delving into synthesizers you really do have the possibility of rewiring people's brains accordingly.

ME: Upon release how has the film been received critically and are you pleased with what you achieved with the film?

JRH: So far it's been turned down by every film festival I've submitted it to. This movie doesn't fit into the modern film festival scene which has no place for a male film-maker making a film about a serial killer who murders women. Even though I feel I've made a very socially conscious film I'm sure it was immediately thrown out as a careless slasher movie.

Also the festival scene has very much become a very incestuous little club that's very hard for a true independent to break into anyway. I think I wasted about six months

John R. Hand (*right*) directs Arnold Odo (*left*) in *Joel* (courtesy John R. Hand).

trying to get *Joel* past these gatekeepers before realizing, "Hey, it's not the flavor of the month, I'm not in the club, it's not happening." So right now I've released the film onto a small number of streaming platforms and the response has been pretty good, very mixed, but I expected that. Some people think I went too far and others don't think it is extreme enough. In the end you just have to make something you're satisfied with and I feel I was able to tell the story of Joel Rifkin effectively.

Chapter Notes

Chapter 3

1. After *The Black Panther*, Ian Merrick directed the horror-thriller *The Demon Within* (2000). Merrick stated during our interview that he was unhappy with the film and the title. The original title was called *The Sculptress*. The film was panned critically at the time. Interestingly, Merrick has a few new projects in the works, including *Blood Tales* and a film called *The Garden of Angels*.

Chapter 11

1. All quotations within this chapter are from an interview with Clive Saunders, London, September 10, 2017.

Chapter 13

1. There is some conjuncture as to how complicit Fugate was in the murder spree. In court, Fugate testified that she was held hostage against her will by a possessive Starkweather and that she was not implicated in any of the deaths, especially those of her family. During the trial, evidence was presented that showed Fugate did have opportunities to escape her "captivity" but chose not to. This immediately cast doubt on her innocence, which was further undermined when she admitted to being involved in the robbery of Robert Jensen and Carol King, during which she held them at gunpoint with a .410 shotgun. From there things get murkier, as both Starkweather and Fugate ultimately blamed each other for the murder of Carol King, while Starkweather admitted sole responsibility for the death of Robert Jensen. Evidence indicates that Fugate was infatuated with Starkweather and wholly aware of the crimes he was perpetrating, including those committed against her family, and that she was complicit in some of the murders, or certainly helped assist him in his crimes. Despite maintaining her innocence she was sentenced to life imprisonment at the Nebraska Correctional Center for Women in York, Nebraska.

Chapter 14

1. The Moors Murders remains one of the most shocking and depraved crimes committed in Britain. Killer duo Ian Brady, and his girlfriend Myra Hindley, murdered five children aged between 10 and 17 years old between July 1963 and October 1975. Some of the children were sexually assaulted. Their bodies were buried on Saddleworth Moor, near Manchester. Brady and Hindley spent the rest of their lives in jail. Dubbed the evilest woman in Britain, Hindley, who claimed she had been reformed and campaigned for release, died in prison on November 15, 2002 (aged 60). Brady was declared criminally insane and confined in the high-security Ashworth Hospital. Brady stated he should never be released and died on May 15, 2017 (aged 79).

2. The James Bulger case is another crime that shocked the British public. In February 1993, two-year-old James Bulger was abducted by two ten-year-old boys, Robert Thompson and Jon Venables, and tortured and murdered. Both Thompson and Venables were convicted of murder on November 24, 1993. In June 2001, both Thompson and Venables were released from prison, to widespread controversy. Thompson has changed his name and little is known about him post-release. Venables has had numerous offenses stacked up against him since his release, and again returned to jail in November 2017 for possessing images of child abuse on his computer. Vincent Lambe's Academy Award–nominated short film *Detainment* (2018) caused uproar in sections of the media when announced and was publicly condemned by James Bulger's mother.

Bibliography

Cettl, Robert. *Serial Killer Cinema: An Analytical Filmography with an Introduction.* Jefferson, NC: McFarland, 2008.
Cooper, Ian. *The Manson Family on Film and Television.* Jefferson, NC: McFarland, 2018.
Coville, Gary, and Lucanio, Patrick. *Jack the Ripper: His Life and Crimes in Popular Entertainment.* Jefferson, NC: McFarland, 2008.
Davis, Don. *The Jeffrey Dahmer Story: An American Nightmare.* New York: St. Martin's, 1995.
Derf. *My Friend Dahmer.* New York: Abrams ComicArts, 2017.
Graysmith, Robert. *Zodiac: The Shocking True Story of America's Most Elusive Serial Killer.* London: Titan Books, 2007.
Harrison, Paul. *Mind Games: Inside the Serial Killer Phenomenon.* Chatham, Kent Urbane Publications, 2018.
Jensen, Jeff, and Jonathan Case. *Green River Killer: A True Detective Story.* Oregon: Dark Horse Comics, 2019.
Keightley, Alan. *Ian Brady: The Untold Story of the Moors Murders.* London: Pavilion Books, 2017.
Kerekes, David. *Killer Komix.* Manchester: Headpress, 1999.
Kerekes, David. *Killer Komix 2.* Manchester: Headpress, 2000.
Kimber, Shaun. *Henry: Portrait of a Serial Killer.* London: Palgrave Macmillan, 2011.
Meikle, Denis. *Jack the Ripper: The Murders and the Movies.* London: Reynolds and Hearn, 2002.
Methews, Tom Dewe. *Censored.* London: Chatto and Windus, 1994.
Moore, Alan, and Eddie Campbell. *From Hell.* Marietta: Top Shelf Productions, 1999.
Newton, Michael. *Waste Land: The Savage Odyssey of Charles Starkweather and Caril Ann Fugate.* New York: Pocket Books, 2014.
Rule, Ann. *The Stranger Beside Me: The Inside Story of Ted Bundy.* London: Sphere, 1989.
Schechter, Harold. *Deviant: True Story of Ed Gein, The Original Psycho.* London: Pocket Books, 1989.
Smith, Tom Rob. *Child 44.* London: Simon & Schuster, 2008.
Sounes, Howard. *Fred & Rose: The Full Story of Fred and Rose West and the Gloucester House of Horrors.* London: Sphere, 2019.
Sullivan, Kevin M. *The Bundy Murders: A Comprehensive History.* Jefferson, NC: McFarland, 2009.
Sullivan, Terry, and Peter Maiken. *Killer Clown: The John Wayne Gacy Murders.* New York: Pinnacle, 2000.
Time Out Film Guide 2011. London: Time Out, 2010, London.

Index

A Is for Acid 5
Ackland, Joss 89, 95–96
Adventures of Sherlock Holmes 84
Aes-Nihil, John 59–67
Allen, Arthur Leigh 18, 22
The Alphabet Killer 7
Anger, Kenneth 62, 67
Angst 54–58, 199
Another Nice Mess 14
Anne Rule Presents: The Stranger Beside Me 5, 142–151, 170
Apocalypse Now 34–35
Appropriate Adult 5
Arendt, Hannah 27
Armstrong, Michael 46
Arnold, Tracy 73–74
Aronofsky, Darren 57
Assante, Armand 85–86
Atlanta Child Murders 4, 42
Avery, Robert 11, 18, 22
Ayer, Debbon 180

Bacon, Francis 31, 119, 126
Badlands 6, 152, 156–157, 165, 175
Baldwin, Adam 131, 134, 138
Barry Lyndon 31
Basco, Dion 118
Batman: Gotham by Gaslight 182
BBFC 76–78
Bean, Alexander "Sawney" 3
The Beast Within 23
Beausoleil, Bobby 59, 67
Becker, Lutz 25, 30
Benedetta 180
Berkowitz, David 5
Beyond the Valley of the Dolls 61
Bianchi, Kenneth A. 111–117, 171
The Big Score 13
Birke, David 132, 173, 176–181
The Black Panther 42–53, 201
Blair, Mark 193
The Blair Witch Project 60
Blockbuster Video 128, 130, 132–134, 136, 138–141
Blood Tales 201
Body Heat 155

Bonin, William 177–180
Bonnie and Clyde 6
Das Boot 57
Boot, Mark 2, 155–156, 167, 174
The Borrower 79, 101
The Boston Strangler 3, 42
Boston Strangler: The Untold Story 8
Bowen, David 193
Brady, Ian 5, 42, 173–174, 201
Braun, Eva 23, 26
Breker, Arno 29–30
Bright, Matthew 2, 7, 111, 142, 166, 169–170
Broken Blossoms 1
B.T.K (film) 8
BTK Killer 4, 177
Bugliosi, Vincent 195
Bukowski, Charles 131–132, 135
Bulger, James 173, 201
Bundy, Ted 1–2, 4–5, 8, 42, 142–151, 168–172, 192, 196, 198
Bundy: A Legacy of Evil 8, 142
Buono, Angelo 111–117, 170
Burke, Michael Reilly 168
Burke, Robert 5
Burr, Ann Marie 148–149
Butts, Vernon 178–179

Cabin 28 8
Caddie 31
Caine, Michael 81–82, 84, 87
Campbell, Billy 142–145
Can You Spare a Dime? 31
Cannibal Holocaust 76
Cannibal: The Musical 122
The Capture of the Green River Killer 42
Cardoza, Manny 14
Carnegie, Margaret Francis 31, 36
Carnival of Souls 197
Caruso, David 5
The Chant of Jimmie Blacksmith 7
Chase, Richard Trento 7
The Chaser 6
Ché 91
Chikatilo, Andrei 7, 89–99

Child 44 7, 89
Christie, John 3
A Christmas Carol 175
Churchill, Winston 29
Citizen X 4, 42, 89–99
A Clockwork Orange 31
Cold Light of Day 42
Collins, Lewis 87
Communion 23
Confessions of a Serial Killer 193
Coppola, Francis Ford 34–35
Corman, Roger 135
Cotton, Peter Gilbert 182
Coward, Noël 28–29
Criminal 120, 122–124
Cromwell Street 5
Cullen, Robert 92

Dahmer (film) 6, 118–129, 132, 176–178, 196
Dahmer, Jeffrey 4, 8, 42, 118–129, 153, 178–180
Dahmer vs. Gacy 118
Davison, Bruce 119
D.C. Sniper: 23 Days of Fear 8, 42
Dead Man 164
The Deadly Tower 7
Dean, Rick 134–135, 137
DeAngelo, Joseph James 175
Dekalog 194
The Deliberate Stranger 4, 42, 143
The Demon Within 201
DeMunn, Jeffrey 89–90, 93–94
De Niro, Robert 101
Deranged 1, 167
Detainment (2018) 173, 201
The Devil's Playground 31
Dr. Jekyll and Mr. Hyde 84
Dr. Lamb 6
Dr. Strangelove 30
The Double Headed Eagle: Hitler's Rise to Power 1918–1933 25
Douglas, Kirk 32

East Area Rapist 175
Easy Rider 34, 39
Ed Gein (film) 2, 6, 100, 105–111,

206   Index

113–114, 123, 153, 157, 166–169, 171–172 175
Ed Gein: The Butcher of Plainsfield 8
Edelberg, Ben 135–137
Elam, Jack 182
Evilenko 89
Extremely Wicked, Shockingly Evil and Vile 8, 42, 143

Fairchild, Max 38
Farina, Dennis 73
Farrington, Debbie 53
Fassbinder, Rainer Werner 192
The Fearless Vampire Killers 62
Feifer, Michael 8
Feigenbaum, Carl 189
Ferman, James 69–71, 76–77
Final Judgment 6
Fincher, David 9, 11, 18
Fine, Billy 14
Fire, Richard 73
Flynn, Scott L. 7
Foster, Barry 83–85
Frankenstein's Bloody Nightmare 197
Freeway Killer 7, 173, 176–181
Frenzy 198
From Hell (film) 7, 84
From Hell (graphic novel) 7, 182–183, 186
Fugate, Carol Ann 152–165, 175, 201

Gacy (film) 5, 111, 130–141, 153, 173, 176–177
Gacy, John Wayne, Jr. 4–5, 42, 118, 122, 130–141, 177, 179–180, 192, 195
The Gainesville Ripper 7
The Garden of Angels 201
Garretson, William 64
Gein, Ed 1–2, 6, 100, 105–111, 113–114, 153, 157, 166–172
George, Susan 85
Gerhardt, Sonja 182–183
Gerolmo, Chris 89–99
The Giant Behemoth 75
Giuntoli, Neil 79, 101–102
Golden, Julia 197
Golden Gate Theatre 14, 16
Golden State Killer 172–173, 175
Gordon, Stuart 73
Graysmith, Robert 18
Green, Seth 5
Green River Killer 5
The Grey Man 7
The Greys (band) 198
Gries, Tom 59
Griffiths, D.W. 1
Gull, Sir William 84, 87–88
Gulpilil, David 24, 32, 36–37
Gyllenhall, Jake 18

Haarmann, Fritz 8, 54
Haigh, John 5
Halloween 120
Hammer Horror 182
Hand, John R. 190–200

Hands of the Ripper 182
Hanson, Scott 9–22
Hanson, Tom 3, 9–22
Happ, Simon 184
Hardy, Tom 7, 89
Harold Shipman: Doctor Death 5, 42
Haxon 3
The Hellcats 13
Helter Skelter 5, 42, 59, 108
Henrikson, Lance 153, 159
Henry: Portrait of a Serial Killer 6, 42, 54, 68–80, 100–105, 110, 112
Henry: Portrait of a Serial Killer Part 2 79, 100–105, 110, 116–117
Hershey, Barbara 144
The Highwayman 42
The Hills Have Eyes 3
The Hillside Strangler 1–2, 100, 110–117, 153, 166, 171–172, 174
Hindley, Myra 5, 42, 173–174, 201
Hinman, Gary 59, 65
Hitchcock, Alfred 198
Hitler, Adolf 2, 23–30, 170
Holton, Mark 130–131, 135–137
Hood, George F. 152
Hopper, Dennis 23–25, 30–41
The House of Long Shadows 46
Howell, C. Thomas 2, 100, 111–117, 172
Howling II 23
Howling III 23
Human Pork Chop 6
Hunter, Bill 33

I'm a Killer 8
Imamura, Shohei 6
In the Light of the Moon 167
Irreversible 112

Jack the Ripper 3, 5, 19, 42 182–189, 81–88
Jack the Ripper (BBC TV series) 82–83
Jack the Ripper (film, 1976) 182
Jack the Ripper (film, 1988) 5, 81–88, 182
Jack the Ripper (film, 2016) 182–189
Jack the Ripper Goes West 182
Jackson, Samuel L. 159
Jacobson, David 6, 132, 176–178, 118–129
Jenson, Robert 201
Jeremy, Ron 114
Joel (film, 2018) 190–200
Johns, Stratford 82
Johnston, Stephen 1–2, 106, 111, 153, 156–157, 166–175
Jones, Bob 10
Jones, Elwyn 82–83
Jones, James Earl 4
Judgment Day: The John List Story 5

Kalifornia 152
Kargl, Gerald 54–58
Kelly, Mary Jane 182–183, 188
Kelly, Ned 31–32
Kemper 7
Khan, Cédric 7
A Kidnapping in the Family 176
Kiéslowski, Krzysztof 194
Killer: A Journal of Murder 7
The Killer Department 92
Killer Pickton 8
Kinski, Klaus 137
Kohnhurst, Michael 79, 103
Koslow, Aaron 21
Kosminski, Aaron 185, 189
Kroll, Jerry 161–162
Krueger, Freddy 75
Kubrick, Stanley 31, 136
Kürten, Peter 142

Lake Berryessa 9, 11, 14, 17, 19
Lambe, Vincent 173, 201
Lang, Fritz 1, 3
The Last Movie 34
Lawley, Sue 45, 51
Leder, Erwin 55, 57
Lee, Danny 6
Lee, Spike 5
Leet, Scott Anthony 177, 180
Le Prince, Louis Aimé Augustin 182–183, 186, 188
Lieberson, Sandy 25, 28–29
Lommel, Ulli 8
Long, Stanley 48
Longford 42
Look Back in Anger 75
Lorre, Peter 1
The Lost World 3
Lucas, Henry Lee 68–80, 100–105, 110, 116–117, 153
Lucio, Shannon 153, 160–161

M 1, 3
Mad Dog and Glory 101
Mad Dog Morgan 23–25, 30–41
Malik, Terence 152
Manhunt: Search for the Night Stalker 5
Manson, Charles 3, 5, 8, 19, 59–67, 108, 111
The Manson Family 59
Manson Family Movies 59–67
The Manson Massacre 59
Mark of the Devil 46
Marlowe 83
Marlowe, Derek 84–85
McAlpine, Hamish 1, 105–106, 111–113, 117, 166–169, 171–174
McDowell, Malcolm 89
McNaughton, John 6, 54, 68–80, 100–101, 105, 109, 116
Mean Streets 197
Memories of Murder 6
Merrick, Ian 42–53, 201
Merrick, Joseph 182
Meyer, Marc 118
Meyer, Russ 61
Miley, Gregory 179

Millennium 159
Molly, Mike 31
Monster 7
Moore, Alan 7, 183, 186
Moors murders 2, 5, 173–174, 201
Mora, Philippe 23–41
Morgan, Dan 23–25, 30–41
MPI 69–71, 78–79, 100–104
Murder in the Heartland 6, 152
Murlowski, John 179
Murray, Bill 101
Muybridge, Eadweard 188
My Friend Dahmer 8, 42, 118
Myers, Michael 120

Natural Born Killers 76, 152, 156–157, 165
Nazi Party 2, 23–30
Nebraska Correctional Center for Women 201
Ned Kelly (film) 31
Nedwick, Manny 21
Neilson, Donald 42–53
Netley, Charles 87–88
Newsnight 45, 51
Niemann, Sebastian 182–189
The Night Train to Mundo Fine 13
The Night We Called It a Day 41
Nightstalker 8
Noé, Gaspar 112
Nosferatu 3

Odo, Arnold 190, 194–195
O'Donnel, Keir 160
Oldman, Gary 89
On the Moors 2
On the Waterfront 75
Once Upon a Time in ... Hollywood 8, 42, 59
Ordinary People 192
Orpheus 40
Out of Darkness 5

Panzram, Carl 7
Parello, Chuck 1–2, 6, 42, 79, 100–117, 168, 172
Paul Sleeps Here 19
Peter: Portrait of a Serial Killer 42
Peterson, Wolfgang 57
Pi 57
Picnic at Hanging Rock 31
Pink Flamingos 60
Pirozzi, John 115
Polanski, Roman 62, 64–65, 134
The Professionals 83
Psycho 1, 3, 106–109, 120
Pugh, William 179

Rachel, Kylie 114
Radar, Dennis 27, 192
Raging Bull 99
Railsback, Steve 1, 100, 108–110, 114, 123, 172
Raising Jeffrey Dahmer 118

Raison, Robert 34
Ramirez, Jeannie 196
Ramirez, Richard 5, 195
Rampage 7
Rattner, Larry 122, 132, 176–177
Rea, Stephen 89, 92, 95–96, 98
Reed, Hal 9
Renner, Jeremy 118–121, 124–129
Reservoir Dogs 76
Ressler, Robert 1, 168
Rifkin, Joel 190–200
Robards, Jason 4
Roberto Succo 7
Rooker, Michael 68–80, 101–102, 116, 177, 180
Rostov Ripper 4, 89
Roth, Bobby 5
Roth, Tim 6, 152
Rule, Ann 142–151

Saddleworth Moor 201
The Sadist 152
Sapienza, Al 161
Saunders, Clive 5, 177, 201
Savini, Tom 1, 169, 193
Schechter, Harold 167
Schmidt, Holger Karsten 185
Schulze, Klaus 55, 57, 199
Scorsese, Martin 101
The Sculptress 201
The Secret Life of Jeffrey Dahmer 193
See No Evil: The Moors Murders 5–6, 42
Sellinger, Dennis 85
Seymour, Jane 82, 85, 87
Shapiro, Paul 142–151
Shaye, Lin 115
Sheen, Martin 34
The Shining 136
Shipman, Harold 42
A Short Film About Killing 194
Sid and Nancy 174
The Silence of the Lambs 1, 107, 167, 171
Silver Dream Racer 84
Slender Man 181
Snodgrass, Carrie 109
Snowtown 7
Speck 7
Speer, Albert 25, 29
Stark Raving Mad 6, 152
Starkweather (film) 2, 6, 152–166, 174–175, 201
Starkweather, Charles 152–165, 174–175
Starstruck 155
Staunton, Imelda 89, 92–93
Stevens, Cat 141
Stine, Paul 16, 21–22
Stone, Oliver 152
Strangled 8
A Study in Terror 182
Summer of Sam 5, 42
Sumpter, Donald 44, 47–49
Sunset Murders 178
Sutcliffe, Peter 5, 19–20

Sutherland, Donald 89, 92, 95–97, 99
Swastika 23–30
The Sweeney 83–84

Tangerine Dream 54, 57, 198–199
Tarantino, Quentin 59, 96
Tate, Sharon 60–62, 64–66
Taxi Driver 121
Taylor, Brent 153, 160–161
Taylor, Judd 5
Ted Bundy (film, 2002) 2, 7, 111, 143, 153, 166, 168–172
Temple, Lisa 78
10 Rillington Place 3, 42, 50
Tenderness of the Wolves 8
The Texas Chain Saw Massacre 1, 3, 106–107, 166
There Is Something About Mary 115
This Is Personal: The Hunt for the Yorkshire Ripper 5
Thompson, Robert 173, 201
Three on a Meat-Hook 1
Thring, Frank 31, 33, 37
Thurman, Uma 101
Till, Eric 5
To Catch a Killer 5, 42
A Ton of Grass Goes to Plot 13, 19
Toole, Ottis 68–80, 101
Torn, Rip 4
Toschi, Dave 21
Touch of Evil 121
Towels, Tom 73–74
Traffic 93
Trouble in Molopolis 23
True Romance 165
Turturro, Nicholas 2, 100, 111–117, 172
2001: A Space Odyssey 25

The Untold Story 6

Vampyr 3
The Vampire of Düsseldorf *see* Kürten, Peter
Van Bebber, Jim 59
Van der Valk 84
Venables, Jon 173, 201
Vengeance Is Mine 6
Verhoeven, Paul 180
The Vikings 32
Visalia Ransacker 175
Von Sydow, Max 89–90, 92

Waleed, Ali B. 71–72
Waleed, Malik 71–72
Walkabout 36
Walker, Alexander 29
Warhol, Andy 62, 67
Waters, John 62, 66
Watson, Emily 5
Weaver, Doodles 21
Weber, Charlie 133, 141
Wedding Crashers 160
Werner, Byron 2, 152–166, 174
West, Dominic 5

West, Fred 5–6, 42
West, Rosemary 5–6, 42
Whitman, Charles Joseph 7
Whittle, Lesley 43–44, 50
Why Does Herr R. Run Amuck? 192
Wickes, David 5, 81–88, 182
Wild Things 109

Williams, Wayne Bertram 4
Windsor, Frank 82–83
Wong, Anthony 6
Wood, Ed 125
Wood, James 7

Yam, Simon 6
Yorkshire Ripper 5, 19–20

Young, Neil 164
Young Poisoner's Handbook 42
Yuzna, Brian 111

Zodiac 7, 9, 11, 18, 42
Zodiac Killer (film) 9–22, 193
Zodiac Killer (person) 3, 9–22, 193

www.ingramcontent.com/pod-product-compliance
Lightning Source LLC
Chambersburg PA
CBHW060343010526
44117CB00017B/2945